DAVID THE KING

PLAN OF THE BATTLE OF REPHAIM.

DAVID THE KING

A HISTORICAL INQUIRY

BY

MARCEL DIEULAFOY

MEMBER OF THE INSTITUTE OF FRANCE

TRANSLATED FROM THE
FRENCH BY LUCY HOTZ

WIPF & STOCK · Eugene, Oregon

Wipf and Stock Publishers
199 W 8th Ave, Suite 3
Eugene, OR 97401

David the King
A Historical Inquiry
By Dieulafoy, Marcel
Softcover ISBN-13: 978-1-7252-8994-9
Hardcover ISBN-13: 978-1-7252-8995-6
eBook ISBN-13: 978-1-7252-8996-3
Publication date 10/29/2020
Previously published by T. Fisher Unwin, 1902

This edition is a scanned facsimile of the
original edition published in 1902.

PREFACE

OUR ideas about David are to a certain extent conventional. Everybody has made for himself a picture of the Psalmist king, and has put into it some of his own prejudices and personality. We have French Davids, English and German ones, Davids who believe and Davids without faith, Jewish Davids, Davids Catholic and Protestant, Davids of the eighteenth and of the nineteenth centuries, all deviating from the original in a marked degree, each placed against a background in accordance with the accustomed surroundings of the painter.

My wish has been to reinstate the hero of the Biblical epic in his own times and environment, or at least to make the attempt.

My task, after all an ungrateful one—the multitude is never pleased with those who endeavour to row against the stream of its convictions — has been rendered easier by a long experience of the East and by direct contact with its inhabitants. When one shares the life of the people, opportunities arise for looking right into their hearts and for learning their true sentiments. No doubt the thirty centuries that divide us from David are a long space of time ; but the Bible is a book which the tribes are still writing. One learns to read it by living in their midst. Such and such a celebrated sheikh of Khuzistan or Syria might be mistaken for Saul or for Joab, a certain ulema or mushtahid reminds one of Zadok or Abiathar ; this chief of Dervishes reincarnates Gad or Nathan, that woman might have been Bathsheba. To the immutability of the landscape, of customs, of civilisation, almost of the language and of beliefs, correspond an immutablity of ideas, just as a mould that never changes always produces the same cast. In such a case, the obstacle to a really historic reconstruction lies rather in the neglect of certain phenomena than in their interpretation.

It is thus that, in many respects, the history of Samuel, of Saul, and of David at the moment when they were thrown together by circumstances would have been traced with less accuracy, and the picture of Israelite society at the time of David would have been incomplete, had I not been able to assign to the prophet world the rank which it already held there, and above all to estimate its influence, by the manner in which it was exercised. The latest researches in the study of nervous diseases and the precise details given in the Bible, have happily enabled me to penetrate into a region formerly closed, to settle certain disputed questions, and to fill important gaps.

It will be no matter of surprise if the figure of the sovereign, put back into a society whose moral standard seems low indeed, rises higher in proportion as the plane of comparison is lowered ; if its features look different because they have been drawn from the life by an unprejudiced historian instead of by one who has looked too much into his inner self and has suffered philosophical speculations to influence him. It is not only the disciple of Samuel whose physiognomy will be modified. Samuel, Saul and the heroine of the celebrated drama which culminated in the death of Uriah, the birth and elevation of Solomon will of necessity appear in a new light.

With regard to a more special subject, a study of the texts and of the different places mentioned in it, following upon my works on besieging and fortification in the Ancient East, has enabled me to reproduce the state of the art of war before and after

David's reign and to give to the victor of Rephaim the position which he deserves in the front rank of famous captains.

The two campaigns and the final battle where the Philistines, completely crushed, saw the end of their power, will be discussed at length. It was a unique, an amazing passage of arms, although it has never before been properly appreciated.

I ought perhaps to have strengthened certain features, to have intensified certain tones; but for that it would have been necessary to enter into the domain of exegesis pure and simple; and I have preferred to rely upon established facts rather than to engage in controversy and to begin myself to theorise. Nevertheless, as in the centre of every pearl, there lies at the bottom of every legend an initial nucleus of formation; I have endeavoured to extract this particle of truth whenever it could be made to yield interesting details or useful information. And again, this is only by exception and such exceptions are always pointed out. With this view, the two principal sources by whose aid the Books of Samuel were composed have been made use of, as one or the other of them seemed to approach more closely to the truth, or to furnish details which appeared to be historical and interesting.

For the ineffable name of God, I have adopted

the form Jehovah, accepted since the seventeenth century. This pronunciation of the sacred tetragram is certainly wrong, but none is known to be certainly right; and it has the advantage over the new ones of being the most usual. I have followed the same rule for proper names, retaining well-known forms even when they are inaccurate. Those who are interested in the real transcriptions will find them in every index; other readers will forgive me saving their eyes and memory a useless fatigue, and for addressing myself to their intellect alone.

MARCEL DIEULAFOY.

CONTENTS

	PAGE
PREFACE	vii

I.

SKETCH OF THE TWELVE TRIBES—SLOW RISE OF JUDAH—
TRIUMPH OF JUDAH 1

II.

ISRAEL UNDER THE JUDGES—THE PATRIARCHAL SYSTEM—
THE JUDGES—THE PROPHETS 15

III.

DECLINE OF ISRAEL UNDER THE LAST JUDGES . . 36

IV.

SAMUEL — HIS VOCATION — ACCESSION OF SAUL — THE
ANOINTING OF DAVID 43

V.

DAVID AT THE COURT OF SAUL—HIS FLIGHT—HIS FIRST
SUCCESSES—DAVID AMONG THE PHILISTINES—BATTLE
OF GILBOA—DEATH OF SAUL—THE WITCH OF ENDOR . 59

VI.

SAUL AND THE PROPHETS 99

VII.

ISH-BOSHETH, KING OF ISRAEL—DAVID, KING OF JUDAH—RESPECTIVE CONDITION OF THE TWO KINGDOMS—MURDER OF ABNER—ASSASSINATION OF ISH-BOSHETH—DAVID, KING OF THE HEBREWS 114

VIII.

TAKING OF JERUSALEM—JERUSALEM AS CAPITAL—CAMPAIGNS AGAINST THE PHILISTINES—ORGANISATION OF THE ARMY—VICTORY OF REPHAIM—THE PHILISTINES OBLIGED TO PAY TRIBUTE—DAVID AS TACTICIAN, STRATEGIST, AND BESIEGER 134

IX.

THE ARK AT JERUSALEM—ORGANISATION OF THE FAITH AND OF THE CLERGY 176

X.

INTERNAL ADMINISTRATION OF THE KINGDOM—THE PALACE—THE GREAT WORKS 197

XI.

THE GREAT WARS—VICTORIES OVER THE ARAMÆANS, EDOMITES, AND MOABITES—BATTLES OF MEDEBA AND HELAM 204

XII.

BATH-SHEBA 211

CONCLUSION 265

NOTES.

	PAGE
A.—The Tribe of Levi	271
B.—Jehovah and Elohim	272
C.—Israelite Artists	274
D.—Historical Value of the VIIIth, Xth, and XIIth Chapters of the 1st Book of Samuel	275
E.—Historical Value of the XVth Chapter of the 1st Book of Samuel	275
F.—Historical Value of the XVIth Chapter of the 1st Book of Samuel	276
G.—Historical Value of the XVIIth Chapter of the 1st Book of Samuel	277
H.—The Faith of David	278
I.—On Writing	279
J.—The Song of the Bow	280
K.—The Ephod of Divination	280
L.—The Organisation of the Clergy	284
M.—The Ephod Bad	291
N.—The Altar	291
O.—The Cherubim	293

DAVID THE KING

I

Sketch of the Twelve Tribes—Slow Rise of Judah—Triumph of Judah

DAVID was born in Beth-lehem, a small town in Judah, towards the middle of the eleventh century B.C. No heavenly signs, no cataclysms announced his advent; no legends sprang up around his cradle.

We learn from tradition that he was the son of Jesse, the grandson of Obed, and the great-grandson of Boaz and of Ruth, a Moabitish woman.[1] We are

---

[1] Ruth iv. 17, 21, 22; 1 Chron. ii. 12-15; Matt. i. 5. According to certain commentators the Book of Ruth is no authority. But there is no reason for doubting the information given in the last verses (17 to 22), especially as it adds nothing to the glory of David. In the Gospel of S. Matthew, Boaz is spoken of as the son of Rahab (Matt. i. 5). It is difficult to understand the desire to identify the mother of Boaz with the harlot of Jericho who rendered certain services to the Judæans during the conquest of the Promised Land. (Josh. ii.; vi. 16, 17). No passage in the Old Testa.nent authorises this hypothesis, and the careful comparison of the dates of the two

also told that he had seven brothers, older than himself,[1] and two sisters;[2] but the birthplace, and even the name, of his mother are unknown. Elsewhere it is said that in his youth he used to take care of his father's sheep.[3] In connexion with the scanty indications afforded by the Books of Samuel and of Ruth, this detail shows that his family was of humble estate.

The elevation of the son of Jesse was thus not favoured either by riches or by the fame of ancient descent. His genius, Samuel's protection, the choice of Saul, were the factors of his great fortunes. But the causes of the establishment of the monarchy and the reasons which determined the Hebrews to confide the hereditary power to a member of the tribe of Judah, were not entirely owing to events contemporary with David; centuries past had a con-

---

Rahabs seems moreover to contradict it. Nevertheless it is certain that it was in order to wipe out the blot which they presumed existed in the genealogy of David and of Christ, that S. Paul and S. James have endeavoured to exalt a woman who was in point of fact a courtesan, a dissembler, and a traitress to her own people (S. Paul, Ep. to the Heb. xi. 31; and S. James ii. 25).

[1] 1 Sam. xvi. 6-10, and xvii. 12. The Book of Chronicles (1 Chron. ii. 13-15) gives only six brothers to David. This is the result of a confusion.

[2] Zeruiah and Abigail. The first was the mother of Joab, of Abishai and of Asahel (2 Sam. ii. 13, 18; iii. 30, 39; 1 Chron. ii. 16), and the second was the mother of Amasa (2 Sam. xvii. 25; 1 Chron. ii. 16, 17). The name of Zeruiah's husband is not known. By some neglect quite contrary to custom, and doubtless arising from Zeruiah's exalted rank, it is always her own name that is coupled in the Bible with those of her children.

[3] 1 Sam. xvi. 11, 19. Compare with the offerings sent by Jesse to Saul and to his eldest son's officers (1 Sam. xvi. 20; xvii. 18).

siderable share in producing them. Just as kingship was the offspring of a long and disastrous experience of the patriarchal system, the selection of the royal tribe was a political phenomenon with roots penetrating the deep recesses of the past.

Researches with regard to the choice and establishment of the Judæan dynasty would be more conclusive could we go back to the early days of Israel and follow his sons in the different phases of their life. Unfortunately the first chapters of the Bible, very sparing of details in the first instance, have been changed and mutilated, and are often allegorical. Nevertheless, a few fragments, whose primitive form can be traced in spite of the "patine" of ages and additions of a later date, give some general indications of the relative importance of the tribes during the pastoral period and afford valuable help in the investigation of those distant times. Among this number are: the genealogy of the twelve ancestors from whom the tribes took their names, the census taken of the tribes,[1] the song of Deborah, the blessings of Jacob and of Moses.

The result of the comparison and accordance of these passages seems to show that the Judæans, subordinate to four more powerful tribes—those of Joseph, of Reuben, of Simeon and of Levi, for a long time occupied an insignificant position. But while the

[1] The numbers given of the combatants in each tribe must be considered as only approximate. It was a question rather of general calculations than of exact figures.

descendants of Reuben, of Simeon and of Levi decline, those of Judah become more powerful and multiply, as the three numberings of the tribes appear to prove. At the time of the Exodus, they follow closely upon the children of Joseph. Great wars take place, the conquest of the promised land is accomplished, and the Judæans continue their progress. In the marches they head the army,[1] during the halts they occupy the right wing,[2] when the trumpets sound the alarm they are the first to strike their tents.[3] On the return of the spies sent into the land of Canaan, notwithstanding the murmurs of the other tribes, they advocate the crossing of the Jordan; and their resolute will imposes itself upon the factious.[4] One feels that they are preparing to dispute the first place.

The division of the Promised Land allows us to classify the tribes once more in order of importance.[5] The drawing of lots mentioned in the Bible is a pious fiction; fate spoke in the name of Jehovah. The truth is that the tribes took in their turns the share which suited them best. The most powerful was bound to have first choice, and each in turn, from the

[1] Numb. ii. 9; x. 13, 14.

[2] They were on the eastern wing (Numb. ii. 3) and as the army was advancing from the south to the north, it is really the right wing that is in question. The children of Joseph formed the left wing (Numb. ii. 18).

[3] Numb. x. 13, 14.

[4] Numb. xiii. 31, 32; xiv. 6-9; Josh. xiv. 7, 8.

[5] Whatever may be the date assigned to the edition of this passage See below, p. 6, &c.

strong to the weak, chose the best out of the remaining portions. The Book of Joshua adds that the Judæans had the honours of the division. Even before consulting the Lord, the people recognised their right to occupy in the Land of Canaan whichever region pleased them best.[1] The historical value of this tradition has been disputed. But at any rate the importance of the portion assigned to the Judæans a portion so large that they could cede part of it to Simeon,[2] and perhaps even the beginning of the book of Judges, bear witness to their prestige, their authority, and their strength.

"After the death of Joshua, the children of Israel asked of the Lord, saying, Who shall go up for us against the Canaanites first, to fight against them? And the Lord said, Judah shall go up: behold, I have delivered the land into his hand."[3]

According to the Bible, Joseph, who had acquired the privileges of the first-born of Israel, Joseph, from whom sprang Joshua, the chief of the invading army,[4] had to bow to Judah, and could only obtain the second lot. Then came Benjamin, Simeon who enjoyed the protection of Judah; Zebulun, Issachar, Asher, Naphtali, Dan, Reuben, Gad, and Levi.[5]

The settling down of the tribes on their apportioned inheritance put an end to the great evolutions of the pastoral age. Apart from a few exceptions and some passing accidents, the relative power and destiny of

[1] Josh. xiv. and xv. [2] Josh. xix. 1–9.
[3] Judg. i. 1, 2. [4] Numb. xiii. 9; Judg. ii. 9; v. 14.
[5] Josh. xvi., xvii., xviii., xix.

each tribe seem from that moment to be bound up with the share which it has obtained. Certain particulars in the history of the Judges and the general descriptions of the tribes in the song of Deborah and the blessings of Jacob and of Moses indicate this, and show by contrast that the slow and continuous effort which brought the fourth son of Jacob to the front was still going on.

The tribe of Benjamin, established to the north of Judah, is valiant, turbulent and redoubtable. It furnishes the skilled archers and the best soldiers of Israel. Gibeah, its capital, which will later on witness the birth of Saul, becomes a strong place and a haunt of the lawless.[1] Its thick walls and its fighting men inspire such confidence among the Hebrews, that on solemn occasions the deputies of the tribes assemble at Mizpeh in its neighbourhood and under its protection.[2] Nevertheless Benjamin cannot drive away the enemies remaining in the very heart of its inheritance, such as the Jebusites in Jerusalem, or the Philistines in Michmas and in Geba.[3]

Simeon becomes absorbed in Judah.[4] In the time of the last Judges it no longer exists as a separate tribe.[5]

---

[1] Judg. xix. 14, &c. ; xx. 4, &c.

[2] Josh. xviii. 26 ; xx. 1, 3 ; 1 Sam. vii. 16 ; xvii.

[3] The Geba here mentioned is not the same as the acropolis of the Benjamites. Many towns built on heights took from their situation the name of Gibeah or Geba (Josh. xv. 63 ; Judg. i. 21 ; 1 Sam. x. 5 ; xiii. 2, 3, 5, 16, 23). [4] Judg. i. 3, 4, 17.

[5] This is at least what may be inferred from the blessing of Moses. Simeon is not mentioned there.

SKETCH OF THE TWELVE TRIBES

Zebulun and Issachar, settled towards the north, produce Judges of no particular notoriety: Tola and Elon.[1]

Naphtali guards the northern marches and gives birth to Barak,[2] who, under the orders of Deborah leads the forces of his tribe and those of Zebulun, at the battle of Megiddo.[3]

It is the mission of the tribe of Asher, like that of its two neighbours Naphtali and Zebulun, to grow at the expense of Phœnicia. All three are lacking in the spirit of adventure, but they get hold of the roads which lead from Tyre and Sidon into Egypt, Arabia, and Chaldæa. By a sort of tacit compromise they leave them open to foreign trade, and in return obtain permission to occupy a zone of Phœnician territory under the title of colonists. The towns of Kitron, of Nahalol in Zebulun, of Acco, of Aphik, of Rehob in Asher, of Beth-shemesh and of Beth-anath in Naphtali, thus become common to the Israelites and to their neighbours in the west.[4]

The verses devoted to Issachar, Zebulun, Naphtali, and Asher in the blessings of Jacob and Moses depict the comfort and peace enjoyed by the younger sons of Leah and of the concubines ever since, commanded by Deborah, they had overcome the Canaanites who overran their inheritance.

Dan, made famous by Shamgar and by Samson,[5]

[1] Judg. x. 1, 2; xii. 11, &c.
[2] Judg. iv. 6, &c.
[3] Judg. iv. and v.
[4] Judg. i. 30-33.
[5] Judg. iii. 31; xiii.-xvi.

but continually harassed by the Philistines and the Amorites of the west,[1] finds a refuge at the extreme north of Naphtali on the southern slope of Mount Hermon, and in order to settle there subjugates the Sidonian colony of Laish.[2] The territory thus abandoned in the south is at once occupied by Judah.

The tribe of Reuben, which had played such a prominent part in the confederation,[3] remains on the left bank of the Jordan. It is devoured by internal disputes,[4] it declines, and falls at last to the lowest rank.[5]

The fate of the other tribes settled in the land of Gilead is very different. Cut off by the Jordan and the Dead Sea from the country on the other side, always at war with Ammon and Moab, they grow soldierlike and prosperous, and distinguish themselves brilliantly under their own judges, Jephthah and Jair.[6] The blessing of Jacob and even more clearly that of Moses, assigning as they do an important place to one of these tribes, that of Gad, agree with history and form a valuable supplement to it. They explain how these disinherited ones triumphed in time over the children of Joseph,[7] how they helped Ish-bosheth, the son of Saul, to recover his sovereignty over the Philistines,[8] and how they

---

[1] Judg. i. 34; xiv., xv., xviii. 1.
[2] Judg. xviii. 7-29.
[3] Gen. xxix. 32; xlix. 3.
[4] Judg. v. 15.
[5] Deut. xxxiii. 6.
[6] Judg. x. 3; xi., xii.
[7] Judg. xii. 1-6.
[8] 2 Sam. ii. 9.

were able to support David against the rebellious Absalom.[1]

The Levites have found their own line. After having put themselves under the protection of Joshua, they remain the allies of Ephraim, and in spite of the jealousies which they excite, and of the disgrace which pursues them,[2] they obtain a great empire over the souls of men. Under Eli[3] they even arrive at the chief magistracy. But their political strength is not equal to their moral influence, and their authority is of too recent a date to be strong and well established.

In fact, only Ephraim and Judah remain conspicuous; for the tribe of Manasseh, notwithstanding the successes of Gideon[4] and the ambitious designs of Abimelech,[5] Manasseh, which will one day see realised in Samaria its judges' visions of royalty, has for a long time past been subject to the tribe of Ephraim.[6]

---

[1] 2 Sam. xvii. 22, 24, 27–29.   [2] See note L in Appendix.

[3] Samuel seems to have belonged to the tribe of Levi. He was descended from Kohath, a son of Levi, whose family had for a long time past been settled in the land of Ephraim, and whose children recruited the ranks of the acolytes of the Cohen or chief of the priests at Shiloh (Exod. vi. 16, 18; Josh. xxi. 4, 5, 10, 20, 21, 26; 1 Chron. vi. 1, 2, 16, 22, 23, 26, 27, 33, 34, 61, 66). Although very early made a member of a college of prophets (1 Sam. iii. 1–20), he also occupied, under Eli, a subordinate position in the priesthood (1 Sam. i. 27, 28; ii. 11, 18, 19, 21; iii. 1, 3, 5, 15).

[4] Judg. vi. 11, &c.; vii., viii.   [5] Judg. ix.

[6] Gideon's saying is well known: "Is not the gleaning of the grapes of Ephraim better than the vintage of Abiezer?" (a town belonging to Manasseh, Judg. vi. 11 and 34). This superiority of Ephraim was a result of the integrity of the tribe; Manasseh was cut in two by the Jordan.

Out of Ephraim sprang many of the leaders of Israel. Joshua, Deborah, Tola, Abdon, Eli, Samuel,[1] are all more or less connected with this tribe. The most famous sanctuaries are found in its territory. Shechem[2] marks the spot from which the Almighty showed the Promised Land to the Patriarch Abraham. Beth-el[3] recalls to memory the first altar raised in honour of Jehovah. Shiloh, sanctified by the "tabernacle of the congregation," becomes a place of general assembly, and the religious capital of Israel.[4] It does not lose this advantage until after the disastrous battle of Aphek where the sons of Eli are killed and the Ark is captured by the Philistines. At Nob, the priests consult the ephod,[5] which has been taken there since the loss of the Ark.[6] And finally, Naioth possesses a college of prophets.[7] The priests and the prophets thus seem to have incorporated themselves with Ephraim, which, jealous of its prerogatives, is often up in arms against the other tribes.[8] But while fighting without profit against their brethren, the men of Ephraim tolerate strangers in the heart of their dominions. They abandon the mountain of

---

[1] Numb. xiii. 9; Judg. ii. 9; v. 14; iv. 4, 5; x. 1; xii. 13, &c.

[2] Gen. xii. 6, 7. For the great celebrity of Shechem, see Gen. xxxiii. 19, 20, and Josh. xxi. 21; xxiv. 32.

[3] Gen. xii. 8; xiii. 3, 4; xvi. 12; Judg. i. 22.

[4] Josh. xviii. 1, 9, 10; xix. 51; xxi. 2; xxii. 12; Judg. xviii. 31; xx. 18; xxi. 19, &c.; 1 Sam. i. 3. For Shiloh, see also below, p. 24, n. 1.

[5] See below for the ephod and the Ark, p. 180-188, and notes K and L.

[6] 1 Sam. xxi., xxii. 9, &c.; xxiii. 6.

[7] 1 Sam. xix. 18, 19, 22, &c.   [8] Judg. ix., xii., xx., xxi.

TRIUMPH OF JUDAH

Beth-el[1] to the Philistines, and then, at first through weakness, and afterwards for fear of losing the advantages of their alliance, they allow the Egyptians and the Canaanites to keep Gezer, Beth-shean, Taanach, Dor, Ibleam, and Megiddo,[2] that open door into their territory, that enforced halting place on the road from Egypt into Syria.

The tribe of Judah is not so brilliant as that of Ephraim, its legendary past is more modest, its sons have never sought for power; but alone among its brethren, Judah never ceases to grow. It conquers the south of the Promised Land. It extends its inheritance, drives away or subjects to its yoke the ancient masters of the soil,[3] and ends by absorbing the descendants of Simeon and those of Dan remaining in the neighbourhood. In time it becomes so powerful that it disdains the other tribes, and isolates itself in its strength, forming a clearly marked division.[4] When the lightning that heralds the storm

[1] 1 Sam. xiii. 2.
[2] Josh. xvi. 10; xvii. 11-13; Judg. i. 27-29.
[3] Judg. i. 4-19.
[4] Judah takes part in none of the great coalitions presided over by the Judges. Deborah (Judg. iv. v.), Gideon (Judg. vii. 23; vii. 1), Jephthah (Judg. xi. xii.), Samson (Judg. xv. 10-14), have never numbered any Judaeans among their troops. It is only when menaced that they take up arms. Judah is introduced into the song of Deborah by the Vulgate owing to an error; and in fact, except for a few verses (Judg. i. 2-10, 17-19; iii. 5-11), and some insignificant passages (Judg. x. 9; xv. 9-12; xvii. 7; xix. 1), this tribe is not spoken of in the Book of Judges. The tribes of the centre and of the north already excluded Judah from the clan of Israel, just as it became the rule to do after the schism. It is thus that even in the inscription of Mesa, the names of Judah and of Jerusalem are missing.

illumines the horizon, all look to Judah for help. But it needs a disaster to make its children draw their heavy sword, and grave crimes to force them to chastise. Then they deliver Israel out of the hands of Chushan-rishathaim, King of Mesopotamia,[1] or again, they march against the Benjamites guilty of having violated and done to death the wife of a Levite ; lay siege to Gibeah, their capital, and bury the crime beneath the ruins of the criminals' den.[2] By following their advance, and by taking into account their tendency to autonomy, one can already foresee that they will leave far behind them the other sons of Jacob ; and that no political transformation will be durable unless they form its pivot. But one more effort, but a few years more, and Judah shall represent the whole of the chosen people, and in the language of men its name shall be substituted for that of Israel.

[1] Othniel led the army of the Israelities in this expedition (Judg. iii. 9-11). Under the pretext that Othniel might signify " Lion of God " and Caleb " Dog of God," certain historians have classed these two personages in the category of legendary heroes. The reason for this is purely one of sentiment. According to the Bible Othniel was the son of Kenaz, the younger brother of Caleb, who had distinguished himself at the end of the Exodus (Numb. xiii. 31 ; Josh. xiv. 6-14). For Othniel see also below p. 33, n. 6.

[2] Judg. xx. 18. The taking of Gibeah dates from the time of Phinehas, son of that Cohen Eleazar of whom mention is so often made in the history of the Conquest. Eleazar, who dies a few years after Joshua, was supposed to be the son of Aaron. It seems, according to these data, that the siege of the capital of Benjamin took place about half a century after the occupation of the Land of Canaan.

TRIUMPH OF JUDAH

"Judah, thee shall thy brethren praise ;
 Thy hand shall be on the neck of thine enemies,
 Thy father's sons [1] shall bow down before thee.

Judah is a lion's whelp ;
From the prey, my son, thou art gone up ;
He stooped down, he crouched as a lion,
And as a lioness ; who shall rouse him up?

The sceptre shall not depart from Judah,
Nor the ruler's staff from between his feet,
Until Shiloh come (*i.e.* the pacification of the country is complete),
And unto him shall the obedience of the peoples be." [2]

---

[1] Or rather "thy mother's sons," &c. Judah is the last of the sons of Leah, and is the fourth son of Jacob. The three eldest, sons of Leah, like himself, and to whom the Bible alludes, are Reuben, Simeon, and Levi. It seems, according to this passage, which agrees perfectly with the information given in the Book of Numbers, that at some time or other, but long before the period of the Judges, the three tribes represented by the three elder sons of Jacob had been the most powerful in the confederation. The great change which had come about in the relative order of the power of the tribes is shown by this verse.

[2] These are the celebrated lines which have given rise to so many controversies and polemics. Some read, "Until Shiloh (the peacemaker) come," and see in it an allusion to the Christ born of the house of David. Others understand by "the peacemaker," David himself, and conclude from that, going from the detail to the whole, that the blessing is of the date of the sovereign to whom the prophecy applies. In point of fact the word translated "the peacemaker" might just as well mean the pacification. This simple change gives quite another sense to the verse. There is no more question of a prophecy, but only of a sort of promise.

"Judah shall fight (retain the ruler's staff) until the complete pacification of the Land of Canaan, and the unification of the tribes."

Thus understood, and whether giving a promise or expressing a desire, this phrase does not necessarily imply the coming to the throne of the son of Jesse, and might very well date back, especially if one puts it into the mouth of a Judæan, to a period much earlier than the reign of David.

Binding his foal unto the vine,
And his ass's colt unto the choice vine ;
He hath washed his garments in wine,
And his vesture in the blood of grapes

His eyes shall be red with wine,
And his teeth white as milk." [1]

[1] Gen. xlix.

II

Israel under the Judges—The Patriarchal System—The Judges
—The Prophets

AT the same time that the tribe of Judah was preparing to take the lead among its brethren, we can trace in the history of the last Judges, the manifestation of a slow but continuous expansion of the moral sense of the people of Israel.

The sentiments of individual protection and of the administration of justice by the state had developed themselves. The Benjamites and the inhabitants of Jabesh-Gilead had experienced bitter proofs of this.[1] The germ of patriotism existed in the common love for the Promised Land.[2] One could feel that the tribes were seeking to draw tighter the loosened bonds which united them, such as language, race, and above all the belief in a heavenly protector, infinite as time, infinite as space, creator of worlds and of living beings ; who thought for his people,

[1] See above, p. 12, n. 2, and Judg. xxi. 8–12.
[2] 2 Sam. x. 12 ; xx. 19.

watched over them, and dwelt in their midst.[1] But except for this new trend indicative of moral growth, the Hebrews were in a stationary or even decadent condition. If they had exchanged their brown tents for the more solid buildings of the conquered nations, they yet retained the legacy of their old traditions, and had abandoned no custom, thrown off no prejudice. Their polygamy, their predatory instincts, their respect for brute force, their ignorance of the plastic arts and their disdain for civilisation still kept them in a state of partial barbarism.

As Joshua had left them, so would David find them.

In the most fertile districts surrounding the inhabited centres, where they were least exposed to inroads of the Philistines, the Amalekites and the rest of their numerous enemies, the Israelites sowed corn and barley and even cultivated the olive and the vine.[2] Fig-trees, pomegranate and palm-trees[3] grew in the well-watered gardens. But the crops of grain and fruit were seldom in excess of the needs of each family. As in the days of the Exodus, the flock was still the true indication of fortune and the standard of wealth.[4] And yet even when barely established on

---

[1] See note B in Appendix.

[2] Deut. xxviii. 39, 40, 51 ; Judg. ix. 8–14 ; xv. 1 ; Ruth i. ii. ; 1 Kings iv. 25. Josephus calls the vine and the fig-tree the kings of trees. The olive was also highly estimated (Hosea ii. 12 ; Joel i. 7, 10, 11).

[3] Exod. xxviii. 33, 34.

[4] When speaking of a very poor man the annalist says that he had

ISRAEL UNDER THE JUDGES

the soil, Israel plumed itself upon its agriculture. The parable of the cake of barley bread—that curious emblem of civilisation, which rolls down from the heights where Gideon is encamped and descends among the nomadic Midianites, overthrowing tents and crushing men, shows with what contempt the tribes remaining faithful to the pastoral system were looked upon.[1]

Among this people of husbandmen and shepherds, the rusticity of the dwellings was in harmony with the hard lives led by all. The house, a rude heap of rough-hewn blocks and earthen bricks, consisted of one or two rooms lighted by the doorway, and divided by means of woollen curtains or carpets ; the whole being covered by a flat roof or terrace of very thick clay.[2]

In the place of honour stood the teraphim, shapeless images of household gods.[3] Here and there were articles of furniture made of palm wood, coarse specimens of pottery, a few goat-skins and sheep-skins. Even in the days of Jehoshaphat, when a wealthy woman of Shunem wishes to arrange a room for the prophet Elisha, she only puts into it for

---

but one sheep (2 Sam. xii. 3). To describe a very rich man, he attributes to him a thousand goats and three thousand sheep, or a great number of flocks and herds (1 Sam. xxv. 2 ; 2 Sam. xii. 2).

[1] This parable occurs in the account of a dream, in which the barley bread cooked among the ashes in reality symbolises civilisation and the Israelites (Judg. vii. 13 to 15).

[2] 1 Sam. ix. 25, 26 ; 2 Sam. xi. 2 ; Isaiah ix. 9 and 10.

[3] Gen. xxxi. 19, 30–34 ; Judg. xviii. 17 ; 1 Sam. xix. 13–16.

furniture a bed, a table, a seat and a lamp. And her delighted guest is most grateful.[1] We can find these same dwellings in any eastern tribe of the present day that has remained purely oriental. The harem of the great Sheikhs of Mesopotamia is as simple and as destitute of luxuries as was the house of the Shunamite.

Such were the houses standing among the vines and spreading fig-trees;[2] serving at the same time for storehouse and cellar, the common shelter for the family and for the flock. Asses, oxen, and camels were, however, relegated to the courtyard. Among the animals used for transport or for labour, the horse would have been looked for in vain.[3]

In every town or village a few houses rose higher than the rest, dominating the uniform mass of buildings. They possessed an upper storey, more secluded than the ground floor and often used for the women's apartments. In this case, the windows were supplied with a lattice of woodwork, resembling the *moucharabiés* of the Arabs.[4] These upper chambers, called *aliâh* by the Hebrews, indicated the dwellings of the rich and powerful. It is the same in Persia, with the

---

[1] 2 Kings iv. 8–12.

[2] 1 Kings iv. 25.

[3] Asses and mules were ridden by the most exalted personages (Judg. v. 10; x. 4; xii. 14; 1 Sam. xxv. 20; 2 Sam. xviii. 9; 1 Kings i. 33, 38). The first horses brought to Jerusalem were taken by David from the studs of Hadarezer (2 Sam. viii. 3 and 4). See below p. 205 n. 4.

[4] 2 Kings i. 2; Song of Songs ii. 9.

balah-khaneh (literally high houses).[1] But whether consisting of one or of two floors, whether belonging to a poor family or to a rich, each house was surmounted by a parapet. In Deuteronomy this was imperatively enjoined.

"When thou buildest a new house, then shalt thou make a battlement for thy roof, that thou bring not blood upon thine house, if any man fall from thence."[2]

This verse shows the important part played by the terrace in Hebrew life. In point of fact, it was only habitable during the evenings and summer nights,[3] when the darkness brought a relief longed for all day, and there was a chance of the cool breeze that sometimes blows after sunset.

Without excepting the two-storied houses, which indeed were as simple in aspect as those of the poorer classes, one would have sought vainly in Israel for a monument, a palace, or a religious edifice affording scope for the display of the taste and intelligence of the builder. The palace was non-existent for want of a king to inhabit it; the religious edifice was but a shelter, sometimes only a tent.

It may be that the sanctuary of Shiloh, which

---

[1] Josh. ii. 15; 1 Sam. xix. 12; 2 Kings i. 2. In the first two texts mention is only made of persons climbing down from a window by means of a rope; but in the third, the upper floor is spoken of by name. The Hebrew word is even given in Judges: "Ehud approached the king, who was sitting in his *aliâh*, and said unto him. . . ." (Judg. iii. 20). This name is perpetuated in the countries where Arabic is spoken. (The English version calls it "summer parlour."—Translator's note.)

[2] Deut. xxii. 8.

[3] 1 Sam. ix. 25, 26; 2 Sam. xi. 2.

played such an important part,[1] contained two or three apartments. They were at any rate austerely simple, for the Hebrews, making a virtue of their ignorance and rudeness, held it culpable to give an imposing aspect to the sacrificial altars, to gravestones, to erect pillars, to construct a religious building of a durable character.[2] They still obeyed the laws of the desert. Their unwillingness to free themselves from the yoke was so great, the influence of tradition was so powerful, that even the prestige of royalty and the power of David were unable to triumph over them.[3] There is nothing surprising in these scruples when one remembers how victorious Rome, from quite an opposite point of view, when at the summit of her glory and enriched by the spoils of the whole world, but dominated at the same time by sumptuary laws, refused for years to allow her theatres to be built of anything but wood.[4]

In the time of the Judges, the Hebrews' knowledge of fortification was as rudimentary as their attempts

[1] Sam. iii. 2 and 3. See above, p. 10 n. 4 ; and below p. 30 n. 3, and also note N in Appendix.

[2] Exod. xx. 25 ; Levit. xxvi. 1 ; Deut. xxvii. 5, 6. For the altars see note N in Appendix.

[3] See below, pp. 176, 177.

[4] It was Pompey who endowed Rome with the first stone theatre (about the year 50 B.C.). Before that, the censors had only authorised temporary wooden theatres, and had ordered the demolition of those whose construction had been attempted with more lasting materials. Pompey placed a temple at the summit of the edifice and the stone benches thus became the seats of a sanctuary. The law did not appear to be violated, and thanks to this stratagem, the building remained intact.

at architecture. The enceintes of Schechem and of Thebez, the ramparts of Gibeah and of Jerusalem, were no doubt simple walls, and even these dated from the days of the Canaanites.[1] Before the reign of David, the people of Israel were ignorant both of the art of strengthening the defences of a place, and of the art of laying proper siege to it.[2]

The simplicity of life showed itself even in dress.

Primitive as the dwelling places and their furniture, clothes were reduced to a few draperies serving to protect the body against excess of heat or cold. Their material was supplied by the textile products of the country—wool, goats' hair[3] or flax, woven separately.[4] There was the *cĕthôneth* of linen, not dyed or prepared in any way, confined at the waist by a loose belt and stopping short at the knees;[5] the *simlah* made of brown or white wool bordered by a band of blue, the colour of the sky, according to Josephus,[6] and having the four corners finished off with heavy tassels;[7] then a thin headcloth kept in its place by means of a cord and covering the hair, which was worn long;[8] and finally, leather sandals furnished with

---

[1] Judg. ix. 43, 46; ix. 51; 2 Sam. v. 7–9.

[2] See below, p. 140, n. 2.

[3] Exod. xxv. 23–26.

[4] Deut. xxii. 11.

[5] From an injunction in Exodus xx. 26, it may be inferred that this garment was very short.

[6] Numb. xv. 38; Jos. "Ant. Jud." iii. 8. 5.

[7] Numb. xv. 38; Deut. xxii. 12.

[8] Leviticus xix. 27. This feature of their style of headdress may be also remarked in Egyptian paintings of the Hebrews (A captive

thongs. Tunics, mantles and headdresses consisted of shawls or pieces of silk wrapped round the body. The very name of the under-garment, *cĕthôneth*, from which is derived the Greek χίτων, the express direction to attach heavy tassels to the four corners of the *simlah* or overdress so as to keep it from blowing about, indicate the shape and object of the two chief articles of clothing. This costume, which is reproduced on Egyptian bas-reliefs, closely resembles that of the Druses and the Maronites.

For the heads of families there was the *meîl*,[1] a mantle or robe, richer and more characteristic; for the priests there was the linen ephod.[2] The women loved gay-coloured tunics,[3] which were also worn by the youths of the well-to-do classes;[4] but the former might be distinguished by a veil falling down over the shoulders. The unmarried daughters of important personages wore long sleeves to their tunics.[5] To the women belonged also the small hand-glasses made of burnished metal, the anklets, the *nezems*[6] or nose jewels, the gold chains and girdles, the necklaces strung with half moons, symbolical of the goddess Astarte.[7] As for rings, bracelets and earrings, they

---

Israelite at Karnak: Rosellini, *Mon. reali*, pl. cxlviii.). The flowing locks of Absalom afford another instance of this fashion (2 Sam. xiv. 26, xviii. 9).

[1] 1 Sam. xv. 27, 28; xviii. 4; xxiv. 5; xxviii. 14.
[2] See note M in Appendix.
[3] Judg. v. 30; 2 Sam. i. 24; Ezek. xvi. 13.
[4] Gen. xxxvii. 3.   [5] 2 Sam. xiii. 18.
[6] Gen. xxiv. 22, 47; Isaiah iii. 21; Ezek. xvi. 12.
[7] Exod. xxxii. 2; xxv. 22; Numb. xxxii. 2; Song of Songs i. 10; Isaiah iii. 16-21; Ez. xvi. 10-18.

seem to have been worn indiscriminately by both sexes.[1]

These jewels, which considering the poverty of the nation were very plentiful, were more than mere ornaments; they formed the sterling wealth, the last reserve, of each family. In those happy times feminine coquetry found itself fully justified by domestic economy.

Like the hand-mirrors, the necklets, bracelets and other articles of jewellery no doubt came from the coast; and like all objects of Tyrian and Sidonian manufacture, bore the double stamp of Egypt and Chaldæa. The only native works of art of which mention is made, the ark, the altars, the tables of shew-bread, the pectoral,[2] the brazen serpent of Moses,[3] Aaron's golden calf,[4] the molten image of silver made for Micah,[5] the golden vases and the ephod of Gideon,[6] were more or less without shape, unless the Bible is wrong in attributing them to the

---

[1] Exod. xxxii. 2; xxxv. 22. There is reason to believe that among the Midianites, who were really closely related to the Jews, the fighting men adorned themselves with jewellery. This custom had either the same origin among both nations, or was borrowed by the one from the other. Even in our own days the young boys belonging to the Arab tribes of Mesopotamia wear, like their sisters, both necklaces and earrings.

[2] See notes N and K in Appendix.

[3] The famous serpent, Nehushtan, which, in spite of its origin, was destroyed by Hezekiah, who thought it was conducive to idolatry among the Jews (Numb. xxi. 8, 9; 2 Kings xviii. 4).

[4] Exod. xxxi. 1, 2-4; Deut. ix. 16.

[5] Judg. xvii. 1-5.

[6] Judg. viii. 26, 27.

Israelites. For even supposing that the Hebrews were indebted to the Egyptians or to their neighbours for certain technical and artistic traditions, they must have lost them at a very early date.[1] The fame of the Judæan and of the Danite,[2] to whose industry were ascribed the first articles of sacred furniture and the sacerdotal ornaments executed during the Exodus; and again, the necessity David and Solomon found of employing Phœnician masters and workmen when they wished to build a palace and a temple at Jerusalem,[3] show how utterly incapable the Israelites were of working in wood, in stone, or in metal.

The plastic arts, more exacting than music, poetry or dancing, need for their prosperity certain political and social conditions of life quite incompatible with the habits of nomads. They need also the stimulus of riches, the protection of kings, and the sanction of religion. And the Hebrews had not yet all abandoned the ancestral tent; and the Hebrews, still poor, were governed from day to day by chosen chieftains whose power was bound up with the circumstances which had brought them to the front;[4] and the Hebrews imagined a Creator so infinitely pure, so infinitely spiritual, so infinitely above the gods of the neigh-

---

[1] Not a single work of art which could be attributed to an Israelite has been as yet discovered. See note C in Appendix.

[2] The Judæan was called Bezaleel, son of Uri, and the Danite, Oholiab, son of Ahisamach (Exod. xxxi. 2 to 4; xxxv. 30, &c.; xxxvi. to xxxix.).

[3] 2 Sam. v. 9, 11; 1 Kings v. 1; vii. 13, &c.; 1 Chron. xiv. 1.

[4] See below, p. 29, 30.

bouring peoples, that they would have feared to debase his worship by adoring him in a materialised form. The religion that tolerated the teraphim, those rude images of the lares and penates, which for that matter bore no sacred character, strictly forbade the representation of divinity or of living beings.

The Almighty had said—

"Thou shalt not make unto thee any graven image, nor the likeness of anything that is in heaven above, or that is in the earth beneath, or that is in the water under the earth. Thou shalt not bow down thyself unto them nor serve them. . . ." Then again: "Cursed be the man that maketh a graven or molten image, an abomination unto the Lord, the work of the hands of the craftsman, and setteth it up in secret. . . ."[1]

When it is remembered that tradition, faithful to the memories of the Exodus, also forbade the construction of religious buildings adorned with mouldings or with columns, that it did not allow the erection of altars on bases of any monumental character;[2] it will easily be understood that the arts had nothing much to expect from Heaven. Neither could they count on powerful earthly patrons; for the Judges and the heads of the tribes and of the different families, the priests and the prophets were bound by custom and by their simple tastes to look with

---

[1] Exod. xx. 4 and 23; cp. Lev. xxvi. 1; Deut. iv. 15-18; v. 8; xvi. 22; xxvii. 15; Judg. viii. 27, 33, 34; xvii. 4-6.

[2] See above, p. 20, n. 2.

disdain on earthly goods, and to scorn the refinements of material life.

"Every man is brutish and is without knowledge; every goldsmith is put to shame by his graven image; for his molten image is falsehood, and there is no breath in them."[1]

Jeremiah, when he pronounced this sentence some centuries later, Hezekiah, who threw down idols and destroyed the serpent Nehushtan,[2] were expressing in their anger the sentiments of the majority of the people and of the most noble representatives of its genius.

Finally, the injunction laid upon the Hebrews by the Philistines not to fashion, or even to repair, objects made of iron, greatly contributed to the ruin of every industry.

"Now there was no smith found throughout all the land of Israel; for the Philistines said, Lest the Hebrews make them swords or spears; but all the Israelites went down to the Philistines to sharpen every man his share, and his coulter and his axe and his mattock, when the edges of the shares and of the coulters and axes and of the mattocks were blunt."[3]

This strange prolongation of the half-barbaric condition of an eminently gifted nation, as well as its oppression by a number of insignificant peoples, was one of the consequences of its social disorganisation

[1] Jeremiah li. 17.
[2] 2 Kings xviii. 4.
[3] Sam. xiii. 19–22.

and of the rivalries thereby produced. Some have erroneously attributed it to racial characteristics. The protracted prosperity of Phœnicia, the greatness of Babylon, of Nineveh and of Carthage, as well as the splendour of the monarchy under David and Solomon, show how mistaken is this opinion. But although not ethnical in origin, the evil from which Israel was suffering was none the less deep-rooted and grave.

"In those days there was no king in Israel: every man did that which was right in his own eyes."[1]

This definition of the patriarchal system, which ends and summarises the Book of Judges, gives a fair idea of the state of political anarchy in which the people of God were content to live, and betrays the secret of their decline. Mention is certainly made of the rights of primogeniture,[2] of the subordination of

[1] Judg. xxi. 25. Cp. Judg. xvii. 6; xviii. 1-3.

[2] The firstborn was the first son of an Israelite by one of his wives (Gen. xxvii.; xlix. 3; Deut. xxi. 15-17). He had certain special rights recognised by custom; becoming at his father's death the head of the family, and inheriting two portions where his brothers received but one (Deut. xxi. 17). Daughters could only inherit when their fathers left no sons (Numb. xxvii. 8). Although the rights of the firstborn seemed absolute, yet there must have been sometimes, under certain conditions, a choice exercised as to who was to become chief of the family. In such a case precedents were found in celebrated examples taken from universally-accepted traditions. It was told how Jacob had acquired the birthright of Esau (Gen. xxv. 30-34; xxvii.); Joseph that of Reuben (1 Chron. v. 1, 2); Ephraim that of Manasseh (Gen. xli. 52, 61; xlviii. 13 20); Kohath that of Gershom, since Moses and Aaron were supposed to be descended from Kohath, second son of Levi (Exod. vi. 16, 18, 20; Numb. iii. 17, 27-32; 1 Chron. vi. 1, 2, 3, 49; xxiii. 6-13); Moses that of Aaron (Exod. vii. 7); Eleazar, son of Aaron, that of his two elder brothers (Exod. vi. 23; Lev. x. 1, 2, 6, 12;

children to the head of the household, of the heads of households to the head of the family or the race, of the heads of families to the heads of the tribes.[1] But besides the fact that the heads of the tribes had not survived the conquest,[2] the heads of families and of houses possessed no definite prerogatives. The authority of the patriarchs was of the same kind as the powers exercised by Arab *sheikhs* or Persian *naïbs*. They command and they are obeyed only within the limits fixed by ancient customs, and above all by the submission or the resistance of those whom they govern. Except for this rudimentary attempt at social organisation, the tribes acknowledged no authority, no kind of hierarchy, no bond.[3] There

---

Numb. iii. 2-4; 1 Chron. vi. 3; xxiv. 1, 2); and, starting from Eli, the descendants of Ithamar, fourth son of Aaron, that of the descendants of Eleazar (see note L in Appendix); finally, David, that of all his brothers. It was thus that Solomon could have been named as David's successor in preference to his brother Adonijah (1 Kings i. 5, 13, 17, 30; ii. 15).

[1] The tribes were divided into families or clans which like themselves bare the names of the original ancestors. It even seems as if each one possessed a species of standard, adorned with a characteristic emblem, around which they ranged themselves when marching or fighting. The families were sub-divided into houses (Numb. i. 2; Josh. vii. 14, 16 to 18). The houses, like the families, had chiefs or heads, of whom frequent mention is made (Exod. iv. 29; Numb. xi. 16, 24, 25; xiii. 5-17; xxv. 14; Deut. i. 13-15; xvi. 18; xxii. 15; xxv. 7; xxxiii. 5; Josh. xxi. 1; xxiv. 1; viii. 6, 14; 1 Sam. iv. 3; viii. 4; 2 Sam. v. 3, &c.).

[2] The heads of the tribes are mentioned in Deuteronomy (i. 15), and after that the Bible only speaks of the heads of the families or clans.

[3] Judg. xvii. 6; xviii. 1-31; xxi. 24. The tribes were even forbidden to intermarry, and maidens inheriting from their parents were not allowed to wed members of any tribe but their own. (Numb. xxxvi.)

were no governors, nor soldiers, nor officers, nor tax-collectors, no police to enforce respect for property, no legislators, no ordinary judges or notaries. Did any litigation arise, it was settled by the elders of the community assembled in council at the city gates,[1] and if their decision was appealed against, the two parties, after the establishment of the priesthood, put themselves in the hands of the priests and the Levites.[2] Business transactions, sales of property, were also completed at the gates of the city, the inhabitants acting as witnesses.[3] Such a system needed neither functionaries nor administrative machinery; but it weakened the Hebrews in face of better governed peoples, and exposed them to all kinds of oppression.

Meanwhile, the tribes were tearing one another to pieces, war and pillage were ravaging the heart of the country, Moab, Edom, Amalek, and Philistia were contending for the mastery over Israel.[4] Judah offered the most determined resistance against the assaults of the enemy, both internal and external; but was suffering from the common evil, and ran the risk of being involved in the general dissolution.

Now and then, when the hand of the stranger grew too heavy, those oppressed arose in revolt, chose a leader and united for a time [5] against the Amalekites,

---

[1] Deut. xvi. 18; xxv. 7, 8, 9; xxxiii. 5; Ruth ix 1.
[2] Deut. xvii. 8-13.
[3] Gen. xxiii. 3, &c.; Ruth iv.
[4] See above, pp. 6-11.
[5] Judg. x. 18.

the Canaanites, or the Philistines. In such a case the deputies of the tribes assembled sometimes in Shiloh, more often at Mizpeh, on the top of a high mountain in the land of Benjamin, and held their councils, protected by the military tribe.[1] The little town whose development had been checked by the want of space, became, for as long as the dictatorship lasted, the residence of the appointed leader and a kind of federal capital;[2] a capital for the time being which nevertheless recalled to mind the unity of the Hebrew race; while Shiloh, where the Ark of the Covenant was enshrined and the oracle of Jehovah consulted, was the religious metropolis and a place of annual pilgrimage.[3]

These elected magistrates, known in history under the inappropriate name of "Judges," and who bore the title of *Shophet*,[4] were above all, military commanders. There were no rules as to the nomination of a shophet; no particular position had to be occupied as a stepping stone to the exercise of authority.

[1] Mizpeh, the present Nebi-Samouil, was in point of fact situated very near Gibeah, the fortified capital of the Benjamites. Judges xx. 1, 3, xxi. 1, 5, 8; 1 Sam. vii. 5, 6, 7. Mizpeh in Benjamin must not be mistaken for Mizpeh in Gilead, which was the place of assembly for the tribes dwelling on the other side of the Jordan (Judg. xi. 11, 34).

[2] 1 Sam. vii. 6, 16.

[3] Joshua had carried the ark to Shiloh, from whence it was never moved except on certain rare occasions, until the day of its capture by the Philistines (Joshua xviii. 1, 9, 10, xix. 51, xxi. 2; Judg. xx. 18, xxi. 9, 19; 1 Sam. i., ii., iii.).

[4] The Carthaginians gave the same name to their magistrates, calling them *suffetes*. The "kings" of Edom did not inherit their office (Gen. xxxvi. 31, &c.); they were also *shophetim*.

THE JUDGES

Heads of families [1] and Nazarites,[2] a man of doubtful birth,[3] a priest,[4] a prophet,[5] and a woman, one after the other attained to the dictatorship. But whatever were their antecedents, one and all were bound to lead the people of God on to battle. Deborah herself was a valiant captain and a skilful general, a kind of Joan of Arc. At the battle of Megiddo, on that famous battlefield whose importance she had fore-

---

[1] Ehud was a Benjamite, chief of the warlike family of Gera (Judg. iii. 15). Gideon, Abimelech, Tola, the uncle of Abimelech, and doubtless Jair also, were all in the same position (Judg. vi. 34, viii. 29-31; x. 1, 3, 4).

[2] Samson and Samuel (Judg. xiii. 4, 5, 7; 1 Sam. i. 25-28, ii. 18, 19). Nowadays there are no more attempts to deny that Samuel was a historic personage. (See Noeldeke, "Hist. Litt. de l'ancien Testament, trad. Soury et Derembourg," p. 62; Renan, "Hist. du Peuple d'Israel," p. 348 and note 3; Maspero, "Histoire Ancienne," 4th edition, p. 308).

[3] Jephthah was certainly not the son of a legal wife. The neglect with which he was treated by his father, the words put into the mouth of his brothers, the unusual promises which he exacted from the deputies of Gilead before accepting the shophetate, would even lead one to suppose that he was the son of a prostitute (Judges xi.), did not the reply ascribed to the deputies seem to contradict this hypothesis (Judg. xi. 7, 8). (In the English version Jephthah is called the "son of a harlot." Translator's note.)

[4] 1 Sam. iv. 4, 18. Eli, however, was not a leader in the field, but more particularly a counsellor with regard to public affairs, and a *bonâ fide* judge in private disputes.

[5] 1 Sam. iii. 19-21; vii. 5, &c., 15, 16, 17; viii. 1, 2. Like Eli, Samuel was more of an administrator than a general (1 Sam. vii. 15-17; viii. 1, 2; xii. 1-4), but he was present on at least one occasion of battle with the Philistines (1 Sam. vii. 7-13). It was, besides, a strict duty of the religious chiefs to appear in the field of action, and following the example of Moses, to implore the Lord in favour of Israel (Exod. xvii. 9-12; Numb. xxxi. 6; Deut. xx. 1, 2). If Eli, prevented by his great age, were not present at the battle of Aphek, he at any rate had sent his sons in his stead.

seen, and during the campaign which resulted in the destruction of Jabin, King of Canaan, she commanded in person Ephraim, Manasseh, Benjamin, and Issachar, the flower of the army, and also, through her lieutenant Barak,[1] Naphtali and Zebulun.

When victorious, the shophet could speak as a master and punish those who were refractory,[2] but before the combat, and even when it was proclaimed, he had no other resource but that of persuasion. Those who were willing answered the call to arms.[3]

---

[1] Judg. iv. 8-10; v. 15. The Hebrew text gives, instead of Manasseh, the word Machir, which seems however to be intended for Manasseh. It is at any rate the version of the Vulgate adopted by Renan ("Hist. du Peuple d'Israel," vol. i., p. 314, n. 1), although he contradicts himself a little later on (p. 361). Long before Deborah, Miriam, sister of Moses and of Aaron, exercised a military command (Micah vi. 4). This admission of women to all kinds of employment is a necessity of nomad life, where constant danger makes it a law to neglect no source of strength. For this reason, women famous for their warlike courage are found in numbers among the Arabs. According to M. Barbier de Meynard, Amrah, daughter of Amir ; Hind, the daughter of Khouss Khansa ; Hind, daughter of Otbach ; Sedjah, the prophetess Moseilama, can all be quoted. I was intimately acquainted with the most powerful Sheikh of Mesopotamia, the Sheikh Mesel, whose mother had made war during the whole of her life. She had been the only general of her husband, Sheikh Djaber, and thanks to her intelligence, firmness, and courage, she had constituted for him a vice-royalty, subject at the same time to Persia and Turkey. It would, moreover, be an error to think of the women of the Arab tribes as condemned like the Persians and the Turks to a degraded domesticity. Dwelling without a rival in the tent of their husband, living with uncovered face, respected and listened to by all, courageous, sometimes cruel, their standard has been in no way lowered by the Koran, which is obeyed by the tribes more in the spirit than in the letter ; and they serve as living types of the Hebrew women in the days of the shophetim.

[2] Judg. viii. 15-17 ; xxi. 9-11.

[3] Judg. v. 2, 9.

THE JUDGES

Then, after all danger was averted, general, officers, and soldiers returned to their fields.[1] And from that day the shophet no doubt had a great reputation, was consulted on difficult points, and kept the tribes in the fear of Jehovah,[2] but he exercised no definite authority.[3] Joshua, after his brilliant victories, retired to Timnath-serah and busied himself with his domestic affairs, claiming no rights over the tribes.[4] Saul himself at first recognised in his royal functions only those of the general, and came back to the plough as soon as he had beaten the Ammonites.[5] The first shophetim were thus nothing but temporary chiefs, whose authority died with the peril that called it into being, and whose very unequal power never extended over the whole of the tribes.[6] Sometimes

---

[1] Judg. viii. 29.

[2] Judg. ii. 8–11, 15–19; viii. 33, &c.

[3] The proposal made by the Hebrews to Gideon to allow him to rule over them with exceptional powers during his lifetime, after his victories over the Midianites, and the reasons given by Gideon for not accepting (Judg. viii. 22–24), as well as the contrary stipulation of Jephthah that he should retain the functions of shophet until his death (Judg. xi. 9, 10) once he accepted the post, and the special title borne by him after his nomination (*ras* or *qasim*, *lit.* head or prince, Judg. xi. 6, 9, 11), show that the earlier shophetim gave up their post as soon as the war was over. But from the time of Jephthah, new tendencies began to show themselves. The Hebrews, who were inclining towards monarchy, had no longer the same repugnance for a lifelong magistracy. Eli judged Ephraim until his death; and Samuel would have remained in power had the tribes not decided to choose a king.

[4] Joshua xix. 50; xxiv. 30.

[5] 1 Sam. x. 26; xi. 5.

[6] Except Othniel (see above, p. 12, n. 1), who is moreover wrongly classed among the Judges, the Bible giving him the title of *môsia* Judg. iii. 9), "saviour" or "liberator," none of the shophetim seem to

there were long intervals between two consecutive shophetim;[1] sometimes one or two were in power together. Jephthah in Gilead, Eli and Samuel in Ephraim, Samson in the west, all seem to have been contemporaries, independent of each other and perhaps enemies.[2] Even in their attempts at organisation the Hebrews seemed to create nothing but confusion.

Alongside of the shophet, who spasmodically represented secular authority, there was growing up at Shiloh, under the protection of the Ark, and with the help of the ephod and its oracle,[3] an undisturbed and centralised power whose influence increased every day. This was the priesthood in the hands of the reputed descendants of Levi.[4] The Ephraimites, who counted Shiloh among their towns, had even appointed a chief priest of this sanctuary to a kind of life-long magistracy. They would, perhaps, have constituted a hereditary theocracy in favour of Eli and his descendants, if the crimes of his sons, the capture of the Ark by the Philistines at the fatal battle of Aphek, and the disasters of every nature which marked his shophetate had not furnished new grievances against the Levites.[5]

---

have ruled over Judah and Simeon. Deborah was the heroine of the north; Gideon was elected by the tribes on the other side of the Jordan; Samson by the Danites, &c.

[1] Judg. ii. 15-19; iii. 31; iv. 1, 2; x. 7; xiii. 1.
[2] Cp. Judg. x. 7 and xiii. 1; then xii. 4-6 and xv. 9-12.
[3] See notes K and L in Appendix.
[4] See notes A and L in Appendix.
[5] See below, p. 36, n. 1.

Then there came back into favour the prophets and the seers,[1] who had been supplanted by the priests. They multiplied and obtained such an empire over the souls of the people, that it was these ragged mendicants, these friends of the humble, who were able to take away the power from the shaking hands of the last judges, and transfer it to the kings. Where victorious captains, those predestined founders of monarchies, had failed, an inhabitant of the village of Ramatha, a simple prophet, was destined to succeed.

[1] See below, § vi. p. 99.

III

Decline of Israel under the last Judges

LONG before the accession of Saul and the passing triumph of Benjamin, the hope of dominating the other tribes had been entertained first by the children of Joseph and then by those of Levi.[1] The descendants of Joseph based their claims on the birthright assigned to their ancestor by very ancient traditions.[2] The men of Levi, guardians of the Ark, and privileged interpreters of the ephod, counted on their spiritual authority and influence over the souls of the people and dreamed of a theocracy. The first one to the rescue when Israel was threatened,

---

[1] Abimelech was a bona-fide king. This is in fact the title given to him by the Bible (Judg. ix. 6). During his reign taxes were collected, a standing army was established, and an attempt was made at administration (Judg. ix. 4, 28). He was succeeded by his uncle (Judg. x. 1 and 2). The shophetate was changing itself into monarchy. The sons of Eli in the priesthood, and the sons of Samuel who had been made judges by their father, were equally destined to rule; but their crimes prevented them from so doing (1 Sam. ii. 12-17, 28, &c.; iii. 11-14; viii. 1-3).

[2] See above p. 27, n. 2.

but living apart, disdainful of its brethren, Judah alone, did not seek for honours, but seemed to bide its time.[1]

And moreover, all attempts at founding a monarchy had miscarried. Whether for fear of future tyranny the nation shrank from confiding its destinies to one particular family or caste, or whether the sons of the Judges all made a point of turning the people against hereditary authority; at any rate, Moses, Joshua, Deborah, Gideon, Abimelech, Jephthah, Eli, Samuel, all of them, generals, priests or prophets, had disappeared without establishing a lasting kingdom or a government that could make itself respected. Fleeting triumphs were succeeded by long periods of bondage. Their neighbours were all their enemies and their masters. Yet in spite of everything, the Hebrews, obedient to the Divine Word, increased and multiplied. The flood streamed out across the ill-defined boundaries of the Land of Canaan lying open to the foreigner; the people of Jehovah poured themselves forth. The Israelites felt their strength when they thought of their numbers; but they realised their weakness when they remembered the victories of their feeble adversaries.

Then they compared their fatal liberty with the successful autocracy of their conquerors. They

---

[1] Othniel did not bear the title of shophet (Judg. iii. 9; see above p. 12, n. 1). As for the shophet Ibzan of Beth-lehem (Judg. xii. 8, &c.), it is fully recognised that he came from Beth-lehem in Zebulun and not from Beth-lehem in Judea. Commentators are agreed upon this point.

thought of the ravages among the tribes and the bloodshed caused by their inherited hatred of authority. They mourned over the sons they had lost to no avail in the never-ending wars; they wept for their daughters who filled the slave markets of the unbelievers. Their enemies had robbed them of everything; even the Ark of the Covenant, that pledge of divine protection, had fallen into their hands after the disaster of Aphek.[1] The Philistines, the Jebusites, the Aramæans and the Amalekites had all established military posts in the heart of the country;[2] and the Hebrews, deprived of their arms, were growing weaker day by day, and could see no end to their misfortunes.

Would not federation, with all its disadvantages, be better than dispersion and anarchy? Would not a centralised government offer conditions of happiness impossible under the patriarchal system, even though it had been amended by the shophets? The people, torn by suffering and anxiety, grew amazed and doubted their God, seeking everywhere for the secrets of strength and victory. They coveted the prosperity of the Philistines and Phœnicians, of the Assyrians and the Egyptians. They longed to grow rich in peace, to be the only masters of their children, of their flocks and of their crops; to have abundance for their families, and security for their tribes. And

---

[1] See below, p. 178.
[2] At Gibeah, for instance (1 Sam. x. 5; xiii. 3, 19, &c.). See above, pp. 6-11.

they began to dream of a sovereign who would pacify domestic dissensions, and who would place himself at their head and fight their battles. But then they called to mind their bitter experience of monarchy and of hereditary power, and saw before them a dark future of oppression. And they were haunted also by the dread of alienating their true king, their only master, Jehovah, the God of the patriarchs, the inspirer of Moses: they feared to excite his jealousy by raising up unto him a rival on earth.[1] Then again, it would be necessary to choose among the tribes one to supply the monarch, and it would never have been allowed to any one of them to rise high enough to dominate the others. The monarchy had become a necessity, and the Israelites were still struggling against their fate.

The apologue of the trees related by Jotham, when he wished to discredit Abimelech, son of Gideon,[2] and the diatribe of Samuel against royalty,[3] are echoes of this crisis. The people were groping about irresolute. On one hand were their most cherished traditions, on the other their most fervent desires; against their hatred of autocrats, was the necessity to live. They hesitated between kings and patriarchs, just as they "halted" between Jehovah and Baal.[4]

[1] 1 Sam. viii. 6, 7, 8; xii. 12, 13.
[2] Judg. ix. 7-21.
[3] 1 Sam. viii. 9, 11-17. See below, on the historical value of this piece, pp. 45, 46, 47, and note D in Appendix.
[4] 1 Kings xviii. 21.

The ox is kept in servitude by the yoke which utilises the violence of his strength for the ploughing of the field and the fertilisation of the fallow land. If his strength were ungoverned, it would become harmful. But the animal, trained into a beast of burden, suffers long tortures. In the same way, social laws, with the authority they assume over individual liberty, are a constraint upon mankind. And therefore man seeks to avoid their discipline, until adversity convinces him of their power for good. When he consents to adopt them, he has already recognised that public prosperity depends on certain strict rules which a nation must obey in order to exist. He submits to these laws in order to protect his native soil, the cradle of the fatherland, and above all, to establish an undisputable authority, capable of levelling all before it, of struggling against overweening ambitions, of preventing internal disputes and of destroying the ferments of dissolution. For the payment of a tithe levied on human wishes, instincts or passions, contributes to the strength of a state, just as a tax on material objects constitutes its riches. Woe to the country which refuses to recognise this moral obligation, or which even allows of murmurs against it. From the effects of a disastrous war it is possible to recover in time; but the end of social anarchy is death.

The need of a security necessary for prosperity and comfort led in the dark ages to the formation of families, of races, and of tribes, phases humanity passes through before dividing into nations. This necessity had stimulated the Hebrews into raising themselves out of a state of anarchy up to the patriarchal system and to the shophetate. But the time was approaching when, after a new crisis, and spurred on by their misfortunes, the sons of Jacob were to make new progress. They were now to evolve the idea of the common fatherland and to abandon their respect for brute force for loftier ideals of duty and honour, paving the way for the advent of Isaiah, of Hosea and of Micah; they were about to place their social organisation, and the victories they had won over their former savage state, under the safeguard of a throne.

From this point of view the genesis of the monarchy among the Israelites merits careful consideration. Its history furnishes an authentic document where one can follow in all its phases the evolution of human society from anarchy to royalty; and better still, it forms a living proof of the vanity of socialistic theories. It is the condemnation of those dreamers who, tired of a constraint sometimes heavy but always beneficial, attempt to overthrow the barriers erected round human passions by our forefathers, when, uniting their efforts, they strove to free themselves from the drawbacks of savage life and were struggling for a better state.

David, when he assembled the tribes under his authority, delivered them from slavery and raised them above the nations to whom they were subject; the schism sufficed to prepare their fall, and threw them back into bondage.

IV

Samuel—His Vocation—Accession of Saul—The Anointing of David

SAMUEL made his appearance in the course of the drama of conscience which was to decide the destinies of Israel. The extraordinary man who was to play the chief part belonged to the tribe of Ephraim, or according to the Chronicles, to the race of Kohath, a division of the tribe of Levi which had been settled for a long time in the land of Ephraim.[1] His mother, whose religious exaltation sometimes rose to the transports of prophecy, had been married for years and had remained childless. At last Heaven answered her prayers, and in an impulse of gratitude she dedicated her firstborn to its service. Elkanah, an ardent follower of Jehovah, made no objection to the wishes of his wife: the child was confided to the care of the priests at Shiloh.

[1] 1 Chron. vi. 1, 16, 19, 22-28; Josh. xxi. 5.

The parents of Samuel lived in Ramatha,[1] a village situated in the territory of Joseph, but lying quite near Gibeah, the fortress of the tribe of Benjamin. They were in such direct contact with the rivals of Judah, that it was only natural that they should sympathise with their views and teach their son to do the same.

The young Nazarite grew up in the neighbourhood of the Ark, in an atmosphere of piety that penetrated his child's nature and impregnated it all the more thoroughly owing to the fact that his origin and education predisposed him to mysticism. He made the acquaintance of the Israelite chiefs when they came every year to offer up a solemn sacrifice,[2] and greatly impressed them by his lofty wisdom, his piety, and his prophetic gifts. "And Samuel grew, and the Lord was with him, and did let none of his words fall to the ground."[3]

Later on, after the taking of the Ark and the startling death of Eli,[4] the seer retired to his native town, where he consecrated an altar. The priests, held responsible for so many evils, lost all their popularity, which was transferred to Samuel. His authority increased, and from Ramatha extended itself by degrees over the neighbouring tribes. If

---

[1] Ramah, or Ramathaim, of the Cufites, nowadays Er-Ram, lies one league to the north of Jerusalem (Robinson, *Researches*, i. p. 458; ii. p. 7, &c.).

[2] 1 Sam. xii. 1, 2-5.

[3] 1 Sam. iii. 19, 20.

[4] For the capture of the Ark, see pp. 146 and 184.

the scandalous conduct of his sons prevented him from establishing a hereditary form of government to the profit of his house, he was at any rate the only one powerful enough to give a master to Israel. And when the Hebrews, driven to extremity by the successes of the Philistines and by the aggravated oppression which forbade them to manufacture arms or even to possess them, resolved at last to unite, trusting to find in the monarchy a remedy for every evil, it was, in fact, to Samuel that they confided the task of choosing a king.

At first he tried to make them abandon their design. "The king will take your sons for his chariots and to be his horsemen; and they shall run before his chariots . . . and he will set some to plow his ground and to reap his harvest and to make his instruments of war. And he will take your daughters to be perfumers and to be cooks and to be bakers. He will take your fields, and your vineyards, and your olive yards, and give to his officers and to his servants. And he will take your menservants and your maidservants and your goodliest young men and your asses, and put them to his work. He will take the tenth of your flocks: and ye shall be his servants. And ye shall cry out in that day because of your king which ye shall have chosen you; and the Lord will not answer you in that day." [1]

But the mind of the tribes was made up. Their deputies replied to the seer that they persisted in their

[1] 1 Sam. viii. 11–19.

desires, that they wished for a master who would give them good government, and that they would never grow tired of the change.[1] Then Samuel retired to consult the Lord, and when he came back among the delegates of the people he requested them all to return to their homes, assuring them that they should soon have a monarch.

Although the contrary has been alleged, this scene and the interesting diatribe which with the parable of the trees [2] sums up the fear of Israel and its ancient grievances against royalty, have an air of great truth about them. It may be certain that they are not borrowed from the same source as the other parts of the same book, and that their form is of later date than the time of Samuel ; but at any rate, they seem to have a historical foundation. In his twofold capacity of priest and of prophet, Samuel dreaded a master fashioned on the model of the Kings of Egypt and of Syria. He feared that the prestige of his God would be injured by the competition of another power. Would not an autocrat crush a nation which held itself accountable to none but the Almighty ; would he not take advantage of the homage reserved for Jehovah and for his ministers, his only earthly representatives? To substitute a kingdom of this world for the sovereignty of Heaven would be an act of ingratitude, of impiety, of apostasy.[3]

---

[1] 1 Sam. viii. 11-19.
[2] Judg. ix. 8-15.
[3] See above, p. 38, n. 1.

There is no doubt that these misgivings, which were felt by all the Israelites, haunted a man so deeply religious. Samuel must have experienced some bitterness, too, at having to resign all authority, the exercise of which, however limited, is always so fascinating; and he must have felt a little hurt when he was asked to divest himself of it. During his magistracy he had gained some slight successes over the Philistines and had concluded an honourable peace with the Amorites. Would his successor be more fortunate? He expresses himself with such frankness on this point that one cannot doubt either the sincerity or the authenticity of the regrets which the Bible ascribes to him.[1]

It is even a question whether, wishing for a lasting work and distrustful of the versatile temperament of the Hebrews, the prophet did not try to provoke resistance. We give a warm reception only to gifts that have been long desired.

In any case his hesitation was but momentary. After having guarded against the caprices of the tribes, he pledged himself to the establishment of the monarchy and was anxious to find a sovereign as soon as possible. Whatever might have been his private

---

[1] 1 Sam. xii. 1, 2-5. From chap. viii. to chap. xviii. certain critics have made numerous reservations. Some verses are considered to be historical, others are supposed to have been changed or interpolated. I will point out the disputed passages in which I have preferred to approach more closely to the text. The reasons for such decisions will be found in the notes at the end of the book. On chap. viii. see note D.

sentiments and his caste prejudices, and in spite of his dreams of a theocracy for Israel and his objections to a temporal power, he did not wish to prolong the life of misery and oppression of his people, he did not wish to condemn them to destruction for want of a shepherd to lead them. He felt that the hand of God was no longer over the tribes, and that the time was at hand when they would be enslaved in their own inheritance, just as their ancestors had formerly been in Egypt. The hatchet was already striking at the roots: in a short time the tree would be in the flames.

A few months later Nahash, King of the Ammonites, laid siege to Jabesh in Gilead. The terrified inhabitants offered in vain to surrender on honourable terms. "On this condition will I make a covenant with you," said the monarch in answer to their supplications, "that all your right eyes be put out, and I will lay it for a reproach upon all Israel." [1]

On hearing this, the elders of Jabesh sent messenger after messenger to the tribes on the other side of the Jordan; and wherever they went, their tale moved the people to tears and lamentations. None, however, dared to affront the Ammonites, none cared to run the risk of a new defeat, to sacrifice themselves for the Gileadites, who had become almost strangers to the rest of Israel; and who only a little while ago, in the time

[1] 1 Sam. xi. 1 and 2.

of Jephthah, had defeated and massacred the men of Ephraim.[1]

But Samuel saw the greatness of the danger. The worshippers of Jehovah were doomed if their last bulwark were to be removed. Between the Philistines in the west and the Ammonites in possession of the eastern bank of the Jordan they would be crushed like corn between the millstones. At his instigation and with his aid,[2] one of the chiefs of the tribe of Benjamin, Saul, son of Kish, raised troops among the people, came down upon the enemy, and delivered Jabesh.

"When Saul stood among the people he was higher than any of the people from his shoulders and upward,"[3] . . . he was handsome, strong, and brave, . . . as gentle and confiding as a child. His forehead shone with a halo of triumph. He was the perfect type of the Israelite hero, the *gibbor*[4] predestined to rule. He belonged, moreover, to the military tribe, to that tribe of Benjamin which occupied among the Hebrews the same special position that Sparta held in Hellas. Dazzled by the glory of a victorious commander, who was his own discovery, the prophet was unable to distinguish between the qualities sufficing for a shophet and the virtues necessary for a sovereign. He named Saul as the elect of God,

---

[1] Judg. xii. 4, 5, 6.
[2] 1 Sam. xi. 7.
[3] 1 Sam. ix. 2; x. 23; xiii. 1.
[4] See below, p. 155, n. 3.

and magnanimously resigned all power. As might have been expected, his choice met with warm opposition among the rival tribes; but it was nevertheless ratified by a sort of plenary assembly.[1] And it is thus that Samuel, the determined adversary of the monarchy, the champion of theocratic government, consecrated the first king to reign over Israel.

The intentions of the prophet were pure, his conduct was generous; but nevertheless he made a mistake. In spite of a profound knowledge of the human heart acquired during his long period of administration, he fell into the error so common to men of intellect, who think they will be able to sway men of action when they take them as auxiliaries. He also, when he chose a successful captain, had counted on the gratitude of a simple and upright soul. He had hoped to keep Saul under his influence, to place the civil power in the religious guardianship of the prophets, and to preserve the supreme authority for his God. With this view, and in order to ensure at the same time for his disciple the efficient support of the different societies of prophets, he had made him a member of the community at Gilgal, of which he was the spiritual father,[2] and had initiated him into the practices of divination.

"Then God gave Saul another heart . . . and the spirit of God came mightily upon him and he

[1] 1 Sam. x. 26, 27; xi. 12, &c.
[2] See below, p. 71, p. 101, n. 1, and p. 102, n. 1.

prophesied. . . . And it came to pass, when all that knew him beforetime saw that, behold, he prophesied with the prophets, then the people said one to another, What is this that is come to the son of Kish? Is Saul also among the prophets? And one of the same place answered and said, But who is their father? (*i.e.*, are not their ancestors the same as those of Saul?) Therefore it became a proverb, Is Saul also among the prophets?"[1]

At first success smiled on the young monarch. But Saul, a member of the military tribe, and chosen as he was for his military virtues, could be and was but a simple soldier. Dazzled by the glory of his victorious sword, vain of the popularity which flourishes around a sceptre, and hoodwinked by his courtiers, he was already on the brink of the abyss into which he was to sink. He despised the counsels of his benefactor, went so far one day as to tear his mantle[2] in a fit of passion, and abandoned the ways of the Almighty. He was on the road to the most fatal despotism. The clear vision of Samuel perceived other symptoms of great gravity. Although his choice had been ratified by an assembly of the heads of the people, all the tribes had not acknowledged Saul; the number of the discontented was increasing, and the king, obstinate in his errors, took no trouble to win back the disaffected. The

[1] I Sam. x. 10, 11.
[2] I Sam. xv. 26–28. Cp. I Sam. xvi. 2. See below pp. 59, 60, 61, the passages concerning the war with the Amalekites.

experiment was only a partial success; if it were continued, it would fail altogether.

Samuel saw his mistake, and rather than allow the Hebrews to fall into a worse plight, he resolved to destroy an imperfect piece of work. From that moment he looked around for a successor to Saul. Thanks to the correspondence he had kept up with the priests and to his relations with the prophets who recognised him as their chief, he was able to sound every man in Israel and to acquire an accurate knowledge of the general state of feeling. He learned that the duration of the monarchy depended upon the tribe which should have the guardianship of the throne, and that the tribe of Judah, in spite of its exclusion from the communion of Israel, and in spite of internal rivalries and the common jealousy of its brethren, was the only one able to enforce obedience.

Such was the destiny of Samuel: to work loyally and of his own free will, against his own interests and well-known preferences. He had fought against the monarchy, and he had created it. He must have shared the sentiments of the rest of Israel with regard to Judah, since he had chosen the first king from among the adversaries of the southern tribe; and yet he was about to offer it the power.

Certain historians, surprised by these contradictions, have regarded Samuel as an enigma; others have taken them as pretexts for denying his opposition to the establishment of the monarchy[1] and

[1] See above, pp. 45 to 48.

afterwards to the government of Saul. Nevertheless, an ample explanation of his conduct lies in his ideal of duty, an ideal so lofty that he sacrificed for the salvation of the tribes the exercise of the shophetate, his personal sympathies, his race hatreds, his prejudices of family and of caste, even to the pride of his infallibility as a prophet. This selection of Judah, for that matter an entirely reasonable selection, is to the credit of the son of Elkanah and Hannah; but it also shows that the race of the fourth son of Jacob, whose continuous progress has been traced,[1] had attained to such power that it forced itself upon the choice of an enlightened and impartial Judge. The triumph of the South was the work of centuries, just as the establishment of the monarchy was the result of the irresistible progress of ideas. The germs of both existed in the seeds scattered over Israel. And the harmony was so complete between the position won by Judah and the aspirations of the Hebrews, that the descendants of Jesse were able to hold their own in spite of the race hatreds accumulated since the Conquest; and to remain in power as long as the monarchy lasted. The work of Samuel was to divine this harmony behind the thick veil which would have hidden it from an intelligence less clear-sighted, from a soul less loyal and true; just as the great act of his life was to sacrifice to its realisation his own power, preferences, and opinions.[2]

[1] See above, pp. 3 to 5 and 11 to 14.
[2] See notes D and E.

As soon as he had decided upon the tribe, the seer pushed his researches still further. Samuel was thus able to learn that in Bethlehem, a village close to his own home, a child was growing up who seemed predestined to fulfil his purpose. At an early age he used to keep his father's sheep, "and when there came a lion or a bear, and took a lamb out of the flock, he went out after him, and smote him, and delivered him out of his mouth." And in the long days passed among his flock in search of the scanty grass of the wilderness, he would compose songs that his skilled fingers accompanied on the cithara.[1] Nature had lavishly endowed him with all the graces of body and of soul. " He was ruddy and withal of a beautiful countenance, and goodly to look upon . . . prudent in speech and a comely person, and the Lord was with him. . . . He was but a youth and ruddy, and withal of a fair countenance." [2]

Poets they all were in Israel, for poetry, very different from the plastic arts, those fruits of civilisation, blossoms as soon as a soul is found to bear its seed, wherever Nature provides a fertile soil. And the birth of poetry is also that of its twin sister music, whose chords seize on the nerves and call forth answering vibrations—music, the universal medium of all living beings, the ancestor of speech, the mother tongue of languages, which out of cries of joy or pain

---

[1] 1 Sam. xvi. 18 ; xviii. 10; Amos vi. 5.
[2] 1 Sam. xvi. 12, 18 ; xvii. 42.

has raised itself to the supremest harmonies without losing its hold on the heartstrings.

The Hebrews were accustomed to compose songs on each remarkable or characteristic event that took place. They were chanted in chorus on the days of solemn feasting and were graven on the memories of generation after generation.[1] The pilgrimage to the land of Canaan, the sojourn in Egypt, the exodus, the return to the Promised Land, its conquest, its division among the tribes, were all thus celebrated. The young shepherd had inherited the treasure of a long line of forefathers, but if he equalled his predecessors in grace and in feeling, he surpassed them in brilliancy.[2] The genius which was to rise on Israel was already dawning.

These accounts thrilled the soul of the old man. He wished to see the youth, to assure himself that he was born a king, and to anoint him in the name of the eternal God. After that death would have no sting. He would have accomplished the work of his life.

Until the accession of Saul, the seer had made a custom of paying periodical visits to the tribes in the neighbourhood of Ramatha. Every year he went "in circuit to Beth-el and Gilgal and Mizpah; and he

---

[1] Writing was already known to the Hebrews, but its use was much restricted (Berger, "Histoire de l'Écriture dans l'Antiquité," p. 134; Renan, "Histoire du Peuple d'Israel," vol. i. p. 374. See note I in Appendix.

[2] The song of the Bow (2 Sam. i. 18, &c.) and the few remaining lines out of the elegy pronounced over the tomb of Abner (2 Sam. iii. 34) are ascribed to David. See note J in Appendix.

judged Israel in all those places."[1] Later on he had effaced himself before the young sovereign, fearful of giving offence to his new-born royalty.[2] From that time he had contented himself with offering certain advice to the king, and had appeared but seldom at court; then, feeling that his opinions were troublesome, and fearing perhaps for his life,[3] he had ceased to come at all, and had shown himself no more in public.[4] The disobedience of Saul and his fits of passion, the disasters which he dreaded, and the desire to see the son of Jesse without awakening jealous susceptibilities or provoking the anger of the monarch,[5] determined Samuel to quit his retreat once more and to start for Beth-lehem with the avowed intention of sacrificing to the Lord, and of calling Jesse to the sacrificial feast.

The appearance in their midst of the man of God caused great surprise among the elders of Benjamin. Samuel passed by Gibeah, the old acropolis of the Benjamites and now the royal city, skirted the heights crowned by Jerusalem,[6] gazed at its lofty walls which Saul had never been able to conquer though they arose before him as an insult and a reproach, and

[1] 1 Sam. vii. 15, 16, 17.
[2] 1 Sam. xvi. 4.
[3] 1 Sam. xv. 26-28; xvi. 2.
[4] 1 Sam. xv. 12, 34, 35.
[5] 1 Sam. xv. 26-28; xvi. 2.
[6] We do not know when the town of the Jebusites took the name out of which we have made Jerusalem; it must have been long before the reign of David (Renan, "Histoire du Peuple d'Israel," vol. i., p. 227).

went on his way to the south. He traversed a grey and stony plain dotted here and there with the melancholy verdure of olive trees and evergreens, and barred by the mountain of Hebron in the distant south; and came at last to the sombre dwellings of Beth-lehem, built on the summit of a rocky eminence.

When the news arrived of the prophet's approach the whole population ran out of the gates and crowded the dusty roads. After meeting him the people turned back towards the town and, followed by the barking of the yellow dogs and the *you-you* of the women remaining on the terraces, preceded by boys and girls bearing in their arms still smaller children, accompanied him to the house of Jesse, where he was going to seek shelter.

Samuel made no confidences to his host. He bade him purify himself and his sons and invited them to the sacrifice. The seven eldest made their appearance, handsome and vigorous, ready to fight against the enemies of the new-born fatherland.

" Hast thou no other children ? " asked the prophet.

" No others old enough to bear arms."

" I wish to know them all."

" What! wouldst thou see the youngest ? He is barely fifteen years old, he keeps the sheep, composes songs, plays on the cithara and excels in the handling of a sling—occupations and pleasures suited to his age and size."

" Send for him."

" He is far away in the desert with his flock."

"Send and fetch him, for we will not sit down till he come hither."

Messengers were sent after David. And in the evening when he presented himself in his shepherd's garb, still covered with the dust of his rapid journey, holding his staff in his hand, his loins girded with a sling, but with a flame of genius shining in his large eyes and the mark of the divine seal apparent in his sovereign beauty, Samuel hesitated no more. He had recognised the chosen of Jehovah.

Taking the horn of sacred oil, he drew the youth towards him and anointed the pure forehead that bent before him.

"David, thou shalt be king."[1]

---

[1] In spite of the discredit into which it has fallen, I have followed the sixteenth chapter of the First Book of Samuel more or less closely. The criticisms directed against it have not convinced me, and I persist in preferring the Biblical version to those which have been gratuitously substituted for it. The motives for my preference will be found in notes D, E, and G in Appendix, as well as the general reasons mentioned above in pages 45 to 48, 52 to 54, and below, p. 61 n. 3, p. 66 n. 1, &c.

V

David at the Court of Saul—His Flight—His First Successes
—David among the Philistines—Battle of Gilboa—Death
of Saul—The Witch of Endor

ONE after the other, Moab, Ammon, Edom, the kings of Sobah and of Philistia, had all been assailed by Saul, and from each campaign he had returned in triumph. In the last war, undertaken on the advice of Samuel, he had hewn in pieces the Amalekites—those inveterate enemies of Israel, those incorrigible plunderers [1] whom the Judges had doomed to destruction without ever having been powerful enough to chastise them.[2] Then he had cut down all the prisoners and had put the vanquished monarch to death. This execution, ordered by Saul against his will at the instance of the prophet, who inherited the

---

[1] 1 Sam. xv. 5, &c.; xiv. 48; xvi. 1; xxviii. 18. See on the Amalekites, Exod. xvii. 8-13; Numb. xiv. 43, 45; xxiv. 20; Deut. xxv. 17, &c.; Judg. vi. 3.

[2] It seems that among the few inscriptions graven on stones, there was anathema against the Amalekites. It will be also noted that it was against them that David directed his first blows. (See below, pp. 87 and 88.)

political traditions of his predecessors, had put an end to the campaign.[1]

And now the son of Kish reigned in peace at Gibeah, leading the simple life of the last Judges. In the morning, on leaving the harem, he would seat himself at the palace gate, surrounded by his servants and a few Benjamite guards.[2] He gave audience there to all comers, heard the news of the day, interrogated travellers, received the verbal reports of his officers, settled any disputes and dealt out justice.[3] Then, when the sun was low in the heavens, he would retire to the women's apartment. At each new moon he would give a banquet, where every officer had his appointed place; he himself sitting right against the wall for fear of assassins.[4] When he went out in public he was preceded by runners.[5] Such were his prerogatives and occupations in times of peace.

Saul, however, was growing restless. Ever since the defeat of the Amalekites he had not seen Samuel, whose observations and counsel he could no longer brook; and for want of a war to conduct, he was becoming a prey to indolence and lassitude, those maladies of Asiatic despots, and was oppressing his household with the heavy burden of his inaction. He

[1] See note E in Appendix.
[2] See below, p. 154, n. 1.
[3] Cp. 2 Sam. xv. 2 with 1 Sam. xxii. 17.
[4] 1 Sam. xx. 25. He was afraid of being attacked unawares from behind.
[5] 1 Sam. xxii. 17.

DAVID AT THE COURT OF SAUL

was growing subject to outbursts of passion, followed by long periods of prostration: the symptoms of a pathological condition whose development had been increased by his admission to the ranks of the prophets.[1] "Now the spirit of the Lord had departed from Saul, and an evil spirit from the Lord troubled him." His officers, who strove with all their means to find entertainment for him, came one day to the king "and said unto him, . . . Let our lord now command thy servants, which are before thee, to seek out a man who is a cunning player on the harp: and it shall come to pass, when the evil spirit from God is upon thee, that he shall play with his hand, and thou shalt be well." [2]

Then they heard, perhaps through Samuel, that a native of Beth-lehem, a young Judæan, was noted for his skill on the cithara, his poetic gifts, his beauty and his courage.[3] He was called David, and he belonged to a respectable family of the town. He was at once summoned before the monarch.

The Bible does not tell us the sentiments of the son of Jesse on the arrival of the royal emissaries. Did he see in this invitation the manifestation of the Divine will? Did he look upon his departure for

---

[1] See above, p. 51, n. 1, and below, pp. 107-110.

[2] It is a question here, not of the spirit of evil, but of a visitation of the Lord upon Saul (1 Sam. xvi. 14, 16, 23; xviii. 10; xix. 9, 10).

[3] This whole picture, though taken from chapter xvi. (see for the historical value of this chapter, note F in Appendix), breathes an inimitable air of candour and of truth. It also contains very precise details with regard to the nature of the evil from which Saul was suffering. (See below, chap. vi., p. 104.)

the court of Saul as a step towards the throne, or did he start for Gibeah all unconscious of his destiny? Whatever his thoughts were he obeyed the call, and set out driving before him an ass laden with bread, a leathern bottle of wine, and a kid, sent by Jesse to Saul, to predispose him in his son's favour. The offering was a modest one, and in harmony with the position of the sender, but the intention sufficed to make it welcome.

In Persia, that museum of Oriental traditions, the custom still exists of these presents from inferiors to superiors, from a humble servant to a powerful monarch. And whether it be a question of a basket of peaches, a bunch of grapes or a draught of fresh water—and whether destined for Darius, Xerxes, or Muzafer-ed-din Shah, the *pesh-kesh* is none the less well received.

"And David came to Saul, and stood before him: and he loved him greatly; and he became his armour-bearer. And Saul sent to Jesse, saying, Let David, I pray thee, stand before me, for he hath found favour in my sight. And it came to pass, when the evil spirit from God was upon Saul, that David took the harp and played with his hand: so Saul was refreshed, and was well, and the evil spirit departed from him."[1]

The office of harpist to the king was not of such an engrossing nature as to prevent its holder from sometimes leaving the palace. The paroxysms were still

[1] 1 Sam. xvi. 21, 22, 23.

infrequent, and the preparations for a war sufficed to ward off the attacks of the king's disease. On such occasions David would return to Bethlehem and resume his pastoral life, once more donning his shepherd's garb.

It is during one of these intervals, and about eight years after the coming of Samuel to Beth-lehem, that the Bible places the episode of Goliath.[1] The Philistines, encouraged by Saul's illness, had made a fresh incursion into the territory of Judah. The king, who had marched against them, took up a position on the slope of the vale of the Terebinth, opposite the enemy. Every morning a gigantic Philistine, heavily armed in the fashion of his country, used to come out of the ranks towards the army of the Israelites and defy their champions to overthrow him. And every morning he returned in triumph, for none were bold enough to take up the challenge.

For forty days the Hebrews had devoured their shame when David, according to the sacred annalist, arrived in the valley of the Terebinth. He was bringing bread for his elder brothers, who had started with the contingent from Judah; and ten cheeses which Jesse, always thoughtful, intended for his sons' officers. David was then twenty-three years old. Although he had never taken part in a battle, and

[1] It is thus, I fancy, that we should understand and fit in chapter xvii., which was no doubt derived from a source containing interesting details, not to be found anywhere else. In any case, the editor of the first Book of Samuel set about their interpolation in a very clumsy manner.

was without any experience of war, he expressed the desire to match himself against Goliath. To those who questioned him, or tried to turn him from his purpose, he spoke of his ambition to kill the uncircumcised Philistine, and thus avenge the army of Israel; but his secret resolution perhaps arose from other motives. Was it not said that the king would give his daughter to the conqueror of the giant? In many ways the Bible stories of the Old Testament bear a resemblance to fairy tales. They have the same naive charm and unexpectedness.

The result of the duel is well known. David, who had never worn armour, and who feared to try a new experiment in the face of such grave danger, would not accept the helmet of brass and the coat of mail offered him by the king.[1] He was an expert in the handling of a sling, and he needed all his agility in order to use one to effect and to ward off the thrusts of Goliath.

When the giant advanced, full of contempt for a weak and unarmed antagonist, David put his hand in a sort of purse hanging from his girdle, took out a flat and polished stone[2] and slung it with such

---

[1] It has been suggested that there is a contradiction between this fact and verse 18 of chap. xvi., which describes David as *gibbor*, "a mighty man of valour." But at that epoch the majority of the Israelites were unaccustomed to the use of defensive armour (1 Sam. xiii. 19–22); and then it is said elsewhere that David had acquired his reputation for courage in fighting with wild beasts. Although the two passages may be taken from texts of different origin, it is thus possible that they are not contradictory.

[2] 1 Sam. xvii. 40, 49; cp. 1 Sam. xxv. 29.

strength and aim that it smote Goliath between the eyes, pierced the forehead, and imbedded itself in the bones of the skull. The Philistine fell prone upon the earth, and his people, seized with panic, fled to Gath and Ekron.

In Susiana, where the sling is in general use, the marksmen, capable of repeating the exploit ascribed to the son of Jesse, are still numerous. Young or old, all men carry a sling, and like David, they look out for smooth pebbles, very flat and well polished, which cleave the air easily and strike on their edge like an axe. In itself, therefore, the episode is not improbable. It deals with the victory of a slinger over a man in heavy armour, with the superiority of well-aimed projectiles over weapons used at close quarters. It might perhaps be that the king, a very skilful slinger, had in after days received all the honours of a feat accomplished in concert with one of the comrades of his youth, Elhanan, son of Jaare-oregim of Beth-lehem. The Bible gives a glimpse of this association.[1] But there can be no possible doubt that the son of Jesse, while yet a youth, fought in the wars against the Philistines, that he was noted for his courage and admirable coolness, and that he took a decisive part in the final battle. This must be unreservedly admitted.

---

[1] 2 Sam. xxi. 19. The tale has certainly been dramatised and embellished; but the chief objection brought against it has not perhaps so much force as is generally thought. (See note G in Appendix.)

On the other hand, the majority of commentators have thought they found such grave contradictions in the chapters dealing with the youth of David that the Vatican Manuscript has endeavoured to solve them by altogether suppressing verse 55 in chapter xvii. and verse 5 in chapter xviii., which seem in flagrant opposition to chapter xvi., if the text be only considered from a grammatical point of view, without taking into account the temperament of Saul.

In chapter xvii. the Bible says that after the flight of the Philistines the king called David and inquired his name, his family, and his origin. The monarch, according to this, did not recognise the harpist who in chapter xvi. is represented as one of his favourites. This would lead one to deny all historical value to chapter xvii. No doubt the fusion of the different texts from which the Books of Samuel were compiled is nowhere else so evident; nevertheless, the above would be too formal a conclusion to arrive at. Saul was a neurotic subject, a prey to fits of *demoniac mania*, and possessed with the delirium of persecution.[1] With the whim of a sick despot, envious and jealous of a triumph in which he had had no share, might he not have feigned ignorance of the conqueror of Goliath, even though he had offered him arms before the combat; might he not have wished to subject him to this childish vexation? Far from

[1] Saul's illness and its true nature will be treated in the following chapter.

being anomalous, would not such conduct be the consequence of his morbid condition, already indicated by his rage on hearing of the siege of Jabesh in Gilead, by the terror which he inspired even in Samuel and by his periods of possession;[1] would it not be a regular symptom, characteristic of coming attacks, the first manifestation of the unnatural hatred he was to conceive for David? The remainder of the narrative gives a certain air of probability to this hypothesis, and changes the so-called contradictions into an evidence of authenticity.

Among the qualities with which Heaven had so lavishly endowed him, David had received the precious gift of winning and retaining affection. He was full of personal charm, one of those rare beings who fascinate the multitude, who inspire devotion just as others inspire hatred, and who are obeyed more through love than fear. He had become the friend of Jonathan, the eldest son of the king; the servants and officers of the palace made much of him, and when they saw him advance, so young and handsome, holding in his hand the head of the gigantic Philistine, his shoulders laden with *spolia opima*, the women and the young girls forgot themselves so far as to sing—

> "Saul hath slain his thousands;
> David his tens of thousands."

The success of David, his great popularity, this

[1] 1 Sam. xi. 6 and 7; xvi. 1, 2 and 3; xvi. 14, &c.; xviii. 10; xix. 9, 10, 23.

enthusiasm, these cries of gratitude, all found a terrible echo in the diseased mind of Saul. The resentment that he had felt on witnessing the fall of Goliath, now took large proportions, and he began to hate his former favourite as much as he had once loved him. His one idea was to rid himself of this youth who robbed him of his glory, and from that day forward he cast an evil eye on David, and could scarcely contain himself when David played to him day by day. And one day " Saul had his spear in his hand, and he cast the spear; for he said, I will smite David even unto the wall." But the blow was badly aimed by a hand trembling with anger, the spear glanced aside, and David fled. After having twice tried to kill him, the monarch gave him the command of a thousand men, then that of his guards, the *râcim*, and sent him to fight against the Philistines in the hope that he might come to his death during an engagement. His desires were disappointed. The son of Jesse escaped from every snare, and his influence over the tribes was increased by the fact of his always marching at their head to bring them back each time in triumph. That was not the aim of Saul. In order to expose him to fresh risks he promised David to choose him for a son-in-law, pressing him to earn this signal mark of favour at the cost of further exploits. For a time he seemed to be softened, but in his festering heart there was only room for rage. One day he even attempted to chastise his favourite son Jonathan, and to smite him with his spear because he tried to speak in defence of David!

Meanwhile the time arrived for the marriage of Merab, the oldest of the princesses. Forgetful of all his promises to the son of Jesse, the king united her to Adriel, one of his officers. The conqueror of Goliath would never have submitted to this supreme humiliation, and to his life of daily peril, had not the friendship which he inspired in all taken a more tender form in the heart of the second daughter of Saul. Michal was fascinated by the handsome poet, the celebrated captain; and he, full of glory, intoxicated with this first love, agreed to every test to prove himself worthy of her. He was barely twenty-four years old!

Saul made a pretence of yielding to his daughter's wishes, but he would only allow the marriage on one condition, both strange and terrible. David accepted it, and paid the required price for his betrothed.[1] Once again the hopes of the monarch were disappointed; death refused to come to his aid. He gave way at last, but without abating his anger; and had it not been for the intervention of Jonathan he would have tried to kill his son-in-law on the very day of the wedding. In any case, the attempt was only put off for a time.

Michal, like all the wives and daughters of chiefs,

[1] In order to rid himself of David Saul employs the same means as are later on adopted by the latter when he wishes to compass the death of Uriah. (Cp. 1 Sam. xviii. 17 with 2 Sam. xi. 14-16. See below, pp. 217-219.)

inhabited the first floor, the aliâh, corresponding to the *bālā-khaneh* of Persian dwellings.[1] One night she was informed of the orders given by the king. David was to be seized before daybreak; the ground floor was already invaded by her father's guards. In all haste she "let him down through the window," took one of the wooden teraphim which were found in numbers in every Hebrew household, and laid it in the empty bed. When Saul's men appeared she pointed to the idol, and pretending that her husband was sick, refused to disturb him, thus giving him time to make good his retreat.

The son of Jesse took refuge with Samuel, his adviser and spiritual master. The seer, who was stricken in years, was anxious to make sure of future protectors for his disciple. He took him to Naioth in Ramah, to one of those communities of prophets placed under his direction, and without any doubt made him a member of the society. This passage is of great importance. It explains how David, at least once in his life, came to abandon himself to a transport whose violence and exterior characters resembled those of the sacred ecstasy;[2] and it shows the importance of the prophetical brotherhoods, since it was necessary to belong to them in order to entertain any hope of ever coming into power. Samuel, Saul, and David are striking examples of this fact.

[1] See above, p. 18, note 1.
[2] See below, pp. 189-193.

FLIGHT OF DAVID—HIS FIRST SUCCESSES 71

In spite of the sanctity of the place and the respect with which the interpreters of Jehovah were looked upon by the Hebrews, Saul, who had discovered the refuge of his son-in-law, sent archers and servants and officers of his household, one after the other, to Naioth, with the strict orders to bring him back dead or alive. And three times his messengers, forgetful of their mission, braving the anger of the king, were seized with the spirit of God, "and when they saw the company of the prophets prophesying, and Samuel standing as head over them, they also prophesied."[1] Saul, who wished at all costs to get David into his power, set out himself to accomplish the arrest, but before reaching Naioth "the spirit of God came upon him also, and he went on, and prophesied, until he came to Naioth in Ramah. And he also stripped off his clothes, and he also prophesied before Samuel, and lay down naked all that day and all that night," in a state of complete prostration.

"What!" cried his officers once more, when they saw their master beside himself, a prey to the delirium of prophesy. "Is Saul also among the prophets?"[2]

---

[1] 1 Sam. xix. 20.

[2] 1 Sam. x. 11, xix. 24. The repetition of this saying has been thought by some to prove that the two verses in which it is given have been taken from different sources. In this case, such is not my opinion. It is a question here of a saying which must have often been repeated. At the most, it would only be another proof of the harmony and of the historical value of these two sources. See below, p. 108, &c.

David, who had been a witness of this strange scene, and whose life was at stake, did not content himself with repeating the words. He made inquiries as to the intentions of Saul. The king, each day more violent, had resolved to kill him with his own hand. Any shelter in the tribes of Joseph and of Benjamin would be unsafe. Out of patience and irritated by such ingratitude, he fled away out of his enemy's reach. He went first to Nob, the home of Ahimelech [1] the priest, great-grandson of Eli, whom he wished to interest in his cause. After the capture of the ark Shiloh had declined in importance, and the tabernacle, the remains of the sacred furniture and the ephod used for divination, [2] had been transported by the priests to Nob. David arrived there, defenceless and famished. He obtained from Ahimelech some loaves of shewbread, [3] the armour of Goliath which he had consecrated in the tabernacle after his victory, [4] and a consultation of the ephod on his behalf, and then set out for the court of Achish, King of Gath. His reception there was not at all satisfactory, and we find him a short time

---

[1] For the priests see note L in Appendix.

[2] For the ephod see note K in Appendix.

[3] The loaves of shewbread were spread upon a table before the Lord, in imitation of one of the essential practices of the Egyptian religion. These loaves were made of unleavened bread. Thus it seemed that they must be purer than ordinary bread (1 Sam. xxi., Hosea ix. 4), and could only be touched or eaten by those who were ceremonially pure.

[4] The Bible tells us that the cohen gave into the hands of David the selfsame sword of Goliath which he had consecrated after his victory. (See end of note G in Appendix.)

afterwards hiding in the cave of Adullam, east of Beth-lehem, in the territory of Judah.[1] The sojourn in a country where his life was in danger, made it incumbent upon him to take defensive measures.

It is easy for us to see that Saul was not responsible for his actions. But David did not possess this key to the king's conduct, and even if he afterwards guessed at the truth, he would none the less have taken precautions against the royal anger. A mad dog is avoided or even stoned, although disease is an excuse for its fury. The fugitive therefore called his brothers and other relatives to his side, swelled their numbers with discontented persons and adventurers who were attracted by his fame, and was soon at the head of about four hundred men. He was becoming for Saul a source of uneasiness, if not of actual danger. The religious section, under the influence of Samuel and hostile to Saul, understood this so well that they sent Gad to make an alliance with him and to invite him to occupy the forest of Hereth, which would bring him nearer to his native town of Beth-lehem, where he had many partisans. This intervention of the prophets shows the tenacity and the perseverance of Samuel in his plans to overthrow Saul and to prepare for the accession of the son of Jesse. It shows also that David, from this moment, was aware of his lofty destinies.

Saul's answer to the action of the prophet Gad was an order for the death of Ahimelech, a completely

[1] For Adullam see below, p. 145 n. 2.

innocent man, and a general massacre of his acolytes, of their families, and even of their flocks. He alleged that the cohen was a party to the rebellion, that he had furnished the fugitive with bread and arms, and had consulted the ephod at his request. Abiathar, one of the sons of Ahimelech, was the only one who escaped from the carnage. He had but one refuge— David's encampment in the forest of Hereth—he hastened there at once, taking with him the prophetic ephod.

The king, blind in his rage, had hoped to terrify his enemies and to discourage their secret adherents, but he had not understood that by massacring the descendants of Eli he would drive the priests over to the enemy and thus deprive himself of the only force that could counteract the influence of the prophets, which they were employing on behalf of the disciple of Samuel. The course of events was quite different from what he had expected. The cohen Abiathar not only transferred from Saul to David all the moral authority of the head of the clergy and the powerful aid of the ephod, but he became the auxiliary of Samuel just at the right moment, purifying a heterogeneous troop by his presence and justifying the recourse to arms.

Those historians whose philosophical tendencies lead them to combat Christianity do not condemn the conduct of Saul and his mad thirst for blood; they defend his actions or deny them, and reserve all their severity for the reputed ancestor of Jesus. If they

FLIGHT OF DAVID—HIS FIRST SUCCESSES 75

are to be believed, David at this period of his life was a good-for-nothing, a rogue, a bandit worthy of the gallows, and as a climax, a creature of the priests! [1] Later on they will accuse him of duplicity, of murder, and of treason. This is unjust. [2]

The thirteenth century A.D. was as wicked and fruitful in crime as any epoch in the world's history. Brigands above, brigands below, brigands in the castle, brigands on the roads. St. Louis, on the eve of the Sixth Crusade, opened the gates of the prisons in order to increase his army; and the recruits, assured of the remission of all their crimes, both past and future, spread themselves out like a savage horde, sacking, plundering, ravishing, and murdering under the protection of the holy emblem attached to their shoulder. Such were their excesses that the Pope demanded a preliminary crusade against the new army of Christ. Is St. Louis to be classed among these strange crusaders? and are the crimes which were the bitter fruit of those troublous times to be condemned with the same rigour as if they had been committed in our own times?

It is the same thing with these Arab tribes, the glory and the honour of the desert. Try to make the nomads of Mesopotamia or of the Hedjaz understand that man has another mission upon earth than that of making war from his birth to his death, of plundering caravans, and of killing their defenders.

[1] Renan, "Histoire du peuple d'Israel," pp. 334, 437, 450, and 416.
[2] See below, pp. 93, 98, 120; notes 1, 4, 1.

Try to teach them that buffaloes, horses, and sheep are not exclusively the property of the strong—that wheat and barley do not spring up ready threshed and winnowed, that they do not grow in sacks on the backs of camels, and that they are not to be reaped at the point of a lance or of a yataghan—it would be labour lost. This only shows that a code of morality is not always drawn up according to the same standard, and that men should be judged not only from one absolute and unvarying point of view, but also after taking into consideration the surroundings among which their lives have been passed. The responsibility of a contemporary of Saul is quite different from that of the Hebrews living after the great prophets, whose mission it was to educate the conscience of the people.

In any case, these reservations only concern the followers of David; the son of Jesse stands in no need of them. He is as far above reproach as is St. Louis. What is, in point of fact, the reply of history and science to the accusations levelled against his memory? Ever since the day when the kingdom was saved by David, he has waged incessant war against the enemies of Israel, always returning in triumph, and as a reward for his services, as a recompense for all the risks he has run, Saul tries to smite him with a spear, commands his death, and forces him to quit a wife whom he loves deeply and whose love is his. David flies from the royal assassin, but the king pursues him with such hatred that, for want of being able to reach him, he strikes at the priests of Nob, at women and innocent children and the cohen of Jehovah, found guilty of having given bread to the son-in-law of the king,[1] of having lent a weapon to the conqueror of the Philistines. And yet the fugitive has committed neither crime nor sin, unless it be a sin to offend a diseased mind, or a crime to take precautions against murder by establishing a guard of relations, friends, and a few soldiers. The soldiers were no saints; in such a case it is not the sober and contented people who offer their services; recruits are rather found among the ranks of the adventurous, the bold, the disinherited. David could not possibly have commanded a picked crew: on that point there can be no dispute. But is he himself to be condemned on account of the moral standard of his followers? Has he ever pillaged Israel? Has he ever engaged in civil war or fomented it? The temptation must have seemed irresistible, the companions whom he tolerated but whom he had not chosen must have urged him on to such a course. There was a famished band to feed, the rapacity of his men to satisfy. Nevertheless, instead of yielding to treacherous counsels, he resists the temptation to revenge, and, far from sinking under difficulties apparently insurmountable, he profits by Saul's crime

[1] That is the plea urged by Ahimelech in his defence. "And who among all thy servants is so faithful as David, which is the king's son-in-law, and is taken into thy council, and is honourable in thine house?" (1 Sam. xxii. 14.)

to cultivate the friendship of the priests ; he exhorts and disciplines his soldiers, he holds out to them but one object, the glory of Israel, he names to them but one enemy, the enemy of the sons of Jacob and Jehovah. Such is his prudence, such is his influence, that each expedition against the nomads is a fresh success for the monarchy whose servant and supporter he still remains. And this wise captain was not yet twenty-five years old, and this able leader, except for Samuel who initiated him and mapped out his career, had only known shepherds and soldiers all his life. In what way could his detractors have improved on his conduct had fate thrown them among such surroundings, had circumstances involved them in similar events, bringing them face to face with a madman bent upon their destruction?

Even if Saul had not heaped insults upon David, any unprejudiced mind would acquit the latter of blame in his behaviour towards the king. Saul, who only reigned by the grace of Jehovah, was abandoned by the priests and the prophets, the interpreters of the Divine will, who had been the very ones to bring him into power. Was this not a proof that the Lord, displeased with his representative, had deprived him of all lawful authority and would one day confide it to the house of Jesse? And again, if it were necessary to say more in his defence, it should be remembered that David belonged to the tribe of Judah, and that his whole being must have quivered with anger when he bowed to the authority of the Benjamite chieftain, when he bent before a sceptre held by one of those children of Gibeah whose fathers had been punished by his ancestors for their crimes.[1]

In any case, the son of Jesse, in obeying the inspirations of his generous heart, acted like a consummate politician. One hasty step, one act of violence, would have compromised for ever his dawning fortunes; whereas his deep wisdom, as much as his courage, daily gained for him new partisans. So true is it that the highest skill of all is that inspired by justice and by duty.

David had succeeded in arousing so much confidence that the towns of Judah, when threatened by the enemy, preferred to appeal to his valour, rather than beg the aid of the king. One day he was informed that the Philistines had crossed into Judah, that they had attacked Keilah, and had pillaged the threshing-floors of the country.[2] He would have marched at once against the invaders had it not been for his men, who feared to meet such formidable adversaries. Then he consulted the ephod, which was kept in the camp by the cohen Abiathar. The ephod was the mouthpiece of Jehovah and David knew that the people's faith in it was boundless. Twice running, the divine oracle advised the expedition. Nothing remained but to obey. The besiegers were hewn in pieces and the Israelites entered the

[1] See above, p. 12, n. 2.
[2] 1 Sam. xxiii. 1. Keilah is named as a town ascribed to Judah, in the geographical indications given in the Book of Joshua (Josh. xv. 44).

re-conquered city in triumph. After having succoured Keilah, the victors had remained there, only too glad to exchange the encampment in the forest of Hereth for the more comfortable houses and gardens. But David felt that in settling himself in a fortress, he ran the risk of being blocked up in it by Saul. Perhaps he feared that a life of ease would have an enervating effect upon his little army—perhaps he was afraid of taking up the attitude of a sovereign.

The woods and the mountains are the common refuge of wild beasts and of the disinherited. He determined to return to his wild retreat; and to overcome all resistance, he once again had recourse to the ephod.

Saul, who had remained unmoved by the siege of Keilah, chose this moment for the assembly of a large army to be employed in the pursuit of his former favourite. Thanks to the forced connivance of the inhabitants, his measures were so well taken that David himself despaired of escape. The Philistines were his unconscious saviours. Hearing that the royal army had started for the south, they promptly made a raid upon the land of Benjamin. The monarch was obliged to abandon the pursuit, but no sooner was he free from anxiety on the score of the Philistines, than he took it up again. He was resolved to seek out David on the highest hill-tops— even "upon the rocks of the wild goats."[1] He came

[1] 1 Sam. xxiv. 3.

FLIGHT OF DAVID—HIS FIRST SUCCESSES

up to him on the heights of En-geddi, not far from the Dead Sea.

"And he came to the sheepcotes by the way, where was a cave, and Saul went in to cover his feet. Now David and his men were abiding in the innermost parts of the cave. And the men of David said unto him, Behold the day of which the Lord said unto thee, Behold, I will deliver thine enemy into thine hand, and thou shalt do to him as it shall seem good unto thee. Then David arose and cut off the skirt of Saul's robe privily. And it came to pass afterward, that David's heart smote him, because he had cut off Saul's skirt,[1] and he said unto his men, The Lord forbid that I should do this thing unto my Lord, the Lord's anointed, to put forth my hand against him, seeing he is the Lord's anointed. So David checked his men with these words, and suffered them not to rise against Saul."[2]

The details of this episode are doubtless not all historic, especially as there is another version which gives different ones.[3] But at any rate we know that David, when hunted down by the royal troops, had the chance of ridding himself of his persecutor, and that he chose to spare him. This trait of generosity,

---

[1] It will be seen later on that David, ever since his first campaign, had felt that as he was destined by Heaven for the crown, he was bound to respect the magistracy to which he aspired.

[2] 1 Sam. xxiv. 1–7.

[3] 1 Sam. xxvi. Comp. xxv. 5, &c. As in the episode of the fight between David and Goliath, the primitive annalists to whom the editor of the Books of Samuel had recourse, had preserved the web of the story and had woven into it certain dramatic details.

so contrary to the customs of the period and even to the spirit of the Old Testament, bears in itself sure proofs of authenticity. It could never have been invented at that time and in that atmosphere where the greatest heroes, following the example of Jehovah, sought rather for revenge than for justice tempered with mercy. To Christianity belongs the glory of having made a law of the forgiveness of injuries. But David had already a glimmering of this sublime form of charity. He felt that vengeance degrades the soul that thirsts for it and soils the hands that wreak it; he understood that God has His own times and ways for meting out justice.[1] And then he had faith, not the narrow and sterile faith that leads to fatalism, but the faith, deep and fruitful, of the prophets of Israel.[2] And as he believed firmly in Jehovah and in the promises of Samuel, he felt no inclination to stain his hands with the blood of his predecessor in order to seize a crown which was his predestined inheritance. Perhaps he also feared to come into power by violent means. "They that take the sword shall perish with the sword" was an ancient saying in Israel well founded on the tragic history of the surrounding monarchies.

In the meantime, Samuel died. The son of Jesse could not join the immense procession which must have followed the prophet to his grave; but in the

---

[1] See the episode of Shimei (1 Sam. xvi. 5-12), and below, pp. 88, 119, 120, 124, 252.

[2] See below, pp. 98, 99, 176, 177, 178, and note H in Appendix.

depths of his retreat, he must have shed some bitter tears. Samuel was not only a venerated teacher, a perfect model of piety, of virtue and of faith; he was also an invaluable support. As long as his protector lived, David found helpers, and sometimes friends, among the men of Judah whenever his adventurous life led him amongst them.[1] But no sooner was the seer dead, than their attitude began to change. The prop was broken, and they were ready to trample on the fallen plant; David soon had a proof of this.

In agricultural countries, the gathering of the fruits of the earth which sum up the labour and hopes of a year, has always been an occasion for rejoicings. These feasts, which, according to the country, are celebrated at the harvest, at the vintage, or at the olive crop, are a rest between two periods, the one at its end, the other at its beginning; they are a relaxation for the body and for the mind, a short holiday before the commencement of a fresh piece of work. They are also an encouragement, a thanksgiving from the master to the servants. Among the Hebrews, where shepherds were so numerous and where the prosperity of the country largely depended upon the quality and abundance of the wool, one of these agricultural festivals took place at the sheep-shearing.[2]

---

[1] I Sam. xxiii. end o v. 23.

[2] I Sam. xxv. The feast of the sheep-shearing is mentioned again in the Second Book of Samuel (xiii. 24.) The other periods solemnised were the Passover, the Feast of Weeks, and the Feast of Tabernacles.

Now shortly after the death of Samuel, Nabal, a very rich man belonging to the tribe of Judah and to the race of Caleb, and who pastured three thousand sheep in the forest of Maon, gathered together his shepherds in the carmel [1] of Judah and set about the shearing of his immense flocks. The son of Jesse, whose little band formed a sort of gendarmerie and protected the tribes against inroads of the Arabs or the Philistines, was accustomed to receive on such occasions a present of flour and of sheep. Until now, everybody had hastened to pay this contribution—a very light one in comparison with the services rendered. Nabal refused it in the rudest terms. David recognised that his credit would be for ever compromised if he did not exact payment. He chose two hundred men, left as many to guard the baggage, and marched straight on the carmel. But Abigail, the favourite wife of Nabal, saw the danger to which the imprudence of her husband had exposed them. Before help could arrive, their goods would be pillaged—their flocks dispersed—their servants killed. Would they themselves escape the massacre? Perhaps in her woman's heart she pitied the misfortunes of the young hero whose beauty, courage, and poetic gifts all men joined in praising.

She hastened to load some asses with two hundred

The two former corresponded to the sowing of the crops and the end of the harvest ; the latter, to the vintage (Lev. xxiii. 19–14 ; Exod. xxiii. 15, 16 ; Deut. xvi. 13).

[1] Carmel signifies garden, a place planted with trees. The carme of Judah is often mentioned (1 Sam. xv. 12 ; xxv. 2, 7).

loaves, two skins of wine, and five sheep ready dressed, five measures of parched corn, a hundred clusters of raisins, and two hundred cakes of figs,[1] and sent them in secret to David. She herself followed close in their train. Seated on a white ass, her veil wrapped round her, attended by a few faithful servants, she hastened along a mountain-path which had been worn in the steep rocks by the streams of winter. David, at the head of his men, was coming down by the same way. At the foot of the carmel, in an abrupt bend of the road, they met face to face. "And when Abigail saw David, she hasted, and lighted off her ass, and fell before David on her face, and bowed herself to the ground. And she fell at his feet, and said . . .

"My lord, as the Lord liveth, and as thy soul liveth, may the Lord withhold thee from blood-guiltiness and from avenging thyself with thine own hand. . . . Forgive, I pray thee, the trespass of thine handmaid: for the Lord will certainly make my lord a sure house, because my lord fighteth the battles of the Lord; and evil shall not be found in thee all thy days. And though man may be risen up to pursue thee, and to seek thy soul, yet the soul of my lord shall be in the bundle of life with the Lord thy God; and the souls of thine enemies, them shall he sling out, as from the hollow of a sling[2] . . . And when

[1] This enumeration is interesting on account of its giving valuable information with regard to the customary food of the Hebrews.
[2] A curious allusion to the manœuvres of slingers. See above, p. 64.

the Lord shall have dealt well with my lord, then remember thine handmaid."

Abigail was young and beautiful; her words, full of subtle flattery, were pleasing to David, and echoed hopes that he had never expressed so openly; she obtained the mercy that she craved.

"Blessed be the Lord, the God of Israel, which sent thee this day to meet me . . . and blessed be thou, which hast kept me this day from bloodguiltiness, and from avenging myself with mine own hand. . . . Go up in peace to thine house; see I have hearkened to thy voice, and have accepted thy person. I will spare the house of Nabal."

Heaven showed less clemency. In the course of the interminable festivities held to celebrate the sheep-shearing, Nabal was struck with apoplexy, and "became as a stone." Ten days later he was dead.

David, who had won Michal by exposing himself to the greatest dangers, was annoyed at her never having tried to join him. Perhaps she was afraid of sharing his adventurous life—perhaps she had forgotten all her former feelings for the outlaw. Jonathan, Michal's brother, whose love for David never failed, was consulted, and gave him no hope of ever seeing her again. On the other hand, Abigail was beautiful; the son of Jesse knew that she was accustomed to an active life, and the step she had taken proved her courage and wisdom. He asked for her in marriage and obtained her hand. Shortly afterwards he gave her for a companion a woman of

Jezreel named Ahinoam, and in accordance with the patriarchal system, they both became his wives. Saul, on his side, had given Michal to one of his officers, Palti, son of Laish, of the tribe of Benjamin.

Henceforth the rupture between the king and his former favourite was irremediable. The chase became so hot and obstinate that David, betrayed and abandoned even by the men of Judah, was driven to take refuge among the Philistines. With all his energy, and with all his courage, he could not struggle against the forces of the king, and the hostility to which he was exposed ever since the death of Samuel. He went to the court of Achish, King of Gath, where he had already asked for shelter when he first fled from Saul.[1] But his situation had changed very much since those days. He now presented himself at the head of six hundred fighting men, in a position to recompense any services that should be rendered to him. Achish understood this, welcomed David and his men, and gave them the town of Ziklag to dwell in. And it is thus that after innumerable vicissitudes, the exile, his family, and his little army found among their worst enemies the retreat denied them by Israel.

This moment was a decisive one for David. We ought to follow him step by step, studying his every act, examining his every thought, for never will he traverse a situation more perilous for his honour, never will he be put to a more cruel test. His first

[1] 1 Sam. xxi. 10, &c. ; xxvii. 2.

anxiety was to assure the existence of his companions in exile. The Amalekites, as terrible to the Philistines as to the Hebrews, were among those nations on whom lay the malediction of Jehovah. Saul had drawn down the anger of Heaven by sparing their king [1]—David did not make the same mistake. It was at them that he directed his first blows, and he struck with a heavy hand. His action was both loyal and well advised, for in defending the borders of Philistia against the incursions of the plundering Arabs, and in acknowledging by a signal service the hospitality of Achish, he also rewarded his soldiers' devotion with the booty, attracted fresh partisans, accustomed them to war, and created a choice band of formidable warriors. It was thus that he trained the future generals of his army, Joab, Abishai, Asahel, and Benaiah, and was able to organise the corps of the *Gibborim*.[2]

Until now David had only had material difficulties to surmount; the hour was approaching when his duty and his interests would find themselves keenly opposed. None among the Philistines doubted his sentiments with regard to Saul. King Achish, in particular, thought that a burning and unquenchable hatred filled the soul of the outlaw. He deemed it clever to invite his guest to march with him against Israel, with the Gibborim for an escort. Now although

---

[1] I Sam. xv. 2, 3, 18, 20, 23, and xxviii. 18. For the Amalekites see above, p. 56, notes 1 and 2.

[2] See below, p. 155, n. 3.

half-civilised nations whose conception of the fatherland is but a vague one, are disposed to be lenient towards crimes committed against patriotism; still the belief in the unity of the race was so profound among the Beni-Jacob, and there was such a broad line of demarcation between the worshippers of Baal, of Astarte or of Chemesh, and the servants of Jehovah, that the duty of every Israelite was to give a prompt refusal to such a request. On the other hand, David was grateful to Achish for the safety and peace he enjoyed after so many reverses, and he was bound to him by the strict ties of hospitality and by a sort of vassalage. He was obliged to choose between his country and his benefactor; he agreed to the proposal of Achish. But while the army was on its way to the plain of Jezreel, he used all his skill to excite the mistrust and jealousy of the Philistines, with such success that their chiefs insisted on his dismissal.

A dreadful spectacle saddened his return. The Amalekites, after ravaging the south of the country of the Cherethites [1] in Philistia, and ransacking the southern portion of the land of Caleb in Judah, had

[1] Would this name of Cherethites (*Krētim* in the text) give any grounds for the belief that one of the tribes of the Philistines, and even the generality of the Philistines, were of Cretan origin? This hypothesis would agree with what the Bible says about the Cherethites, whose name it sometimes applies to the Philistines (Zeph. ii. 5; Ezek. xxv. 16); and also with an old tradition (Gen. x. 14; Cp. Amos ix. 7) which makes the Philistines come from the island of Caphtor or Crete.

advanced to Ziklag, and had plundered and burnt the town. The women, the children, and the flocks had been carried off; Abigail and Ahinoam, the Jezreelitess, were among the captives. The Gibborim were overwhelmed with grief. A storm of rebellion rose among them. The obedient soldiers, the faithful companions of good and evil days, began to accuse their chief, holding him responsible for the catastrophe; and were even ready to stone him. Instead of attempting a defence which would never have been listened to by an excited horde, maddened with grief, David summoned the cohen Abiathar, requesting him to bring the ephod and to cast the Urim;[1] then, in accordance with the commands of the oracle, he led off the mutineers in pursuit of the Amalekites. Advancing on the south by forced marches, he came on the morrow to the brook Besor, where he left the baggage in the charge of those who lagged behind, and hurried on at the head of four hundred men picked out from among the most hardy and courageous of his followers. Soon they came up to an Egyptian slave, half dead of starvation. His master, an Amalekite, had abandoned him because he was ill and could not keep up with the rest. David gave him bread and figs, questioned him, and from his information was able to overtake the robbers. He surprised them eating, drinking, and dancing in the midst of the spoils of the Judæans and the Philistines, charged them forthwith, and defeated

[1] For the *urim* and the *ephod*, see note K in Appendix.

them with great slaughter. A few slaves who had thrown themselves on the camels at the first alarm were the only ones to escape. The pursuit had been conducted with such spirit and boldness, the surprise of the Amalekites was so complete, that the Israelites were able to recover their women and children and all their possessions, and to lay hands upon the immense booty found in the camp. In addition to glory, they had won wealth.

Difficulties arose at the moment of dividing the spoils. The combatants wished to refuse any share to those who had stayed behind with the baggage. David judged otherwise: "Ye shall not do so, my brethren, with that which the Lord hath given unto us. . . . I will not hearken unto you in this matter, for as his share is that goeth down to the battle, so shall his share be that tarrieth by the stuff: they shall share alike." It was but just, for the guard of the camp was changed at every battle. And accordingly, says the Bible, "it was so from that day forward, that he made it a statute and an ordinance for Israel, unto this day." As for the hero of the day, he divided his share of the spoils into two portions. The one constituted his war fund; he gave the other to the chiefs of Judah who had befriended him when he was being pursued by Saul. Those of Beth-el, Ramoth, Hebron, Jattir, Siphmoth, Hormah, and many other villages and encampments, profited by his bounty, and could bear witness to his generosity.

The conduct of David during his exile among the hereditary enemies of the Hebrews is beyond all praise. This period of his life betokens one of the finest intellects and most upright consciences that have ever graced humanity. Exposed to perilous trials that might have made the strongest mind falter, torn by strong passions and conflicting interests, thrown into a social atmosphere where the refinements of honour were either unknown or scoffed at, he pursues his course without hesitation or pause. He advances with head erect and proud bearing, laughing at difficulties, surmounting obstacles, and displaying every day new qualities generally thought incompatible. In the most critical situation for his honour, or in danger of a military rebellion, he triumphs sometimes by ingenuity and finesse, sometimes by decision and firmness. Compromise with conscience, faltering, an error of judgment will be looked for in vain; he will ascend his destined throne without stain and without remorse. It is the disciple of Samuel, the *protégé* of the priesthood, it is the forerunner of the great prophets who will seat himself there, and lean upon the ark of the covenant in Jerusalem, no longer the city of the Jebusites. And yet his actions have been looked upon as crimes. Does he refuse to march against Israel in the following of the Philistines, he is styled *supremely cunning*, just as he has been set down as a *bandit*, a *plunderer*, a *soldier of fortune*, an *unscrupulous bravo*, and a *robber*. Does he divide among the elders of Judah the booty taken from the Amalekites, he corrupts them and commits an *arrant piece of roguery*.[1] But the generosity of this rogue should at least be acknowledged, since according to the rules of war, more rigorously observed in the days of antiquity than in our own times, the spoils of the enemy are legitimate property acquired by the victor. He was thus distributing his own wealth, differing in this from so many who prefer to be liberal with that of others. But what avails it to dwell on this? The detractors deliberately shut their eyes to plain facts; and to a mind unwarped by prejudice or passion the life of David is too eloquent to need a champion.

While the son of Jesse was triumphing over the Amalekites, and making them pay for the pillage of Ziklag, the Philistines who had continued on their way to the fountain of Jezreel came up with the army of Saul. The field of battle was admirably chosen. The fighting would take place on the territory of Issachar, near Mount Gilboa,[2] in the great plain extending from Mount Tabor to the gulf of Saint-Jean-d'Acre. Across it ran the road which, by means of the fords across the Jordan, put Aram and Chaldæa in communication with the sea. The Hebrews used to stop travellers and demand a ransom, plundering them when they refused to pay toll. If they could obtain possession of the valley of Jezreel the Philis-

---

[1] Renan, "Hist., &c.," pp. 334, 338, 412, 427, 437, 450. See above and below, pp. 74, 75, 98, 120.

[2] 1 Sam. xxix. 1; 2 Sam. i. 6, 21.

tines would cut the Israelites into two branches, and would become their substitutes for the acquisition of the dues paid by the caravans either voluntarily or upon compulsion. The Canaanites and then the Midianites had already had the same object in view; but they had been cut in pieces, the former by Deborah, the latter by Gideon, on battlefields in the close neighbourhood of the one where the two armies were about to engage.[1]

The result of the battle of Gilboa was disastrous for the Israelites. At the beginning of the action Jonathan, Abinadab, and Melchishua, the sons of Saul, were killed. The old king stood firm against all onsets. Surrounded by the enemy, he was retreating inch by inch, fighting to the last, when an arrow struck him. Fearing to fall into the hands of the uncircumcised, he begged his armourbearer to kill him. And, as the officer hesitated, he threw himself resolutely upon the point of his sword.

The Philistines, who found him lying near his three sons, ruthlessly stripped him of his armour and distributed it as precious trophies among the temples of Ashtaroth;[2] they cut off his head and nailed his limbs to the ramparts of Bethshan, which had fallen into their power. Nevertheless, the inhabitants of Jabesh, who had formerly been succoured by Saul,[3]

---

[1] Judg. v. 19; vi. 33. This battlefield was the one occupied by Kleber on the 16th of April, 1799.

[2] Astarte. The text puts the name in the plural (1 Sam. xxxi. 10).

[3] 1 Sam. xi.

and who since that time were greatly attached to the royal house, crossed the Jordan, marched all night, bore away the bodies of the monarch and his sons, and carried them to Gilead, where they burnt them and gave them honourable burial.[1]

Before the combat Saul, seized with terror and tortured by remorse, abandoned by the sacerdotal caste whose chiefs he had massacred, deprived of the help of the prophets who were still faithful to David, had in vain attempted to consult Jehovah.[2] To calm his pangs his servants sought for a woman "with a familiar spirit" who could foretell the future, and in spite of the persecutions levelled against false prophets[3] they succeeded in finding one at Endor, in the neighbourhood of Jezreel. In the night the old monarch, accompanied by two officers, had visited her in disguise, hoping to invoke the shade of Samuel. And the spirit of the prophet, reluctantly answering the summons to earth, had predicted disaster to the army, the death of the princes and of the king, the end of the dynasty and the accession of the son of Jesse. "The Lord hath rent the kingdom out of thine hand, and given it to thy neighbour, even unto David. Because thou obeyedst not the voice of the Lord, and didst not execute His fierce wrath upon Amalek, therefore hath the Lord done this thing unto thee this day. Moreover the Lord will deliver Israel

---

[1] 1 Sam. xxxi. 12, 13 ; 2 Sam. xxi. 12 ; 1 Chron. x.
[2] 1 Sam. xxviii. 6, 15.
[3] 1 Sam. xxviii. 9. Cp. 1 Sam. xv. 23, and 1 Kings xviii. 40.

also with thee into the hands of the Philistines; and to-morrow shalt thou and thy sons be with me. . . ."

This conjuration has been much discussed. It is agreed that the account of it is very ancient and must have been promulgated by David. As for the story itself, it is generally considered apocryphal. This conclusion is too dogmatic; if we follow the version of the Bible, there is at least an air of probability about the tale.

"When the woman saw Samuel she cried with a loud voice, and spake unto Saul, saying, Why hast thou deceived me? for thou art Saul. And the king said unto her, Be not afraid, what seest thou? And the woman said unto Saul, I see a god (according to Josephus, 'something Divine') coming up out of the earth. And he said unto her, What form is he of? And she said, An old man cometh up and he is covered with a robe. And Saul perceived that it was Samuel, and he bowed with his face to the ground" (without looking at him) "and did obeisance."

There is no question here of an apparition of Samuel, as seems to be thought whenever the truth of the tale is discussed, but only of a spectre which the sorceress alone sees, or pretends to see, and which speaks by her mouth. There is a considerable difference between the two. The days are now gone by when the attacks of hysteria to which the Israelites were subject were classed as the tricks of charlatans.[1] Perhaps in days to come it will be possible to dis-

[1] The subject is treated in the following chapter, p. 103.

tinguish clearly between the real phenomena and the stage effects accompanying the consultation of oracles. We can already say that the good faith of the pythoness[1] was generally as great as that of her clients. The trickery belonged rather to the domain of the priests, who hypnotised her and suggested her answers. It is thus possible that either the witch of Endor divined or recognised Saul in his disguise, that she read his secret heart and foresaw his fall; or else that Saul, over-excited by the preparations of the sorceress, fell into one of those trances to which he was subject, saw Samuel in a vision, and interpreted the echo of his own thoughts. After the event a precision was doubtless given to the words ascribed to Samuel which they did not possess when first pronounced.

However that may be, the episode merits consideration, for it shows Saul living his last years in a state of practical excommunication. "And when Saul inquired of the Lord, the Lord answered him not, neither by dreams, nor by Urim, nor by prophets."[2] The king is afraid and suffers under the ban laid upon him by the prophets and the priests. None of the interpreters of Jehovah will come to his aid,

---

[1] The pythonesses were, in fact, women attacked with acute hysteria. (See below, p. 107, n. 1.)

[2] The ordinary and legitimate means of divination, those which Jehovah was Himself supposed to make use of.

Dreams did not need a medium. (Numb. xii. 6; Judg. vii. 13; 1 Sam. iii. 1-18; 2 Sam. vii. 4; Jer. xxiii. 25, &c.) The Urim (see note K in Appendix) was the special oracle of the priests.

and rather than remain thus isolated from the supernatural world, he has recourse to one of those soothsayers who have in all ages been persecuted by the prophets, and against whom he himself has launched a decree of death.[1] It was the impiety of Saul that brought down upon him the contempt of the ministers of religion, while David on the contrary had their warm approval. The prophets and the priests took a decisive part in bringing about the accession of the son of Jesse, because of his upright life, his earnest faith and purity of doctrine; the slightest faltering would have lost him for ever in their eyes.[2] And yet those same historians who describe David as a *clerical*[3] deny the sincerity of his beliefs and accuse him of hypocrisy.[4]

[1] 1 Sam. xxviii. 9. The texts condemning false prophets are numerous. (Deut. xiii. 1; xviii. 20; 1 Kings x. 19, &c.)
[2] See above, pp. 81, 82, and below, pp. 176, 177, 178, and note H in Appendix.
[3] See above, p. 75, n. 1.
[4] Renan, "Hist., &c.," pp. 449 and 450.

VI

Saul and the Prophets [1]

THE sovereign who expiated the defeat of Gilboa by a voluntary death was a man of no exceptional power of mind, but he had the warlike virtues of his predecessors; the outset of his career and the last moments of his life even bear witness to a generous

[1] Care must be taken not to confound the *rôê* or *seer* with the *nabi* or prophet. At the time of Samuel, and for some centuries later, the *seer* is he who enters into communication with God by means of the inward word (see below, p. 103, n. 1 and p. 104, n. 4) without any preliminary initiation or apparent trouble (Amos vii. 14). The example of Samuel, a seer, is equally decisive. The *prophet* is the member of those communities which are abou to be discussed and in whom the spirit of God makes itself manifest by an exaltation whose characteristics will also be described. Later on the term *rôê* or seer was abandoned and that of *nabi* or prophet was used indiscriminately, so that it is no longer possible always to preserve the distinctions which are however established by the comparison of numerous passages in the Bible (see 1 Sam. ix. 8, 9, 16–19; x. 5–13; Amos vii. 14, &c.).

In order to avoid any misunderstanding, I am anxious to specify that the only concern of this chapter is with outward manifestations, with the *apparent* characteristics and effects of the transports of the prophets, with their *human* side, the only one that can be examined by a historian.

heart and a proud spirit. Nevertheless he led a miserable life, spent in alternate periods of dejection and of anger, and came very near to being the ruin of Israel. These striking discrepancies will, however, be reconciled when we trace, in accordance with the Bible, the origin of the attacks to which the king was subject and the transports of the disciples of the prophets, and recognise their true nature.

From the very beginning of the history of the people of Israel, we find mention of certain privileged persons on whom the spirit of God came. Moses,[1] Miriam, sister of Moses, Eldad and Medad and the other sixty-eight chiefs of families chosen to guard the tabernacle, were certainly seers, or prophets in the later sense of this word.[2] The fame of the predictions ascribed to Balaam was widespread.[3] Shortly after the conquest, Deborah, a prophetess, became chief magistrate. After that mention is only made of obscure visionaries of about the same date as Gideon.[4] We know, besides, that the prophetic spirit slumbered during the period of the Judges, when the sacerdotal caste, established around the Ark at Shiloh, had obtained pre-eminence in religious matters.[5] But it awoke towards the end of the shophetate of Eli, at that troubled epoch which embraced the capture of the Ark, the decline of the

[1] Exod. xv. 20; Numb. xxvi. 60.
[2] Exod. xv. 20; Numb. xi. 24-29.
[3] Numb. xii., xxiii.; xxiv. 3, 4.
[4] Judg. vi. 8-11.
[5] For the organisation of the clergy see note L in Appendix.

priests attached to its service, and the youth of Samuel. The heirs of the seers, whom the most ancient texts describe as being few and scattered among the tribes, now grew in numbers and in influence, organised themselves and formed communities.[1] From that moment they vied with the priests and Levites, counterbalanced their authority and soon became powerful enough to promote the success of Samuel, their spiritual father,[2] and to raise him to the shophetate. Later on they helped him to found the monarchy in favour of Saul, one of their members; and then, again inspired by Samuel, they disinherited the chosen candidate who had betrayed their trust, and transferred the power to David, whose initiation among them also seems certain.[3] Children of no particular tribe, the fruits as it were of seed fallen from heaven and scattered at the pleasure of the winds, the prophets spoke in the name of Jehovah and claimed to be His direct interpreters. Poor in the goods of this world, with no appointed place in the religious hierarchy which had grown up around

[1] The earliest traces of the existence of these communities of seers are to be found in the First Book of Samuel (x. 5, 10, and xix. 18). They are afterwards spoken of in the Books of the Kings (1 Kings xx. 35-43; 2 Kings iv. 1, 38; vi. 1, 2; ix. 1).

[2] 1 Sam. xix. 20. Cp. 1 Kings xx. 35; 2 Kings iv. 1 and 38-41; vi.; ix. 1. The term employed by the Bible to designate the disciples is "*son*," which seems to indicate that the position of the superior with regard to the seers of his community was that of spiritual father. The title given to the head of a community in speaking of him or addressing him was that of "*Man of God*" (2 Kings iv. 7, 9, 40, 42; v. 15).

[3] See above, p. 70 and p. 71.

the tabernacle, they lived together, eating in common when unmarried [1] and never quitting the solitude to which they confined themselves, except to communicate to the race of Abraham the commands of its God. Their colleges, subjected to the control and to the authority of a superior or spiritual father, were regular centres of initiation where traditions were preserved intact and the headquarters of an active propaganda. In the time of Samuel, the Bible speaks of communities of prophets at Gilgal and at Ramatha,[2] but they doubtless existed in many other places.[3]

The body of the prophets, in the recruiting of its adepts as well as in its religious and prophetic practices, differed greatly from the priesthood, which was confined to the tribe of Levi, and centralised first at Shiloh, then at Nob, and which was attached in turn to the Ark and to the prophetic ephod. Then again it was not, like the priesthood, exclusively an appanage of the male sex. The enthusiastic and impressionable women who were admitted to its ranks had left a certain stamp upon its character which was never entirely effaced.[4]

[1] 2 Kings iv. 1, 38-41 ; vi. 1 and 2.

[2] The prophets met by Saul near Gibeah, on his way to Gilgal, were certainly coming from the latter town, which in the time of Elisha was still a famous prophetical centre (1 Sam. x. 8 ; 2 Kings ii. 1 ; iv. 38). For Ramatha, see 1 Sam. xix. 18-24.

[3] Perhaps in Beth-el and Jericho (2 Kings ii. 3, 5, 18).

[4] Besides Miriam, the sister of Moses, and Deborah, the Bible speaks of several prophetesses (2 Kings xxii. 14 ; Nehem. vi. 4 ; Isaiah viii. 3 ; Ezek. xiii. 17 ; Acts xxi. 9).

When in a state of prophetic ecstasy,[1] the initiated travelled through the country in a long file, shouting, dancing, and gesticulating to the sound of citharas, flutes, cymbals and tambourines, predicting the future, divining secret thoughts, speaking in the name of God. Then they expressed themselves in a kind of allegorical verse, and to judge by the pieces which have reached us, it would seem that their songs, composed according to almost invariable rules,[2] were divided into portions analogous to the strophe and anti-strophe of Greek lyrics.[3] Besides feverish

---

[1] There were three kinds of revelation: the *inward word*, the *vision* and the *dream*. In the first case there was no outward change in the state of the prophets, nor any disturbance in the exercise of their intelligence and of their will (Numb. xii. 6–8; Judg. iv.; 1 Sam. ii. 1–10; iii.; xv. 28, 29; 2 Sam. xii. 9–12; xxiv. 13; Jer. i. 1, 2; Hos. i. 1; Rev. i. 10, &c.).

[2] Prophecies consisted of: (1) an exhortation, (2) an accusation and reproaches, (3) threats of punishment, (4) promises of rewards for repentance and conversion (Abbé Vigouroux, "Man. bibl." v. ii., p. 462).

[3] This question has been very closely studied by M. D. Muller ("Die Propheten in ihrer ursprünglichen Form," Wien, 1896), who even believes that the Greek lyrics were influenced by poets of Semitic origin. He supports his thesis by the comparison of very curious texts, and by the fact that the singers in the first competitions were women of Phœnicia, and also by the word $\beta a\lambda\acute{\eta}\nu$, which is repeated as a refrain in a chorus by Pindar and which has no sense in Greek, whereas it is easily explained by the Hebrew *bâalim*, gods. It would be another proof in favour of the theory which I have so long maintained, and which seems nowadays to be admitted, on the influence of the civilisation of the Phœnicians on the Greeks, whether of the Mycenian or classical period, and on the numerous crossings during these two periods between the conquerors of the soil and the Phœnician colonists who came to settle in Greece (Dieulafoy, "Art ant. de la Perse," v. iii. § vi., and v. iv. § iv., and "Comptes rendus de l'Ac. des Ins., annee 1895," pp. 245–248).

excitement and the need for vociferation, religious and poetic exaltation, vehemence and even eloquence of declamation and an irresistible desire to preach and foretell the future, the prophetic ecstasy, such as it is described in the Bible, was physically characterised by a brilliancy of the eyes, by convulsions of the face and of the limbs, so violent in some as to give the appearance of madness; [1] and morally, by the denunciation of innocent pleasures, by a horror of ornaments and of gay-coloured garments.[2] Nevertheless certain great geniuses such as Deborah, Samuel, Nathan, Hosea, Amos, Micah, Elisha, Elijah, and so many others who were the glory of their order, stand out from the multitude of prophets, with whom they had nothing in common except religious zeal and ambition for the glory of Israel. Ardent patriots, severe moralists, passionate monotheists, they made use of their disciples to defend their doctrine, to maintain justice and righteousness; presiding over their pious exercises, their songs and their dances, without ever taking an active part in them.[3] They had no need of an artificial excitement in order to establish their dominion over men's souls.[4] These eminent minds, these powerful

[1] 1 Sam. x. 8–11; xviii. 8–12; xix. 20–24; 1 Kings xviii. 26–29; 2 Kings ix. 11; Jer. xxix. 26; 1 Corinth. xiv. 23.

[2] Isaiah iii. 16–24; xxxii. 11.

[3] 1 Sam. xix. 20.

[4] Revelation manifested itself among them by the inward word. They addressed themselves to the people by means of discourses, regular sermons, which they revised and repolished up at leisure and either pronounced themselves or transmitted through their disciples. (Abbé Vigouroux, "Man. bibl." pp. 463, 469, 470.)

SAUL AND THE PROPHETS

intellects are not referred to in the following observations, which only concern the humble representatives of the army of the prophets and one illustrious member of their ranks—King Saul.

Every one knows of the care and science that have been devoted of late years to the study of nervous diseases and their epidemic manifestations. Their history has been reconstructed from documents and illustrations ; their different forms have been examined and classified. The result of these patient researches is a very clear definition of the striking features of that strange malady known by the technical name of acute hysteria—*la grande hystérie*.[1] Now these same features, these same signs, are equally characteristic of the outward manifestations of the ecstasy of the prophets. The attacks were, as a rule, mild and much attenuated ; but the contagion, of which one finds flagrant cases, cannot be denied any more than the apparent nature of the accidents and of the symptoms. It is impossible not to be convinced of this, after a careful consideration of the accounts taken from the sacred annals, and of the descriptions of the epidemics that have occurred in modern times. Such profound analogies are to be traced between the transports of the prophets and certain of these manifestations, after an interval of three thousand years, that we might almost wonder

---

[1] Notwithstanding the similarity of names, care must be taken not to confound *la grande hystérie* with hysteria in the ordinary sense of the word.

whether we have not here a series of prints from a primitive picture.

These epidemics, some of which, like the work of the convulsionists of Saint Médard (Paris, 1731), are too well known to need repetition, all bear in fact a close resemblance to each other in certain points. Among the most ancient, we may note the *choræa*, or St. Vitus's dance, and the tarantism which raged in Germany and in Italy towards the end of the fourteenth century; then the long series of possessions: the possessions of the nuns in Germany (1550–60), of the daughters of St. Ursula at Aix (1609–11), of the Ursulines of Loudun (1632–39), and of the nuns of Louviers (1642). Later on came the work of the convulsionists (Paris, cemetery of Saint-Medard, 1731), the preaching mania (Sweden, 1841–42), the American "revivals" and "camp-meetings" (1850–86), and then again the possession of the inhabitants of Morzine (Haute Savoie, 1861), that of Verzégnie, which broke out after a "retreat" preached in great pomp by the Jesuit Fathers (Frioul Italien, 1878), and the possession of Jaca in the north of Spain, which is every year renewed on the 25th of June on the day of Saint Orosia, patron saint of the town.[1] To these plagues and scourges we may add the paroxysms of Mussulman convulsionists and the daily attacks which are so carefully observed in hospitals; and which are

---

[1] I have borrowed the majority of these examples from the excellent work of Dr. Richer: "Études cliniques sur la grande hystérie," with a preface by Professor Charcot.

contagious and might easily become epidemic.[1] Finally, in the domain of religion, we may compare the accounts of the prophets in the Bible with those of the prophetic manifestations of the first centuries A.D.,[2] and of the spirit of prophecy which awoke among the Huguenots[3] when exasperated by the revocation of the Edict of Nantes, and driven into a state of frenzy by the *dragonnades* (1686-1725).

These first comparisons show that in different degrees, the prophet, the *nabi* of the Bible, had all the outward appearance of a neurotic subject whose neurosis assumed the characters of these epidemics of *grande hystérie*, which repeatedly occur in history, and at a distance of centuries from these striking examples. It is an interesting fact that the soothsayers, the sorcerers, and false prophets, who maintained a formidable competition with the interpreters of Jehovah, and whom neither exile nor massacres could destroy,[4] had the same ethnical origin as the prophets ; and that their transports simulated the

[1] The pythonesses, the priests of the Cabirii and probably those initiated into the great mysteries, were also hysterical subjects. The descriptions of different authors and the representations left on vases prove this beyond a doubt. I have not included these cases in the above list on account of their not offering such striking examples of contagion and epidemics as the ones I have chosen, and the comparison would therefore not be so exact or so searching.

[2] Glossology and montanism.

[3] The interesting work of M. Camille Rabaud ("Les Petits Prophètes Huguenots"), which appeared in the *Revue Chretienne* in 1896, may be consulted on this subject.

[4] Exod. xxii. 18 ; Lev. xix. 26, 31 ; xx. 6, 27 ; Deut. xviii. 10-15 ; 1 Kings xviii. 15-40 ; xxii. 13-23 ; 2 Chron. xviii. 14.

same outward characters and inspired an equal confidence among the people.

These conclusions are confirmed both by the general terms of the verses devoted to the attacks of Saul and by the details they furnish.

First of all there comes the introduction of Saul into a community of prophets. In obedience to the commands of Samuel, the young Benjamite goes to meet the prophets of Gilgal, mingles with their troop, and is at once seized with the spirit of God.[1] We thus learn in what manner were recruited the sons of the prophets, and how the outward signs of ecstasy were manifested for the first time. Other convincing and decisive proofs of the contagious nature of the outward phenomena of prophecy are to be found in the transmission of the gifts of Moses to seventy elders,[2] and in the search for David among the *nebüm* of Ramah, during which the archers and officers of Saul, although not prophets, all fell into prophetic transports.[3]

On the other hand the Bible says that whenever the king, in one of his fits of melancholy or of rage, asks David to take his harp, the sounds of the instrument have a soothing effect upon him until the day when, jealous of the musician, he abandons himself to fits of homicidal fury upon hearing the melodies which formerly drove away the evil

---

[1] 1 Sam. x. 10, 11, and see above p. 51, n. 1.
[2] Num. xi. 24-29.
[3] 1 Sam. xix. 20-24. See above, p. 70.

spirit.¹ Now, long before recent experiments, it was known that singing and the music of flutes or of viols brought relief to persons attacked with St. Vitus's dance or with tarantism, and had a calming effect upon demoniacs. But it was just as well known that music, instead of being beneficial, gave rise to terrible paroxysms when it was associated with painful remembrances in the minds of the possessed. This was the case with Saul.

The singular attitude of the king after the death of Goliath, when he feigns not to recognise his own harpist,² is but the well known prelude to an attack. His obstinate and irresistible desire to strike his former favourite dead, his attempt to kill his son Jonathan, guilty of defending David, the massacre of the priests of Nob, of their families and of their flocks, because the cohen Ahimelech has succoured the object of his bloodthirsty hatred, are all the effects of the frenzied delirium and homicidal mania of a hystero-demoniac. The very aversion felt by the sovereign for the prophets and the priests,³ his benefactors and his teachers, may be compared to the morbid repulsion inspired by the ministers of the faith in those possessed—the parallel is a striking one

---

¹ 1 Sam. xviii. 10, 11. The Bible attributes this change to Saul's disobedience to the commands of Heaven. The spirit of God has left him; an evil spirit fills the soul of the king, who retains from his initiation an unsettlement of his whole being that predisposes him to the wildest ravings (1 Sam. xv., xvi. 1; xxviii. 6, 16, 18).

² 1 Sam. xvii. 58. See above, pp. 67 and 68.

³ 1 Sam. xv. 26-28; xvi. 34, 35; xxii. 11-19.

—when the epidemic does not excite religious feeling to the intensest degree. In this domain, everything runs to extremes.

Finally, the uneasiness of the monarch on hearing of the thrice-repeated manifestations of prophecy among his servants, his emotion on approaching the college of prophets which has sheltered David, and on the other hand, his fall to the ground, his torn garments, his cries, his contortions, his disordered movements and his prostration of twenty-four hours when the attack is over, are all just as characteristic as the preceding symptoms. They correspond to the premonitory symptoms and classical phases of an attack of *hystéro-demonopathie* in the exact technical sense of the word, an attack perfectly analogous with the *demoniac* outbreaks alluded to in the first verses.

It is no longer a question of isolated attacks of epilepsy answering to the fatal "divine evil" of the Latins, common also in Greece and in Egypt;[1] we have here a body of evidence, a collection of precious documents which allows us at a distance of thirty centuries to make a complete and exact diagnosis of the condition of Saul; and after thousands of years to connect the great efflorescence of prophecy in its outward aspects and human sides with the epidemics of choræa, tarantism or possession of later ages. These fresh researches also show how the prophetic spirit favourably predisposed the minds of men even

[1] See above, p. 104, n. 4.

when it did not take hold of them ; and how a moral intimacy was created between the seers and the bulk of the Hebrews which led to the harmony and fusion of their different wills.

Such are the scientific and natural reasons for the rapid progress of the communities of the prophets, for their ascendancy over the people and for the extent of their influence in politics, an influence so decisive that their co-operation was necessary for the acquisition of power, and was only to be obtained at the cost of a preliminary initiation.[1] They occupy an important place, even by the side of causes of a religious nature.

Saul made no resistance to this fascination ; from the first moment of contact his nerves vibrated in unison with those of the disciples of Samuel. "What! is Saul also among the prophets?" cried the people in surprise. First of all the attacks were transient, with long respites between ; he had one, for instance, on hearing of the siege of Jabesh by the Ammonites, and a second when he tore the robe of Samuel, who tried to compel him to chastise the Amalekites with greater severity.[2] Then the disease became aggravated, the fits followed closer one on another. He was no longer responsible for his acts, was on the verge of insanity ; and became a prey to a fixed idea even in his calmer intervals.

---

[1] See above, pp. 51, 70, 101.
[2] 1 Sam. xv. 26, 28. On this episode see above pages 51, 59, 60, and the notes referring to them.

Now one can see how a simple offence against his *amour-propre* was sufficient to rouse the anger of Saul. One can understand the blind fury of the monarch when his free will disappeared during an attack; and can imagine the animus of his pursuit of the unconscious provokers of his anger; one can tell how entirely undeserved was his wrath and how baseless his grudge.

But we should also acknowledge the greatness of David as shown by the results of this inquiry, and the sincerity and veracity of the Bible with regard to Saul, whose disease it does not understand; and with regard to his victim, whose respect for the sovereign authority, whose generosity and long-suffering are beyond praise. These descriptive qualities, this remarkable fidelity in the specification of the outward characters of prophetic manifestations, this impartial estimate of the relations between Saul and David, are all precious indications of the historical value of the accounts of the constitution of the monarchy. They prove that the documents relating to this period, one of the most critical in the history of the tribes, reflect in their number and their value the sentiments of the high responsibilities assumed by the people when they petitioned for a king.

It would be an important result only to have shown Samuel, Saul, and David in their true light, to have established the essential features of their characters and to have read aright the prominent acts of their lives; but above the interest attached to all progress in knowledge of the truth, there lies a great lesson. Only yesterday, whole chapters of the First Book of Samuel were considered apocryphal or distorted from their original sense. Common sense was invoked against them, they were contradicted in the name of human reason. And behold, the progress of a science far removed from philological or historical criticism, shows the unsoundness of these fine arguments, and restores to the Biblical narrative its value and its scope. Human wisdom is shortsighted and human reason frail; it is an adventurous enterprise to build upon them as a foundation.

VII

Ish-bosheth, King of Israel—David, King of Judah—Respective condition of the two kingdoms—Murder of Abner—Assassination of Ish-bosheth—David, King of the Jews

THE very night of the defeat of Gilboa, an Amalekite attached to the royal household had hastened towards Ziklag. He arrived there on the third day. Brought before the exile, he made known to him the tragic issue of the battle, and in the hope of securing favour and importance, he boasted of having killed Saul. As proof of the exploit, he brought the gold bracelets and the diadem which he had taken from his master's body.[1]

Any other than David would have warmly welcomed the messenger of good tidings; for the death of the old monarch favoured his hopes and made his ambitions legitimate. Such at least were the very natural sentiments ascribed to him by the Amalekite,

[1] 2 Sam. i. 1 to 10; 1 Chron. x. 3, 4. It was a lie. The Bible says (1 Sam. i. 31) that the king, rather than fall into the hands of the Philistines, begged his armour-bearer to kill him, and that upon the latter refusing to strike he committed suicide.

when he accused himself of the death of Saul. But the Israelites were overcome, it was their defeat that was the price he would pay for power—from the hands of a traitor that he would receive it. Such thoughts could never be harboured by the man who when he had Saul at his mercy had let him go unscathed.[1]

From the day that Samuel took him into his confidence, David had formed a lofty conception of the dignity of the crown. He had understood that in order to inherit it in all its brilliancy, it was necessary to surround it with respect and to guard against the tarnishing of its lustre. It mattered little that Saul was unworthy; he shared in its sanctity, his person became sacred. By despising the king he would be injuring the prestige of the supreme charge for which he was destined. If he allowed a crime of *lèse-majesté* to go unpunished, he would encourage the violation of his inheritance. Whatever name they may bear, all the different governments and administrations of one country are closely related. This was recognised as a supreme law by the ancient Persians in their religious code. They worshipped as a divine genius not the monarch, who received such honours from fawning courtiers for other reasons, but the sovereign glory and the authority over the corporal world granted by Ormazd to their kings.[2]

---

[1] See above, p. 81.
[2] Dieulafoy, "Acropole de Suse," pp. 407, 408, 409.

Thus, far from rewarding the Amalekite, David had him put to death for having laid hands upon his master and for having struck the earthly representative of Jehovah. Then he ordered his people to mourn with tears and fasting for the death of Saul and Jonathan and for the great misfortune of the house of Israel, whose children had perished in such numbers at the hands of the Philistines. He himself rent his clothes and cried aloud and wept, and fasted until even, forgetful of the danger to which he was exposing himself in mourning over the conquered in the presence of their conquerors. Then he took up the harp which he had neglected for the sword, and composed the song of the bow, which the children were in after days to repeat, in commemoration of the monarch and of the heroes fallen with him on the mountain of Gilboa. Sublime verses, which expressed all his piety towards the anointed of Jehovah, which revealed all his tenderness for Jonathan, to whom he was bound by ties that no emergency had been able to destroy.

"Thy glory, O Israel, is slain upon thy high places.
How are the mighty fallen!
Tell it not in Gath,
Publish it not in the streets of Askelon;
Lest the daughters of the Philistines rejoice,
Lest the daughters of the uncircumcised triumph.
Ye mountains of Gilboa,
Let there be no dew nor rain upon you, neither fields ot offerings,
For there the shield of the mighty was vilely cast away,
The shield of Saul, not anointed with oil.

From the blood of the slain, from the fat of the mighty,
The bow of Jonathan turned not back, and the sword of
  Saul returned not empty.
Saul and Jonathan were lovely in their lives,
And in their death they were not divided;
They were swifter than eagles,
They were stronger than lions.
Ye daughters of Israel, weep over Saul,
Who clothed you in scarlet delicately,
Who put ornaments of gold upon your apparel.
How are the mighty fallen in the midst of the battle!
Jonathan is slain upon thy high places.
I am distressed for thee, my brother Jonathan:
Very pleasant hast thou been unto me:
Thy love to me was wonderful,
Passing the love of women.
How are the mighty fallen,
And the weapons of war perished!"[1]

It was a very disturbed inheritance that was left by Saul to his last son Ish-bosheth, then thirty-eight years old. During his lifetime, in spite of his title of King of Israel, he had only been able to establish his authority over Joseph and Benjamin. Judah tolerated him, the tribes of Gilead remained grateful to him for the deliverance of Jabesh,[2] but were not always ready to obey. The Hebrews of the north may even have been unaware of his existence. He was a chief who had risen by his victories, with much less power than many of the shophetim, and only differing from his predecessors in having adopted a *protocole* establishing his right to found a dynasty.

[1] 2 Sam. i. 17, &c. On the song, see note J in Appendix.
[2] 2 Sam. v. 4.

Abner, the *sarsaba* or general of his troops, had hastened to invoke this right among the subject tribes; and in spite of defeat, the investiture received by Saul remained the strength of Ish-bosheth and the great obstacle to the accession of David. But the storm that had struck the crest and beaten down the finest branches of the royal tree was represented by the prophets and the priests as a sign of the anger of Heaven and the condemnation of an impenitent sovereign. They went about saying that the Almighty had withdrawn His hand from over the house of Saul, that heredity could not prevail against the will of God. It was necessary that this terrible downfall, predicted by Samuel, should become a lesson and an example for future monarchs. Henceforth there would be room for two upon the throne. Jehovah would occupy the seat of His elect, Jehovah would govern, the king would obey. This king was David. Long ago he had been singled out and chosen; and the dispenser of crowns, the supreme master of men and of their kings, had granted him the rights of the heirs of Saul.

Then there was great vacillation in the minds of the people. The men of Ephraim and of Manasseh, kept back by fear, inclined towards idolatry, and jealous also of the hegemony towards which Judah was tending, remained for the most part faithful to the son of Saul, whereas those of Hebron and of the southern towns were in favour of the exile. The priests and the prophets had sown the good seed in their pious hearts; the wisdom, courage and generosity of the son of Jesse had conquered the most prejudiced, the fruit was ripening, the harvest was at hand.

David, aware of this balance of opinions, remained as prudent as ever. He sent emissaries to the elders of Judah. All brought him back good news; the people longed for his coming. Then the exile quitted Ziklag with his two wives, Abigail widow of Nabal of the Carmel, and Achinoam of Jezreel, and set out for his tribe. Some days later he entered Hebron and was there proclaimed king over the house of Judah. This great event took place about the year 1050 B.C. David was close on thirty years of age.[1]

Faithful to his policy, his first act as a king was a homage to royalty, his first words were messages of thanks to the Gileadites who had taken down the bodies of Saul and his sons from the walls of Bethshan and had piously buried them in the woods of Jabesh. After showing himself inexorable towards the murderer of his persecutor, he praised the faithful subjects who had honoured the sovereign power in the mutilated bodies of the princes. It was an assurance for them that there was but one soul in Israel, even should there be two heads, and that the generosity of the son of Jesse would only be equalled by his justice. In order to appreciate

[1] 2 Sam. ii. 10, 11; v. 4, 5; 1 Kings ii. 11.

the grandeur of this action, not only the sufferings of David should be considered; above all it must be remembered that Gilead formed part of the Israelite confederation from which Judah and Simeon had been excluded. It was an enemy hostile to the supremacy of the south and one from which a child of Bethlehem had nothing to hope. It would thus seem as if such conduct must provoke unanimous praise. And David would in fact be praised, had not his great and noble figure been thrown into the arena of religious polemics. But passion is blind, and this magnanimity has been described as "the equivocal art of profiting by every crime without ever directly committing one."[1]

The accession of David struck a fresh blow at the tottering power of Ish-bosheth. Since their last successes, the Philistines, masters of Beth-shan and of the upper course of the Kishon, had reached the right bank of the Jordan, closing up the valley of Jezreel and thus isolating Benjamin and Joseph first from Gad, then from Zebulun, Naphtali and Asher. The inheritance of Saul was now menaced not only from the north. In the south, Judah was becoming a source of uneasiness.

In this extremity, in spite of the precarious situation of his party, Abner did not lose heart. Almost directly after the Battle of Gilboa, the sarsaba had led Ish-bosheth through the ranks, encouraging the soldiers and reviving their zeal. Then he had crossed

[1] Renan, "Hist d'Israel," v. i. p. 438.

the Jordan, hoping to baffle all pursuers and to find support among the Gileadites who had just given proofs of fidelity and daring in snatching the bodies of the king and of the princes out of the hands of the Philistines. From Mahanaim, where he had installed the son of Saul and established the seat of government,[1] Abner put fresh spirit into the tribes on that side of the river, entered Geshur, recrossed the Jordan, drove away the Philistines from the towns they occupied in the territory of Ephraim and of Manasseh, opened up the entrance to the valley of Jezreel, and placed the tribes of the centre and of the north under the rule of Ish-bosheth. This concentration was effected slowly and seems to have gone on for two years without any attempt on David's part to hinder it.

The two rivals now faced each other; the collision was imminent.

It was Abner who spurred his master on to action. This fact does honour to David. Always respectful towards the house of Saul, and with a firm faith in the promises of the Lord, he had no wish to conquer a kingdom which was promised to him. But when forced to defend himself against a direct attack, he gathered his troops together and put them under the orders of his nephew, Joab son of Zeruiah, a skilful and faithful lieutenant. He was already subjecting himself to the strict rule which he observed during the whole of his life, never to command in person in

[1] 2 Sam. ii. 8, 12.

a civil war, no matter what issues might be at stake on the field of battle.[1]

The two armies met near the pool of Gibeon, five or six miles to the north-west of Jerusalem. For a long time the victory was undecided; towards evening the troops of David had the advantage. Abner beat a retreat. Closely pursued by Asahel, brother of Joab, he managed to kill him, profited by the emotion caused among his assailants by this death, rallied the Benjamites and established himself with the flower of his army in a strong position on the top of a hill in the neighbourhood of Gibeon. Joab did not dare to risk an attack; Abner on his side could do nothing but remain on the defensive. It was therefore agreed between the two generals that Ish-bosheth's men should retire in peace, abandoning the victory to their adversaries.

Abner's defeat decided the fate of the war. One more effort would have precipitated the fall of Ish-bosheth; David did not attempt it. He preferred to temporise and to wait until the unanimous wish of the tribes should call him to reign over Israel, displaying in the flush of his manhood a rare combination of courage and wisdom in perfect balance, without ever an excusable movement of impatience or an exaggerated prudence to weight the scale and destroy the equilibrium.

This state of dumb hostility continued for about two years, during which the kingdom of Ish-bosheth

[1] See below, p. 234.

grew weaker and weaker. Its true chief was prolonging the death-struggle by his courage, but his master rewarded his devotion with royal ingratitude. One day, he thought fit to accuse Abner of criminal relations with a concubine of the late king. The reply was such as he had provoked.

"Am I a dog's head that belongeth to Judah? This day do I show kindness unto the house of Saul thy father, to his brethren and to his friends, and have not delivered thee into the hand of David, and yet thou chargest me this day with a fault concerning this woman."[1]

It was too much. In spite of the decline of his party, the sarsaba of the army of the north was still a formidable adversary, in a position to discuss the terms of his submission. He resolved to make overtures to the King of Judah before he found himself at his mercy.

David refused to enter into negotiations unless they gave him back Michal, the wife for whom he had paid, as he said, with the heads of a hundred Philistines. Abner, who was on the watch for an opportunity of a meeting with the chief of Judah, sent for her at once, and in spite of the tears and supplications of her new husband, took her himself to Hebron. Joab had been purposely despatched on a punitive expedition against some Amalekite robbers. Preliminaries were soon settled. The terms of the understanding arrived at between

[1] 2 Sam. iii. 7, 8.

David and Abner are not known, but it is easy to guess at their general sense and significance. The army of the south did not yet possess a sarsaba. It was doubtless agreed that Abner should retain his title and thus become the commander-in-chief of the Israelite forces. His reputation for valour and his military talents fully qualified him for the exercise of these high duties.

Directly he returned, Joab heard of Abner's visit, and soon discovered the secrets of the interview. He understood that in exchange for a kingdom, Abner had borne back the promise of a post high enough to counterbalance his own influence. His anger was violent both against Abner and David; for in addition to jealousy he felt the pangs of hatred for the murderer of his brother, and the fear of dishonour should he not exact vengeance.[1] He endeavoured to persuade the king that the sarsaba had come to spy upon him, that he had beguiled him with promises in order to penetrate his projects; and he reproached David for having allowed him to escape when he might so easily have killed him.

David, who looked upon the execution of a defenceless enemy as a crime, charged him to respect his guest. Joab paid little heed to these

---

[1] In the ancient world, the point of honour did not consist in exposing oneself to the blows of the insulter to avenge an offence, but rather in striking the one who had struck. David, of all the Old Testament heroes, seems to be the only one who had an elevated conception of honour and the right to vengeance. (See above, p. 82, n. 1.)

injunctions. With the help of his brother Abishai, he laid an ambush for Abner, took him by surprise and wounded him in the groin. It was thus that Abner had killed Asahel. A tooth for a tooth, an eye for an eye.

There was great excitement in Israel. The king was in danger of being accused of a crime from which, in point of fact, he could derive no profit, and which he had endeavoured to prevent. In the presence of the elders of Judah he pronounced terrible imprecations on Joab and Abishai; and he solemnly asserted his guiltlessness before the Lord, invoking the testimony of the murderers in his favour. Then, not judging this sufficient reparation, he ordered his court into mourning,[1] and on the following day, walked behind the corpse of Abner to the grave, where he uttered lamentations and composed an elegy in celebration of the virtues of the murdered man, contrasting them afresh with the perfidy of those "children of iniquity" who kill by treachery.

"Should Abner die as a fool dieth?
 Thy hands were not bound, nor thy feet put into fetters:
 As a man falleth before the children of iniquity, so didst
   thou fall."[2]

His protestations were so decided and so loyal,

---

[1] For the mourning garment or *sack*, see below, p. 222, n. 1.

[2] 2 Sam. iii. 33, 34. This elegy and the song of the bow are fragments of great antiquity. There are good reasons for attributing them to David. See note J in Appendix.

that they convinced even those devoted to the house of Saul.[1] Nevertheless the young king was blamed for allowing the insolent audacity and disobedience of the sons of Zeruiah to go unpunished. It was forgotten that Joab was more than his lieutenant, more than his nephew; he was a well-proved friend who had never failed him in the hour of need, and who until then had received his full confidence and had faithfully participated in every project. The sovereignty of his house was not so well assured that David could afford to destroy a strong support. There were so many outside enemies to fight against; was it necessary to raise up others in the tribe of Judah? Then, if he had punished Abner's murderer, he would have seemed to seek for a pretext to get rid of an inconvenient accomplice, of a man whose power annoyed him, whose services were a burden on his gratitude. For that matter, he expressed himself very clearly. "I am this day weak though anointed king; and these men the sons of Zeruiah be too hard for me; the Lord reward the wicked doer according to his wickedness."[2] And in point of fact his affection for Joab and for Abishai was from that moment strangely weakened.

David is not the only sovereign who has experienced similar hesitation with regard to a criminal. Darius I. reigned over a people accustomed to the worst forms of tyranny, and nevertheless it is well

[1] 2 Sam. iii. 36. [2] 2 Sam. iii. 39.

known with what precautions he surrounded the execution of Orœtes, the satrap of the maritime provinces who was in open rebellion against his authority.[1]

In any case, the death of Abner did not greatly modify the situation of the two parties. In abandoning Ish-bosheth, the sarsaba did not listen only to the voice of his anger. He felt that the disaffection towards the dynasty of Saul was becoming general, and his interview with the King of Judah was not so much a token of his personal feelings as of the weariness of the tribes engaged in an unequal struggle, and of their desire to group themselves around a monarch who could command respect. If the Hebrews had abandoned the rule of the Judges and had resigned themselves to a heavier yoke, it was only to enjoy the benefits of a more powerful government.

Nevertheless two Benjamites, Baanah and Rechab, wished to make one last effort. But the troops were demoralised, and Ish-bosheth lacked the moral support given by an heir-presumptive, for Mephibosheth, son of Jonathan, and the last prince of the blood royal, was lame in both legs. They soon felt the vanity of the struggle. Then, coming to the conclusion that their king was of no importance except to David, and that the only way they could make use of him was to give him up dead or alive to his rival, they resolved to assassinate him. This design, easier of execution than an abduction, was also more

[1] Herodotus, iii. 127, 128.

decisive and more in keeping with the brutal customs of the Benjamites.

The tale of the murder is epic in its melancholy simplicity. The two conspirators come to Mahanaim,[1] towards noon, in the greatest heat of the day. There is no shade in the streets or in the courtyards. Every living being seeks for shelter from the blinding rays of the sun; men and beasts give themselves up to sleep. The silence and peace of a necropolis reign over the slumbering town. Baanah and Rechab set out alone, reach the palace gates and cross the threshold. Instead of guards and officers, of an army of serving-men, they find one slave. This woman, leaning against the wall, is winnowing wheat, and she too has fallen asleep over her work.

What a strange medley of carelessness, of fatalism, or of blind confidence, to be found in a king threatened with desertion, surrounded by traitors, but still powerful because he possesses a kingdom and is in command of an army! It is to the maidservant who every day prepares his bread that the monarch entrusts the charge of watching over his life.

The assassins pass by this strange guardian without waking her up, penetrate into the royal apartment, surprise their master in his sleep, cut off his head and quit the palace. They march all night, reaching Hebron in the morning. They are shown into David's presence, and say to the king: "Behold the head of Ish-bosheth the son of Saul thine enemy

[1] See above, p. 121, n. 1.

which sought thy life; and the Lord hath avenged my Lord the king this day of Saul, and of his seed." [1]

Just as he had treated the murderer of Saul, so did David treat the murderers of Ish-bosheth. Another opportunity for disparaging the judge and for treating him as an assassin has been vainly sought in this act of justice. It has been pretended that he wished for the death of Baanah and of Rechab in order to bury with them the proofs of his complicity. These pitiable arguments are amply refuted by the king's generous and loyal nature, by the previous sentence on the Amalekite, by the uselessness of the crime, and by the Bible itself, which is always severe on the faults of David. Alexander is not accused of having participated in the murder of Darius Codomanus, and yet, in a parallel case and for a similar crime, he ordered the execution of the regicide. David is as innocent as Alexander. Baanah, Rechab, and Bessus were armed by the same circumstances and the same desires. For it is often the case that the great events of history are the reaction of previous causes upon human passions, and that the moral nature of men varies as little as the physical. When a government is in the throes of death, then audacity is born in the heart of criminals, and even if their position debars

[1] 2 Sam. iv. 5-7. This version of the death of Ish-bosheth is completed with regard to one detail by means of the Septuagint. The Hebrew text is mutilated and is sometimes incomprehensible. It speaks of "wheat" but does not say that a woman was winnowing it and that she had fallen asleep over her task.

them from hopes of power, yet in their keen pursuit of the quarry and their eagerness for the spoils, they are none the less ready to precipitate the catastrophe.

Long before Samuel went to Bethlehem the cause of the south had been won, but no event had taken place to consecrate the supremacy of Judah and its inheritance of the birthright. When he poured the holy oil on the forehead of David, the prophet was anointing the fourth son of Jacob. The Battle of Gilboa, the defection of Abner, the assassination of Ish-bosheth, were the last episodes of a struggle whose issues were preordained, and the fruits of former centuries. The wisdom of Samuel and the genius of David had hastened its climax, just as the accession of Saul had stayed for a day the rise of the men of Judah without preventing it or making them belie their destiny.

From that moment deputations poured into Hebron. First of all came certain families of Judah and Simeon, who had followed the house of Saul and also some of the Levites, led by Jehoiada, the head of the sacerdotal race, and by Zadok, head of the clergy of Gibeon and of the elder branch of the house of Aaron, which had been supplanted by the younger ever since the time of Eli.[1]

The Benjamites presented themselves in small numbers. They still hoped a prince would arise among themselves. On the other hand, the tribe of Zebulun rallied itself at once, without any reserva-

[1] 1 Chron. xii. 27, 28. For Zadok, see note L in Appendix.

tions, and was the only one to go over in its entirety to the side of David.[1] Then the movement grew more pronounced, and all Israel petitioned the King of Judah.

"Behold we are thy bone and thy flesh. In times past, when Saul was king over us, it was thou that leddest out and broughtest in Israel, and the Lord said to thee, Thou shalt feed my people Israel."[2]

David had reigned at Hebron for seven years and a half; for two and twenty years he had waited for the fulfilment of Samuel's promises,[3] without ever having compromised their realisation by neglecting to avail himself of the help afforded by events, without ever having betrayed his destiny by an imprudent or hasty step. He preferred to gather fruit in its due season, when perfect ripeness detaches it from the tree and lets it fall into the outstretched hand. He feared to indulge in the pleasures of an early harvest, for he knew that meant an unripe and perishable crop. In advance of philosophers and of legislators, his conscience had again taught him that power is a delegation of the intrinsic and imprescriptible rights of human societies. To snatch it by

---

[1] 1 Chron. xii. 23-40. Josephus, "Ant. Jud.," vii. 2.

[2] 2 Sam. v. 1, 2. Josephus ("Ant Jud.," vii. 2), who was inspired by the Chronicles (1 Chron. xii. 23-40), says that the movement of concentration was slow. It doubtless lasted for several months.

[3] 2 Sam. ii. 10, 11; v. 5; 1 Kings ii. 11. On comparison of these verses with the preceding ones, it will be seen that David was then between thirty-seven and thirty-eight years of age.

force needs the help of accomplices; and the instigator of the outrage soon finds himself faced with the alternative of goading the people into revolt without being able to satisfy insatiable appetites, or of breaking with dangerous partisans at the risk of succumbing to their attacks. Evil breeds evil, and good cannot come out of crimes. These are, perhaps, mere commonplaces, an everyday and unaspiring code of morals despised by subtle intellects; but the conscience of the son of Jesse was as simple as his heart and soul, as his faith and his trust in Jehovah.

At last the hour appointed by the Almighty was at hand. David had no longer any scruple. Samuel had chosen him, Judah had acclaimed him; God had granted his dearest wish, he was called to the throne by a formal invitation from the Hebrews given of their own free will.

If the triumph of the south were the work of a long succession of generations, if royalty were the fruit of the agreement between the people and their last shophet, David at any rate was the principal builder of its fortunes; Samuel had laid the foundations of the edifice, David completed it, from the base to the summit. How he must have congratulated himself on his forbearance, on the day the glorious task was accomplished! What joy must have been his when he tasted the sweets of his victory over the ardours of youth and the impatience of his associates! With what just pride and satisfaction must he have looked upon the monument whose crowning point he had at last achieved!

Shortly afterwards the elders of the tribes came to Hebron and consecrated before the Lord the compact made with David. And it is thus that the shepherd of Beth-lehem, the humble son of Jesse, rose to be the first among the people of God, and founded a dynasty so lasting as to survive for more than five hundred years. During these five centuries Judah will not retain its supremacy over the tribes of the north. The dissensions that had been appeased by David will once more break out, bringing the greatest misfortunes upon the people; the sons of Israel, led astray by their passions, will undo the faggot bound together with such care. But during the reigns which gave it the foremost place among its brethren, the glorious pages of their history were dictated by Judah. It will brave Assyria, will struggle against Egypt, and its kings will survive the kings of Israel, until the day when the dynasty of the house of Jesse shall be buried by Nebuchadnezzar beneath the ruins of Jerusalem.

VIII

Taking of Jerusalem—Jerusalem as Capital—Campaigns against the Philistines—Organisation of the Army—Victory of Rephaim—The Philistines obliged to pay tribute—David as Tactician, Strategist, and Besieger

HEBRON, the ancient Arba (Kirjath-Arba) of the Canaanites,[1] was justly considered a town of great antiquity. It dominated the vale of Mamre, celebrated in tradition ever since Abraham had pitched his tents there on his return from Egypt.[2] It lay, moreover, in the neighbourhood of the cave of Machpelah, which was supposed to be the tomb of the patriarch and his wife.[3]

Hebron had been the first city to declare for David; for seven years and a half it had sheltered him in the early days of his kingship; and in addition it occupied the centre of the tribe of Judah, the only one that had taken part against Saul. Yet the young sovereign

---

[1] Gen. xxiii. 2. Nowadays El Khalil (the town of the) *Well Beloved*, the surname of Abraham among the Arabs.

[2] Gen. xiii. 18. For the situation of the vale of Mamre, see Gen. xviii. 1.

[3] Gen. xxv. 8, 9; xxiii. 1, 2, 19.

TAKING OF JERUSALEM

had the wisdom to resist all these important reasons for retaining it as his permanent residence.

Near Beth-lehem, his native town, to the south of Gibeah,[1] the Benjamite fortress that had become the capital of Saul; south-west of Mizpah, where the deputies of the tribes met in conclave, rose a rocky height, crowned by a fortified crag. This was Mount Zion, this was Jerusalem,[2] still in the hands of the Jebusites. The position seemed impregnable and able to resist a long blockade, for the rocks which supported the walls of the town enclosed a spring.[3] And, as a fact, the citadel of the Jebusites had triumphed over every attack.[4] Saul himself had not dared to undertake its siege. And yet it was Jerusalem that David determined to make his headquarters; giving proof in so doing of the keen political sense

---

[1] See above, p. 6, n. 2.

[2] The names of Jerusalem and of Zion seem to be very ancient, and of a prior date to the occupation of the country by the Hebrews. Jerusalem meant *place of safety*, and Zion perhaps signified *fortress*. The town was occupied by a Canaanitish tribe named *Jebusim* (Josh. xv. 8; Judg. xix. 10; 1 Chron. xi. 4). Josephus ("Ant. Jud." vii. 3), agreeing with Genesis (xiv. 18), states that the early name of David's capital was Salem, whose meaning he recognises in the sense of place of safety. In this case, it would be the name given to the celebrated Bay of Salamis, which without any doubt bears a name of Semitic origin. (See with regard to these borrowed words and the influence of Phœnicia on archaic Greece, p. 103, n. 3.)

[3] A small spring called *Gihon* and known nowadays as the fountain of the Virgin, situated to the south-east of Jerusalem. It was at the fountain of Gihon that Solomon, by the express orders of David, was anointed king. (See below, p. 248.)

[4] The positon of the citadel was so strong that the taking of the town was always an extremely difficult military operation. See below, pp. 161 and 162, n. 1.

and the clearness of vision which characterise the true statesman. Although he had been placed in authority by delegates from all the tribes, there yet remained some hostile and turbulent minorities whose internal feuds continually hindered the work of union.[1] For two and a half years, perhaps three, he had endeavoured to consolidate a government that still lacked strength, he had attempted to win over the disaffected and had seen the vanity of his efforts. So long as he did not establish a political centre independent of the past, and in harmony with the new administration, he would never break down the barriers between the national and the foreign elements which composed the tribes,[2] he would never allay the jealousies born of an exaggerated autonomy; and his sovereignty, battered and disputed, would be torn asunder between the centre and the south, between Israel and Judah. He must needs be as thoroughly impartial as was his God.

But if by remaining in Hebron he risked offending the former partisans of Saul, neither could he as a

[1] 2 Sam. iii. 39; v. 10, 12, 13; xvi. 11; and chap. xxii.

[2] Besides the Canaanites who had remained in scanty numbers, and had gradually got absorbed among the tribes, and in addition to the towns lying in Israel and still in the hands of strangers and enemies, there also existed confederations analogous to those of the Gibeonites, who had accepted the Hebrews and had made a covenant of alliance with them. (Josh. ix. and xi. 19.) It was these strangers that David wished to amalgamate with the Israelites; and he strove to gain his object by admitting into his guard Hittites such as Ahimelech (1 Sam. xxvi. 6), and Uriah (2 Sam. xi. and xxiii. 39), and by loading the Gibeonites and even the inhabitants of Jabesh with favours (2 Sam. xxi.; see above, p. 119).

Beth-lehemite, as king of Judah, uncrown the metropolis of the south to the advantage of a town of Joseph or of Benjamin. On the other hand, the heir of Moses, of Joshua, of Deborah, was bound to complete the work of the shophetim, to drive away the enemies of Jehovah from Jerusalem, and to pluck out the painful thorn from the heart of Israel.

If only success attended his enterprise, the annexation of a long-coveted place would furnish him with a glorious pretext for abandoning Hebron, and for founding in a neutral position on the rocks of Zion a capital which would symbolise the homogeneity of the people of God.

Emboldened by long impunity, and knowing of old the incapacity of the Hebrew officers and their ignorance of the art of besieging, the Jebusites scoffed at David's projects. They boasted of defending the place with a garrison composed of the blind and the lame.[1] The attack was none the less decided upon. David collected his best troops, constructed the necessary apparatus for a siege on the models of Assyrian engines, then established himself on the plateau of Rephaim, to the north-west of the fortress.

The royal army was soon in possession of the lower part of the town; its difficulties began at the foot of the citadel. To excite his men to victory, David promised all kinds of rewards for the most valiant, and reserved the office of sarsaba, left vacant in Israel since the death of Abner, for the chief who

[1] 2 Sam. v. 6, 7.

should beat down the Jebusites and snatch the first shield from the palisade erected on the top of the wall.[1] It can be seen by this detail that the king intended to rush the assault, and to take the place by storm. But he was obliged to renounce the escalade and to resign himself to the slower tactics of a methodical siege. Operations for the attack were begun. A few weeks later, a curtain was demolished. Joab, at the head of the Gibborim, sprang into the breach and occupied Jerusalem in the name of the king of Israel.[2]

The Bible gives very few details with regard to the taking of Jerusalem, and one is reduced to conjectures which, however, seem bound to be more or less correct. The point of attack, as will be presently shown, was

---

[1] The text is defective. The word translated by "shield" and which is read by the Septuagint and by many commentators as meaning "buckler" would apply to the shields placed in front of the battlements by the Assyrians, as a sort of fence or rough wall, and which served to protect them while they fought. (Dieulafoy, "Acropole de Suse," pp. 198, 209, 210, and figs. 58, 59, 66, 72, 110, 111, 112, 114, 115, 116.) The word translated as buckler by the Septuagint only occurs in one other place (Psalm xlii. 7). In that passage it has been given the meaning of cataract or water-course, which has allowed of all kinds of theories relative to precipices or fissures of subterranean aqueducts which might have played a part in the taking of Jerusalem. The Chronicles (1 Chron. xi. 6) are silent on this subject.

[2] The fortress of the Jebusites had never been occupied by the Hebrews. A verse in Judges (i. 21) and a verse in the First Book of Samuel which seem to contradict this fact, only allude to the lower town or to suburbs, outside the fortifications. In any case, in all other passages the Bible states clearly that until the day that David took Jerusalem, the town had remained in the hands of the Jebusites (Josh. xv. 63; Judg. i. 21; 2 Sam. v. 6). Josephus ("Ant. Jud." vii. § iii.) expresses the same opinion.

TAKING OF JERUSALEM

doubtless chosen to the north-west of the enceinte.[1] The siege must have been a long one, and the town must have been entered by the breach after a final assault.[2] On the other hand, as it was almost impossible to run galleries and dig chambers for mines under the rocks supporting the ramparts, the Israelites, to destroy the curtain, must have had recourse to the battering-ram or to sapping. This point is noteworthy, for it bears witness to the immense progress made in a short time by the Israelites, of which fresh proofs will be found in the narratives of the sieges of Rabbah in Ammon and of Beth-Maacah.

Rabbah in Ammon, which was also taken by Joab, was a formidable fortress, somewhat after the Chaldæan pattern, furnished with massive ramparts, completed by a citadel and protected by a ditch both broad and deep, fed by a branch of the Jabbok. Here again, as it was impossible to mine under the Jabbok,[3] it was necessary after filling up the ditch, and building a road across it wide enough for the passage of the troops and war engines, directly to attack a curtain and to make a breach in it.

At Beth-Maacah, David's officers threw up earthworks commanding the ramparts, and were thus no doubt enabled to break down the upper defences of two neighbouring towers and the curtain that they flanked; and they were about to set the sappers to

---

[1] See below, p. 161 to 163.
[2] Josephus, "Ant. Jud." vii. §§ iii. and iv.; 1 Chron. xi. 6.
[3] 2 Sam. xi. 1, 7; xii. 27, 28, 29. See below, pp. 209, 220.

work at the foot of the wall, when the place surrendered.[1]

Now, till that moment, the Hebrews, who were equally lacking in skilful officers and in the materials for conducting a siege, had never taken a fortified town except by surprise or by treachery. It was thus that Ai, Beth-el, Shechem, Thebez, Gibeah in Benjamin had fallen.[2] And then again, if the disdainful attitude of the Jebusites is any guide, their successes in besieging must have been very insignificant.

The siege of Jerusalem thus marks the beginning of a new era corresponding to the accession of David. Henceforth, the engineers of Israel will yield the palm to none. The causes and origin of their triumphs should be well noted, for they confirm the estimate of the young king's military genius which may be gathered from a study soon to follow of the Battle of Rephaim, where the victor showed himself to be the equal of some of the greatest captains.

Joab, the jealous chief who had assassinated Abner in defiance of David's orders, nevertheless received the prize of his victory,[3] and was created sarsaba of

---

[1] 2 Sam. xx. 15. See below, pp. 239 and 240.

[2] Ai was taken by means of an ambush successfully laid for its defenders (Josh. viii. 1-21). Beth-el was carried by stratagem and by surprise (Judg. i. 23-25), as was also Schechem (Judg. ix. 43-49). Thebez repelled an attempt to take it by storm and the besiegers tried in vain to burn its gates (Judg. ix. 50-52); the united tribes were only able to master Gibeah in Benjamin by laying an ambuscade for its defenders (Judg. xx. 29-41).

[3] 2 Sam. xx. 23; 1 Kings i. 19; 1 Chron. xi. 6; Josephus, "Ant. Jud." vii. § ii.

the Israelite army. His services were rewarded, and his pride and ambition were satisfied. As for the monarch, he "dwelt in the stronghold, and called it the city of David."[1] History has not ratified the conqueror's decree. Jerusalem, the city of the Jebusites, with its arid rocks, has become something better than the town of one man; it is the fatherland of the souls of men, and for centuries to come it will remain the metropolis of the thinking world.

The Hebrews had at last a capital, and in this capital reigned a king in name and in reality. The man who had accomplished their political unity rose, in point of fact, far above the ancient shepherds of the people such as the shophetim and Saul. He was the first to extend his authority over all the sons of Jacob and the first to deserve the title accorded to him.

This position of acknowledged and supreme chief of a monarchy created fresh obligations for David. If the scattered tribes were able to live without laws or common ties, without establishing foreign relations, and with no other care than that of defending themselves from one day to another against the aggressions of the Philistines, the Moabites or the Amalekites; it was quite another matter with a duly constituted nation which owed duties to its different members, and which would have suffered from its isolation. David understood this. He was already on friendly terms

[1] 2 Sam. v. 7, 9; 1 Chron. xi. 5, 7; Nehem. xii. 37; Josephus, "Ant. Jud." vii. § iii.

with the King of Moab, and with Talmai, King of Geshur. The former had sheltered his parents in the course of his strife with Saul,[1] the latter had given him his daughter Maacah as a wife.[2] He was anxious to extend the circle of his relations, and he sent ambassadors to the chiefs of the neighbouring monarchies.

Nahash, king of the Ammonites,[3] and other sovereigns gave them a favourable reception, Hiram King of Tyre distinguishing himself by the warmth of his welcome. It was the first link of an alliance in which the Israelites and the Phœnicians found an equal profit. The tribes sent the surplus of their agricultural riches into the great commercial cities and received in exchange industrial objects which they were unable to manufacture. The two countries also had common enemies, the Philistines, who coveted with equal ardour the coasts and splendid seaports of Phœnicia, and the issues into Asia and the fertile lands held by the tribes. With the hope of rendering this union still closer, Hiram sent to Jerusalem architects, masons and carpenters, whose help had been asked for by the new monarch, and gave them logs of cedar wood to bring with them for the royal dwelling.[4]

---

[1] 1 Sam. xxii. 3.

[2] 2 Sam. iii. 3 ; xiii. 37. Geshur was situated in the deserts of the south-west (Josh. xiii. 2 ; 1 Sam. xxvii. 8). It was by the daughter of the King of Geshur that David was the father of Tamar and Absalom. The alliance between David and Talmai really dated three or four years back ; but it formed part of the same policy as the others.

[3] See below, pp. 206, 207, n. 1.

[4] 2 Sam. v. 9, 11 ; 1 Chron. xiv. 1.

JERUSALEM AS CAPITAL

Masters and men set to work, and soon the heights of Zion were crowned by a palace which looked as if it had been transported from Phœnicia.[1] The rocks, formerly so bare, were now covered with buildings; and the chiefs of Israel, fired with the zeal of emulating their sovereign, built round about the old acropolis, "from Millo and inwards."[2]

When we remember that before the reign of David the Hebrews were ignorant of the rudiments of all the plastic arts, and that they possessed no monument on which their national genius could have had a chance of exercising itself,[3] it is easy to understand the decisive influence and paramount importance of this first manifestation of architecture. The prestige the king derived from it was immense; never had there been seen or imagined in the Land of Canaan anything to compare with it in riches and in splendour. But this artificial and forced expansion of the arts in a country ill-prepared for their culture had unfortunate artistic consequences. While successive invasions of the Hellenes, the Greeks and then the Dorians were soon to emancipate the ancient Pelasgic states from the bastard traditions brought by the ships from Tyre and Sidon,[4] the tribes of Israel were tightening the

---

[1] The palace stood on the heights of Zion, towards the south-eastern angle of the Haram of the present day.

[2] David consigned the Jebusites to the low town and gave the lands surrounding the palace to his most faithful servants. Joab, it would seem, had the lion's share (1 Chron. xi. 6, 8). It was his by right, as the hero of the siege.

[3] See above, pp. 15 to 26.

[4] See above, p. 103, n. 3.

bonds that pressed on them. They had forgotten Egypt, and would become henceforth the captives of Phœnician civilisation.

Persia under the Achemenidæ offered an analogous example of subordination in art.[1] This phenomenon should be considered as a simple effect of inertia. The projectile shot into space keeps on its given course, unless a foreign force causes it to swerve. The Hebrews were even less capable than the Persians of modifying the artistic impulses received from abroad.

The Philistine princes did not follow the example of Nahash and of Hiram. The narrow band of territory to which they had been confined by the Pharaohs no longer satisfied them—they wanted breathing room, and the dream of increasing at the expense of the Hebrews never lost its attractions. They had already driven away Dan and pushed back Joseph and Benjamin; it was now their ambition to reach the Jordan, to obtain the mastery of the roads into Egypt, Phœnicia and Aram. The foundation of the kingdom of Israel, the accession of a young king, the capture of Jerusalem from the Jebusites, not only hindered the success of their plans, but were events of great gravity and fraught with menace.

The Philistines were anxious to crush the Hebrews without giving them time to increase in power. They hastened to assemble their troops, crossed the frontier

[1] Dieulafoy, " Art antique de la Perse," v. ii. §§ v., vi., vii. ; v. iii. and "L'Acropole de Suse," pp. 292 to 303 and chap. xi.

JERUSALEM AS CAPITAL

near the town of Ekron, and marched on the new capital.[1] They had concentrated so rapidly and had made such a sudden irruption that David, taken by surprise, quitted his residence. Had he been so imprudent as to shut himself up in a place badly provided, badly fortified, and defended by an insufficient garrison, he would have run the risk of being surrounded there and cut off from all communication with the Judæans in the south and the men of Joseph in the north. Instead of hastening to meet the invaders, the young king took up a position in the district of Adullam,[2] near Beth-lehem. It was a sure retreat, and difficult of access; and he was thoroughly acquainted with its defensive

[1] An examination of the plan of campaign shows that the Philistines had Jerusalem in view. Their expedition was therefore of later date than the capture of this town by David. Moreover, Josephus states this expressly, and gives the same motives for their aggression as those which I have traced. Josephus, "Ant. Jud." vii. § iv.

[2] The Book of Samuel (2 Sam. v. 17) only says that David went down to the *hold* or strong place. There is a gap in the text which is filled up by another passage (2 Sam. xxiii. 13), considered by critics to belong to the account of the same campaign. It is specified there that the hold was in the district of Adullam. Mention of this is again found in the Chronicles (1 Chron. xi. 15). Another passage, considered on good authority to be correct, speaks not of the *hold*, but of the *cave* of Adullam (1 Sam. xxii. 1). It cannot be supposed, in fact, that David at this period had built a fortress in the technical sense of the word: he had doubtless defended the approaches to the cave by means of abbatis and rough walls. In any case, the spot was so well chosen that Rehoboam later on built one of his "cities of defence" upon it (2 Chron. xi. 7).

The cave of Adullam has been thought to have been found in the neighbourhood, and to the east of Beth-lehem. It is the exact situation assigned to it by the Bible (Gen. xxxviii. 1; Josh. xii. 22, xv. 33; 1 Sam. xxii. 1; 2 Sam. xxiii. 13, 14; 1 Chron. xi. 15; 2 Chron. xi. 8).

resources, having taken refuge there when fleeing from the anger of Saul.[1] It was, above all, an excellent position for the organisation of resistance, for harassing the enemy, and for watching their tactics.

As David had foreseen, the Philistines attempted to isolate his capital. While the bulk of their forces had encamped on the plateau of Rephaim, in front of Jerusalem, a detachment started for Beth-lehem, laid siege to it, and closed the road to the south. The allied princes had wished to fight under the eyes of their protecting gods, and had placed their images in the midst of the camp. But the Immortals love the peace of the sanctuary, and find pleasure only in pure victims presented on the altar. Following the example of Jehovah-Sabaoth at the Battle of Aphek,[2] where the ark had been taken and the sons of Eli had met their death, neither Dagon nor his brethren intervened in the struggle. They had eyes and did not see the Hebrews coming; they had arms and did not strike them. The Philistines, attacked at Baal-perazim, were, in fact, defeated, and their wooden gods, abandoned to their fate, swelled the booty of the conqueror. They were at once burned,[3] as a punishment for their audacious attempt to match themselves against the Lord of Israel. The defeat

---

[1] See above, p. 73.

[2] See above, pp. 38, 44, and below, p. 184.

[3] 2 Sam. v. 21; 1 Chron. xiv. 13. The burning of idols was commanded by the Law (Deut. vii. 5; ix. 21).

of Aphek was avenged; the capture of the ark was fully expiated.

The Bible does not give David's motives for being the first to attack; it is equally silent with regard to the details of the battle of Baal-perazim. We can gather that the king watched the enemy for some time, waiting for a favourable opportunity. It was towards the end of spring or the beginning of summer, at the time of the ripening of the corn, when the mountain springs dry up, and the Israelites suffered much both from heat and from thirst. Nevertheless, they endured in patience, cheered by the example of the king who shared their fatigues, and bore as they did the most cruel privations.

The sacred annalist relates that one evening, David, thoroughly worn out and tortured by thirst, cried out in anguish, "Oh, that one would give me water to drink of the well of Beth-lehem, which is by the gate!" Three Gibborim at once quitted the camp, crossed the Philistine lines, drew water from the well, and returned to their master, bringing with them the water so ardently desired. But David, fearing perhaps to excite longings that he could not satisfy, refused even to moisten his lips with it. "Be it far from me, O Lord, that I should do this: shall I drink the blood of these men that went in jeopardy of their lives?" And he took the cup presented to him and poured its contents on the ground in honour of Jehovah.[1]

[1] 2 Sam. xxiii. 13-17.

At last the long-hoped-for occasion arose. David surprised the Philistines, and God "broke His enemies before Him like the breach of waters."[1]

But if the battlefield remained to the Hebrews, hostilities were by no means terminated. The following year, at the time when kings are used to go to war, the Philistines returned, more numerous and more threatening, resolved on one supreme effort. On his side, David was fully prepared for an assault which he foresaw would be decisive. He seems to have had round him from twenty to thirty thousand well-seasoned, young, and vigorous soldiers.[2] This number, a conjectural one, is taken from documents that check each other, and it may be accepted as at least some indication.

The Israelites fought for several months with varying success. In one encounter the fighting grew so fierce that David, carried away by his courage and obstinate resolve to conquer, dashed

[1] 2 Sam. v. 20. This is the literal translation. "Baal-Perazim" means the "Lord of breaches." The Bible seeks to connect this word with the phrase used to depict the defeat.

[2] The number of 30,000 men is to be found in the first verse of the sixth chapter of the Second Book of Samuel. But this verse undoubtedly belongs to the end of chapter v. In order to occupy the battlefield of Rephaim, and to retain enough troops to effect the movement which decided the fate of the battle, David must have been able to dispose of from twelve to fifteen thousand combatants. These figures seem to indicate that from the beginning of the campaign the Israelite army consisted of little less than double the number of soldiers. Finally we are told (2 Sam. xvi. 22) that Absalom, even when taken more or less unawares, and independently of the troops remaining with David and following him, was able to lead 12,000 men in the pursuit of his father.

into the thick of the enemy. A tall Philistine, clad in heavy armour, threatened him with his brazen spear, and was about to strike when Abishai, son of Zeruiah, saw the danger, threw himself in front of the king, smote the giant and stretched him dead on the ground.[1] It is easy to see from this incident, and from the heroic acts which must have so often distinguished the chiefs of the army,[2] how desperate the struggle was.

The Philistines, who continued to pursue the same plan of isolating the northern tribes from those of the south, succeeded at last in pressing back the Hebrews to the south and west of Jerusalem, and once again occupied the plateau of Rephaim. But, taught by the disasters of the preceding campaign, they had now become very wary; and they profited by the natural features of the ground to such avail as to render their position almost impregnable. Having achieved this result, they must have begun to think about completing the investment. If they had succeeded in so doing, David shut up in Jerusalem, or driven back to the east or the south with troops weakened and demoralised by long campaigns,—unable to levy a fresh contingent,—would soon have found himself at their mercy. It was imperative, at any cost, to break through the circle in which the Philistines were threatening to imprison him, and to press them back towards the west.

[1] 2 Sam. xxi. 15-17.
[2] 2 Sam. xxi. 18-22, xxiii. 8-19 and 21; 1 Chron. xi. 13-24; xx. 4-8.

Reduced to this terrible necessity of risking his throne and the political existence of Israel in one supreme engagement, David conceived, almost under the arrows of the enemy, the plan of battle described in the Second Book of Samuel. The victorious manœuvre which this memorable day saw carried out on the plateau of Rephaim was quite unprecedented, and history has never yet recorded its superior. It will be better judged after a general glance at the military position of the enemies of the Hebrews and that of the Hebrews themselves at the accession of the son of Jesse.

Among primitive peoples a battle resolves itself into an interchange of projectiles, followed by direct attacks of one troop on the other. Like the bull, like the wild boar at bay, the man who is forced to attack, or to defend himself, faces the enemy and charges straight ahead. Soon there is a general struggle, a hand-to-hand fight where the victory is won by brute force, by boldness, by the confidence given by previous successes and the courage inspired by the presence of a chief; by the contempt for danger or the fear of torture. But there is no bond between these different qualities of the body or of the soul; no single will directs them. Each individual throws himself on an adversary, and the battle comes to an end when a number of single defeats bring about general confusion and one side is put to rout. The military chiefs, the kings, whether taking part in an action or presiding over it, do not guide its course.

The commanders of a fleet prepare the battle, give the signal, and—if they throw themselves into the fray—play the same part as their lieutenants. Later on, the nations whom the extent or the fertility of their territory exposed to frequent aggressions, sought to repel them without interrupting the course of social life, and entrusted the defence of the common patrimony to the most vigorous members of the community. Then soldiers arose, for whom war became a profession. The Egyptians had camps for their training. The troops manœuvred there in times of peace, and the officers learnt to make them form in line and go through the different evolutions, and were taught themselves to use the instruments of war to advantage. To the Chaldæans we owe the plan, the profile and the systematic flanking of fortified enceintes, and also the means of investing a stronghold, of approaching it and of penetrating into it by the breach. The Assyrians, the Susanians, and those Persians taught by the Chaldæans, emulated the latter and produced military engineers of the first order, very sagacious, very learned, whose principles and methods have hardly been improved upon.[1] But the art of besieging, together with the elements of tactics and the rudiments of strategy, formed the limit of their military knowledge. Neither the Chaldæans nor the Egyptians, nor the nations brought up in their school, had any notion of the art of preparing a plan of campaign or of battle, and of

[1] Dieulafoy, "Acrop. de Suse," chaps. iv.-vii.

executing on the field a series of manœuvres appropriate to each situation, whether thought out beforehand or inspired by circumstances. Their generals still busied themselves with setting traps and preparing ambushes, or strove to bring to the struggle an army superior in courage and numbers to that of the enemy. Even if they took no pleasure in the sight of pain, they nevertheless tortured their prisoners; for cruelty was a sovereign weapon, and terror a force and an essential point in their warlike policy.[1]

In Greece, at the time of the Persian wars, the Spartans themselves, though well accustomed to fighting, were incapable of adapting an operation to the natural features of the field of battle or to the position and manœuvres of the enemy.[2] At Thermopylæ, at Salamis, at Platæa, at Mycalē, on sea as on land, they content themselves with fighting bravely and dying like heroes. The Athenian chiefs, more prudent and more intelligent, were little superior to the vaunted generals of Lacedæmon.[3] And yet the moment was approaching when Hellas and Rome

---

[1] The bas-reliefs and inscriptions illustrating and relating the exploits of the kings of Assyria are eloquent, as also are certain passages in the Bible (Josh. viii.; Judg. i. 7, xii. 5, 6, xx. 48; 1 Sam. xi. 2, xv. 16–33; 2 Sam. xii. 31, xxi. 1–9). On this point, the Israelites, even in the time of David, were in no way behind any of their contemporaries (1 Sam. xv.; 2 Chron. viii. 2, xii. 31).

[2] Herodotus, ix. 62, &c.

[3] Herod.: for Salamis, see viii. 44, 61, 86, 91, 95, and the passages relating to the part played by Themistocles; for Platæa, ix.; for Mycalē, ix. 102.

were about to carry the art of destruction to the highest degree of perfection. Then came the Barbarians, and until the end of the twelfth century each encounter seemed modelled on the struggles of the peoples of earliest history. The Crusades brought about a temporary revival, but darkness soon reigned anew. The English, during the Hundred Years' War, had recourse once more to strategical operations. The supreme victory was about to be assured to them by the skilful disposition of their troops, by their choice and fortification of different positions and their judicious use of various weapons, when Joan of Arc arose before them.[1] The Maid of Domrémy and the shepherd of Beth-lehem were both visited by the God of combats, Jehovah-Sabaoth. It was but a flash of light; and until Frederick II., the fate of a battle was generally decided by an attack on the front in conjunction with serried ranks and clumsy evolutions.[2]

The sons of Jacob, whose pastoral life had lasted

[1] It seems that at the battle of Patay she ordered an oblique charge on the enemy's left. The English, taken unawares, hesitated. They understood too late that they were to be turned, and endeavouring to change front in order to receive the attack in the proper way, were surprised in the midst of the manœuvre by the French, who turned to the left and penetrated their lines.

Du Guesclin had already, at the battle of Cocherel, made Thomas de la Houssaye, at the head of six hundred cavalry, execute a vast turning movement out of sight of the enemy, and had greatly contributed to the victory by this manœuvre. But there was only question there of an incident and not of a masterly combination on which a whole plan of battle was depending.

[2] For Frederick, see below, p. 169, n. 1.

for a very long period, did not escape the general law. They had daring and individual courage ; Benjamin was distinguished for its skilful archers and a certain experience in matters of war—but they were poorly armed, ill-protected, and also badly officered. The political anarchy which satisfied them seemed an invincible obstacle to the constitution of an army on a footing with that of their neighbours. All the Hebrews were fighting men, not one of them was a soldier.

Nevertheless Saul had turned to account the military aptitudes of the Benjamites and had recruited partially out of his tribe a small army of three thousand men,[1] and the body of the *râcim*, who were in permanent service. *Râcim* is generally translated by *runners*. It was more a question of bodyguards whose duties were to watch over the sovereign, to escort him, to carry out his orders, to arrest or even kill those who had deserved his anger.[2] David, after his exploits and his marriage with the Princess Michal, no doubt became captain of the *râcim*. This is enough to show in what esteem this picked body was held by the king.

Saul had also wished that the troops should have a permanent chief and, following the example of the

---

[1] I Sam. xiii. 2 ; xxiv. 3 ; xxvi. 2. Cp. xiv. 52, and xxii. 6, 7 ; I Chron. xii. 29 ; Josephus, "Ant. Jud.," vi. § 7.

[2] I Sam. xxii. 17. In this same verse the *râcim* are called *the king's servants*. All the acts attributed to the *king's servants* should thus be attributed to the *râcim*. (I Sam. xvi. 15, 17 ; xviii. 22-26, and no doubt xix. 19-21.)

ORGANISATION OF THE ARMY

neighbouring monarchs, he had named a sarsaba or generalissimo.[1] Abner, his cousin-german, was the first to occupy this post in Israel. At each new moon the sarsaba and the captain of the *râcim* were invited to the king's table, where they dined with him and the crown prince. They were evidently the first after Saul and his son Jonathan.[2]

David did better than his predecessor. His earliest partisans, the celebrated *Gibborim*,[3] were divided into three companies of about two hundred men, each company being subdivided into ten platoons. Abishai, Joab's brother, was at their head.[4] Compelled to

---

[1] Cp. 1 Sam. xiv. 50, 51, and 1 Sam. ix. 1. See also 1 Sam. xvii. 55; xxvi. 5; 2 Sam. ii. 8.   [2] 1 Sam. xx. 5, 25, &c.

[3] 1 Sam. xxiii. 33; xxv. 13; xxviii. 2; xxx. 9, 10; 2 Sam. xxiii. 8–39; 1 Chron. xi. 10–46; xxviii. The literal signification of *Gibbor* is "hero." There is an evident identity between the corps of the Gibborim and that of the Gittites (2 Sam. xv. 13, 19, 22; xviii. 2). The former companions of David must have sometimes been designated by the name of Gittites, either on account of the sojourn of David and his Gibborim in the land of Gath (1 Sam. xxvii. 2) or from the fact that during this sojourn a large number of Gittites had enrolled themselves among the Gibborim (2 Sam. xv. 19–22), or else because the Gittites passed for being men of exceptional height, strength, and courage (1 Sam. xvii. 24; 2 Sam. xxi. 18–22)—perhaps for all three reasons. Finally, the Gittites, like the Gibborim, had been constituted during David's exile, had followed their chief when he returned to Hebron (2 Sam. xv. 18), and consisted of 600 men. Moreover, the Gittites are called Gibborim by the Septuagint and by Josephus.

[4] 1 Chron. xi. 20. Cp. 2 Sam. xvi. 9. Abishai, if one reads the text aright, had under his orders three chiefs who were each in command of nine lieutenants. The corps was thus divided into three battalions corresponding to the two wings and to the centre, and each battalion into ten companies, for the chief of the battalion was at the same time the chief of the first company. The names of all the officers who served in the Gibborim during the reign of David have been preserved (2 Sam. xxiii. 8–39; 1 Chron. xi. 11, &c.)

take up arms by the necessities of their adventurous life and subjected to strict discipline, well officered at every step, they had been the instruments of his first successes. When he became king, he surrounded himself with his companions in exile, the heroes of Keilah, of Ziklag, of Gibeon, and increased this solid nucleus with contingents raised among the tribes. While respecting the patriarchal tradition of the entire nation as an army, he regulated the calls to arms, limited the periods of service and partitioned the troops into divisions of a thousand men and sub-divisions of a hundred.[1] He was thus able to constitute a *bonâ-fide* army with a chief named by royal warrant for each strategical group, possessing even a corps of engineers, as is proved by the victories of the Israelites over such well defended fortresses as Jerusalem, Rabbah in Ammon and Beth-Maacha, and recognising as its supreme chief or *sarsaba* Joab, son of Zeruiah, who was promoted to this post on the taking of Jerusalem, as a reward for this success. This was unprecedented. Finally, the king surrounded himself with guards, the Cherethites and the Pelethites (Kretim-Pletim[2]) who were recruited among

---

[1] The detailed plan of the army deduced from the Chronicles (1 Chron. xxvii. 1-15) relates to a theoretical organisation, which perhaps was never realised—certainly not at this period of David's life. I have kept to the information given in the Books of Samuel, which I consider to be good guides. See for the division into army corps and groups of 1,000 and of 100 men, 2 Sam. xviii. 1, 2. Cp. 1 Chron. xii. 14; xxviii. 1; Numb. xxxi. 4, 5, 14; 1 Sam. viii. 12; xiii. 2; xviii. 3; 2 Kings xi. 4, 9, 16.

[2] 2 Sam. viii. 18; xv. 18; xx. 23; 1 Kings i. 38, 44. This was a

ORGANISATION OF THE ARMY

the Philistine principalities and among the Carites[1] whose adventurous life predisposed them towards the role of mercenaries. These he placed under the command of a former officer of the Gibborim, the most faithful and most devoted of all his friends, Benaiah[2] the Levite, son of Jehoiada. These foreign guards,[3] more trustworthy in an insurrection than the national troops, are always sought after by autocrats.

It is, moreover, proved by the course of events that owing to David's persevering efforts, to the many grades between the generals and the soldiers, and to the technical training of the Gibborim and the Cherethites and Pelethites, the orders given on the field of battle were transmitted and carried out without delay. Striking progress is shown by this organisation—the difference is indeed great between the army of Israel and the three thousand Benjamites commanded by Saul!

It was not only a question of having the soldiers, it was also necessary to give them weapons both offen-

---

special body, quite distinct from the Gibborim or Gittites, and was under the orders of the Levite Benaiah, son of Jehoiada. For the Kretim or Cretans, see above, p. 89, n. i. The Pletim, like the Kretim, must have been Philistines, but of another principality.

[1] 2 Sam. xx. 23; 2 Kings xi. 4.

[2] For Benaiah, who became sarsaba of the army after the death of Joab, see 2 Sam. viii. 18; xx. 23; xxiii. 20-23; 1 Kings i. 8, 10, 26, 32, 36, 44, &c.; ii. 30, 34, 35, 46; iv. 4; 1 Chron. xi. 22-24.

[3] It is difficult to say when the foreign or Cretan guard was formed. It seems at least that Benaiah was not put at its head until after the Moabitish war, which came after the wars with the Philistines, and that the post was a reward for his achievements in the campaign against Moab. (Cp. 2 Sam. viii. 2; xxiii. 20; and viii. 18.)

sive and defensive, projectiles, chariots,[1] battering-rams and shields similar to those of their adversaries. The Hebrews had always lacked them, though the time was past when the Philistines forbade them to forge iron, when Saul and his son Jonathan were almost the only ones to wear a helmet and a sword. The king therefore summoned workmen skilled in the manufacture of engines of war, supplied his troops, and when they were duly provided, he erected an armoury among the buildings of the citadel.[2] From that moment, owing to his foresight, the Israelites could attack the best armed troops of the neighbouring countries without being at a disadvantage, and were able to besiege and to subdue fortresses which, before the accession of David, would have resisted all their efforts.

Such was the state of military science when David was chosen by the tribes; such were the training and composition of the troops and such the engines and the armour which this prince had at his disposal a few years after his accession. It is of the utmost importance to establish these different points before attempting the study of the battle described as follows in the Second Book of Samuel[3]:—

---

[1] The Israelites had always been beaten on flat ground, on account of their not possessing any chariots of war (Josh. xvii. 18; Judg. i. 19, iv. 3). It was David who endowed the army with these formidable engines (2 Sam. viii. 4 and xv. 1; 2 Chron. i. 14).

[2] Song of Songs iv. 4.

[3] 2 Sam. v. 22–25. See also 1 Chron. xiv. 15, 16, 17, although the passage is less clear than in the account in 2 Samuel.

"The Philistines came up yet again, and spread themselves in the valley of Rephaim. And when David inquired of the Lord, He said, *Thou shalt not go up*[1]*:* make a circuit behind them over against the *bekaim*[2] (mulberry or balsam) trees. And it shall be, when thou hearest the sound of marching in the tops of the trees,[3] that then thou shalt bestir thyself: for then is the Lord gone out before thee to smite the host of the Philistines.

"And David did so as the Lord commanded him: and smote the Philistines from Geba[4] until thou come to Gezer."

This is clear and precise. And therefore, with the help of the topography of the district to complete the account given in the Bible with regard to certain details, it is possible to reproduce with some assurance the chief phases of the action.

First of all, where must the battlefield of Rephaim

---

[1] Several versions add (verse 23) after *thou shalt not go up*, a word meaning *to meet them*, *i.e.*, attack them in front. These versions thus endeavour to make still more prominent the order to execute the turning movement upon which the whole fate of the battle rests.

[2] Even the ancients were uncertain as to the meaning of *bekaim*, and the Aramaic version simply says "trees."

[3] This sound of footsteps is the sound made by Jehovah in walking on the tree tops, when at the moment of attack he places himself at the head of the Israelites. It should be understood as a soft and gentle murmur (Cp. 1 Kings xix. 12).

[4] The text gives the reading Geba (Gabaa), but in the Chronicles (1 Chron. xiv. 5, 13-16) the name Geba is replaced by that of Guibbeon, the Gibeon of the Vulgate. The best translators consider this as the better reading. From a geographical and strategical point of view either is possible.

be located? There does not seem to be much doubt as to the answer.

A glance at the map of Judæa shows the long chain of mountains running from north to south, with summits crowned by Beth-el, Jerusalem, Beth-lehem, and Hebron, and whose crest separates the Mediterranean slope from the long depression formed by the Dead Sea and the bed of the Jordan. Jerusalem occupies the southern extremity of a kind of promontory between two ravines, that of Kedron to the east, that of Hinnom to the west and south. The northern quarters of the town are joined by a gentle ascent to a plateau which stretches from the north-east to the south-west and branches off to the south, dominating the vale of Hinnom and running along the road to Beth-lehem.[1] It is the expansion of this plateau, situated, according to the Bible, above Jerusalem at the end of the ravine of Hinnom and bounded to the north by the frontiers of Judah and Benjamin, that was doubtless called by the Israelites the plateau or plain of Rephaim.[2] In its greatest dimension, follow-

[1] According to the Book of Joshua (xv. 7, 8, xviii. 16), the frontier passed by the confluence of the two ravines of the Kedron and of Hinnom, sloped upwards and ran along the crest of the latter; rejoined a line along the summit and followed this line in a westerly direction. At certain dates it even seems as if the frontier passed to the east of Jerusalem (Josh. xv. 63). M. Clermont-Ganneau, one of the best authorities on the subject, thinks that the frontier of Judah and Benjamin traversed Jerusalem. According to him the valley of Hinnom should be identified, not with the ravine bounding Jerusalem in the west, but with the hollow running from south to north which divides the town in two portions, and is known as the Tyropæon.

[2] A slight error is made in placing the plateau of Rephaim to the

ing a north-east south-west direction, a rectangle could be described about two and a quarter miles long by nearly a mile wide. There is quite sufficient space for the position and evolutions of two small armies.

Two much-frequented roads crossed each other on this plateau. The one, starting from the port of Joppa and joining the road to Philistia near Ekron, led by Jericho to the fords of the Jordan; the other, the route to Egypt, came from Hebron and Bethlehem and ran towards Gibeon, Shechem and Aram, uniting the men of Judah and Simeon with the Benjamites, the sons of Joseph and the northern tribes.

The strategical importance of this position, demonstrated by the numerous sieges undergone by Jerusalem, is in fact considerable. Even supposing that

west of Jerusalem; to the west there is neither a plateau nor plain in the proper sense of the word. The plateau defined in the Bible appears to be situated north-west of the town, at a distance of some hundred metres above the position assigned to it. The mistake arises on account of the frontier of Judah and Benjamin having been carried a little too much to the west. M. Clermont-Ganneau questions whether the plateau or plain of Rephaim did not lie to the south of Jerusalem, at the junction of the valley of the Kedron and the valley generally known under the name of valley of Hinnom. In this case the name of Rephaim would also apply to the plateau whose limits I have defined. Besides all the reasons, either already given or to follow in the succeeding pages, it is not to be supposed that the assailants would have posted themselves in a position unfavourable for the manœuvring of their chariots and dominated in addition by the heights and the citadel of Jerusalem. In any case, even supposing that the battle took place in the plain situated south of the town, it would only be on certain points of no tactical importance that this change would affect the manœuvre carried out by David.

the enemy did not intend to besiege Jerusalem, they had only, when once masters of the plateau, to cross the Kedron towards the east and obtain possession of Beth-lehem in the south, in order to invest the capital, to cut off its means of communication, to consummate the separation of the south from the north, and to retain an excellent line of retreat to the Mediterranean. Did they wish, on the contrary, to obtain possession of the place? As it is only possible to attack it from the north-west, there was all the more reason for camping in the neighbourhood of the approaches to the town. These advantages are so evident that Joash, King of Israel, Nebuchadnezzar, Titus, and Godfrey of Bouillon all prefaced the operations for the actual siege of Jerusalem by taking possession of the plateau of Rephaim and by putting its northern expanse into a state of defence.[1] All

---

[1] The sieges sustained by Jerusalem while capital of Judah were numerous. The city of David saw before its walls:—

First.—Shishak (or Chechonk), King of Egypt, who occupied it about five years after the schism (Maspero, "Hist. anc. des peuples de l'Orient," 4th ed. p. 361). The means by which he took possession of the city are unknown.

Second.—Joash, King of Israel, in the reign of Amaziah, King of Judah (2 Kings xiv. 1 to 15; 2 Chron. xxv. 23). The place was taken.

Third.—Rezin, King of Syria, and Pekah, King of Israel, in the reign of Ahaz, King of Judah. The siege was raised (2 Kings xvi. 5; Isaiah vii. 1).

Fourth.—Sennacherib, King of Assyria, in the reign of Hezekiah. The siege was raised (2 Kings xviii. 13, xix.; Isaiah xxxvi.).

Fifth.—Nebuchadnezzar, in the reign of Zedekiah (2 Kings xxiv. 10, xxv. 1–8; Jerem. xxii. 19, xxxvii., xxxix., lii.).

With regard to the situation of the lines of the besiegers, it depended on the position of the breach. Joash, it is said (2 Kings xiv. 13; 2 Chron. xxv. 23) made a breach between the gate of Ephraim and the

four alike established their front line there, parallel with the greater side of the north-east south-west rectangle, of which mention has been made; the natural features of the surrounding country, as well as the importance of occupying the roads to Jericho and to Gibeon rendering this a matter of necessity.

The Philistines, who had the same object as the Israelites, the Chaldæans, the Romans, and the Crusaders, and who, in order to attain it, followed methods of attack very similar to those of their successors and made use of weapons and engines almost identical with those of the latter, had like them, and for the same reasons, made themselves masters of the plateau of Rephaim and of the road to Beth-lehem. Then, in obedience to the more or less imperative obligations which imposed themselves on the besiegers, they also were obliged to draw up their troops in the north-east south-western direction indicated above, on horseback on the road from Gibeon to Jerusalem and on that from Jerusalem to Joppa and Ekron.

After a study of the ground, if reference be made to the account given in the Bible, it will be found to confirm the dispositions described above. It is first of all stated that the Philistines, wishing to retain

---

angle, *i.e.*, on the north front between the middle of this front and the north-west angle. For the Chaldæans, it was decided by the escape of the besieged by the gate opposite to the attack, " by the way of the gate between the two walls, which was by the king's garden," and their flight in the direction of Jericho (2 Kings xxv. 4). As for the Romans, we have the very precise testimony of Josephus. He says that the attack was directed against the north-western salient angle of the enceinte.

command of the Israelites, moved back their line of battle to the ridge terminating the plateau. We are told, in fact, that David would have had to "go up" to attack them. Moreover, it may easily be deduced that their left wing was supported by the heights traversed by the road from Jerusalem to Gibeon when it enters the land of Benjamin on leaving the plateau of Rephaim; and that their right was defended by a ravine and by clumps of trees or shrubs, the *bekaim* of the text, situated at the extremity and on the south-western slope of the plateau.[1]

There can be no hesitation either as to the points where the two wings of the Philistines ended, or with regard to the position of the forest of *bekaim*. Firstly, because the formation of the ground and the direction of the two roads going from Jerusalem towards the north and towards the west, whose issues on the plateau it was necessary to command, obliged the besieging army to establish itself along a line drawn from the north-east to the south-west; secondly, because the front line, as has just been seen, had been drawn up as far as possible on to the ridge; and thirdly, and above all, because of the conclusive evidence afforded by the fact that the Philistines, completely put to rout by the flank attack directed against their right wing, fled in the opposite direction

---

[1] The hollow into which David plunged is clearly indicated in the plans of the environs of Jerusalem. At the present day clumps of trees still grow in the ravine which, in my opinion, he followed in order to turn and surround the right wing of the Philistines.

to the attack, taking the only way left open, and regained their principalities by Gibeon and Gezer, in spite of the difficulties, the windings, and the length of the road. It is thus clear that the wood of *bekaim* trees was opposite to the spot where the road from Jerusalem to Gibeon penetrated the mountains of Benjamin, and more or less near the road from Jerusalem to Joppa, since from the moment of the first attack this latter road, *i.e.*, their true line of retreat, was closed to the defeated army. On the other hand, David could only mask his attack by throwing himself into the ravine bordering the plateau towards the south-west. Every consideration and every piece of internal evidence thus unite in determining within narrow limits the extreme points attained by the two wings of the Philistines and in tracing the exact position of their front line. No special mention is made in the Bible of chariots of war. They were greatly dreaded by the Israelites, and would be easy to manœuvre on the battlefield of Rephaim; the Philistines must no doubt have had a number of them in their ranks. They would have probably massed them in a trapezium behind the centre and the right.

Such was the excellent position of defence assumed by the Philistines, when, after long preparations, full of confidence, but not forgetful of the disastrous surprise which had brought the preceding campaign to a close, they awaited the Hebrew attack.

On his side David, who knew himself to be spied

upon by the enemy, and who could not hope to succeed again in an ambush, must have left Jerusalem with great parade, rallying to him the troops encamped to the east of the town. This is not explicitly stated in the Bible, but can be inferred from the conduct of the operations. The Israelite army advances to the sound of the trumpets of war. Although thinned by death, by sickness and deserters from the ranks, it still consists of ten or twelve thousand men.[1] This number barely suffices for the length of the field of battle between the roads from Jerusalem to Gibeon and from Jerusalem to Ekron.

According to custom, the Hebrews draw up opposite to their adversaries.[2] Soon the archers and the slingers spring forward, the infantry supporting them. And while the Philistines, deceived by this demonstration, concentrate their attention on the attack and only think of watching these first movements and of their preparations for the combat, David manœuvres behind the curtain of the troops deployed at his front.[3] He cannot think of charging the enemy's centre nor its inaccessible left wing, protected by rocky buttresses. But on the

[1] See above, p. 148, n. 2.

[2] This very rational formation, which was usually adopted in ancient times, is, moreover, described in the First Book of Samuel xvii. 3.

[3] This was a tactical necessity. The disappearance of a portion of David's troops would have alarmed the Philistines. In parallel cases every general plans an open and energetic attack at the front.

VICTORY OF REPHAIM

right wing there is a deep ravine, studded with thick brushwood which will serve his daring projects. Then, invoking the commands of Jehovah, he quits the field of battle, followed no doubt by the Gibborim and some picked soldiers, perhaps from three to four thousand men.[1] He reaches the south-western slope of the plateau, turns to the right, climbs up towards the north, profits by the unevenness of the surface and the slope of the ground along which he is advancing in order to conceal his flank movement from the Philistines, and reaches the forest of *bekaim* unnoticed. He penetrates into it, forms again for the attack, and then at a signal silently agreed upon, given and transmitted,[2] crosses the skirts of the wood, surprises his adversaries, charges them in the flank and in the rear, and occupies their line of retreat in great force. The Philistines, already menaced at the front by the rest of the Israelite army, fall back in disorder upon their left, and are obliged to fly by the only way left open, the road from Jerusalem to Gibeon. It is only after reaching Gezer, when the

[1] The question might be asked whether the turning movement was not begun during the night. The sound of marching in the tops of the trees would answer in this case to the rustling produced among the leaves shaken by the breeze which sometimes, in the East, begins to blow when day is breaking. I do not think so. (See above, p. 159, n. 3.) David, who knew that the Philistines were on the alert, would have feared with good reason to have been surprised in the act of manœuvring if he had not lulled the vigilance of the enemy by showing himself with the Gibborim on the field of battle. The combat was certainly begun and carried on in broad daylight.

[2] Perhaps by shaking or waving branches of some of the trees. See above, p. 159, n. 3.

pursuit is slackened, that they are able to take once more the road to Ekron and Philistia.

These are the chief lines, broadly sketched, of the Battle of Rephaim. What are the consequences, from a strategical point of view, that we may legitimately infer from them?

The several evolutions of a complicated and hazardous nature which decided the fate of the battle, would betoken, even at the present day, when successfully conducted, a consummate general, experienced lieutenants, troops well accustomed to manœuvres, mobile, and, above all, disciplined almost into unconsciousness, so contrary is it to our instincts not to meet peril face to face. Does not Marshal Bugeaud declare that a soldier in time of war is more frightened at a danger on his flank than at one ten times as great in front of him? And again, does not the theory of besieging partly depend upon the observation made in every age that a man placed behind a parapet always fires, whatever may happen, in a direction at right angles to the front which he is defending?

In point of fact, the Israelites had just effected in the face of the Philistines a turning and enveloping movement, that is to say, an operation of war considered to be one of the boldest, most skilful, and difficult, attempted by forces similar in number to those of the Hebrews; but at the same time very efficacious and brilliant when successful. It was the favourite manœuvre of Frederick the Second, and the one on which his military reputation rests.[1] This prince gained, under the same conditions as David and with an army scarcely more numerous, the battle of Mollwitz (April 10, 1741) and the much better known battle of Rosbach (November 5, 1757), where twenty-two thousand Prussians defied the allied troops of fifty-six thousand soldiers, and killed or wounded one-seventh of their effective force.[2] Napoleon, although he preferred to direct his efforts against the enemy's centre so as to cut its lines in two, a manœuvre considered impracticable at the present day of long-range guns, had recourse sometimes to turning movements, particularly at Montenotte (April 12, 1796), Jena (October 13, 1806), and Borodino (September 7, 1812). Finally, at Reichsfontein and at Saint-Privat (August 18, 1870), the Prussians outflanked one of the wings of the French army and

[1] He had first of all to substitute the formation in three ranks, which was lighter and more easily manœuvred, for the old formations in four ranks.

[2] In the morning Frederick attacked the left wing of the allies, commanded by the Comte de Saint-Germain. While they were skirmishing he entered a hollow at right angles to the front of the two armies and was thus able to conceal his turning movement. Suddenly towards the evening the Prussians appeared on the right of the Franco-Austrian army, and poured a volley into its flank, while their cavalry prevented it by repeated charges from forming for battle.

The battle of Rosbach, so celebrated in history, compares eminently with that of Rephaim. Not only does the ground upon which Frederick manœuvred resemble in its character the battlefield of Rephaim, but the leading ideas of the two actions are analogous, and while the number of troops engaged makes no difference with regard to the importance of the manœuvre, the movements executed by the Israelites and by the Prussians are identical

surrounded it, re-enacting without knowing it the battle of Rephaim.

In each of these battles the assailing army owed the victory to the same co-operation of circumstances. Attacked on its weakest side, the adversary was either unable to modify its order of battle, or when it attempted to do so, was caught in the act of formation. In both cases, the troops surrounded are in point of fact either lost or at least very much exposed, and the rest of the army is doomed to certain defeat, unless it be possible to stop the march on the flank and the changes of front preceding the attack which are always very dangerous—so dangerous that their failure on the plains of Pharsala (June, 48 B.C.),[1] as at Austerlitz (December 2, 1805), brought disaster to formidable assailants greatly superior in numbers to the armies attacked.[2]

[1] Pompey was in command of forty-five thousand foot soldiers and seven thousand horsemen. His right wing stood against a stream whose steep banks formed an excellent defence. He had therefore moved his cavalry to the left, intending by its means to outflank the enemy's right wing and cut off its retreat. Cæsar understood his adversary's plans and favoured their execution. His army consisted of twenty-three thousand infantry and of only one thousand cavalry. Antony was in command of the right wing, Calvinus of the centre, and Sylla of the left wing. He had placed, as a bulwark to receive the shock of the cavalry, six cohorts of veterans hidden behind his right wing. Pompey, on the commencement of the action, orders his cavalry to surround Cæsar's right wing. The latter profits by the turning movement necessitated by the manœuvre, to bring forward the six cohorts in reserve. The cavalry, surprised by this flank attack, are put to rout, separated from the rest of their army, which, hotly attacked and deprived of part of its forces, beats a retreat in complete disorder.

[2] The battle of Austerlitz bears a close resemblance on every point to the battle of Pharsala. Like Cæsar, Napoleon, who had divined

PHILISTINES OBLIGED TO PAY TRIBUTE

An idea of the immense strategical import of this operation may be gathered from these few examples. But the technical value of a manœuvre does not only depend upon its conception; the importance of the forces in action, the difficulties of execution and the result obtained, must also be considered. On this head, and considering the times and the place, the victory of Rephaim is unsurpassed. It is a question, not of comparing the fifteen or twenty thousand soldiers manœuvred by David with the numberless armies of the Napoleonic epic, but of estimating the effort achieved by the Hebrews and the Philistines. The conditions under which this campaign was undertaken, the importance of the interests at stake, the long preparations of the combatants, all combine to show that it was an immense effort on both sides. The Philistines, defeated in the preceding campaign, menaced anew and determined to strike a decisive blow, summoned all their allies to their aid, enrolled Egyptian officers,[1] and led their best troops into the field of operations. On his side, David, warned in

the intentions of the Austrio-Russians, had stripped his right wing in order to attract the enemy, and had carried back behind this point a strong force composed of the guard and of Davout's corps. Kutussof, deceived by the apparent weakness of the right wing of his adversary, plumed himself on his design of turning it. But, by precipitating the march of the troops ordered to outflank the French, he left a gap in his columns. This was the moment for which the Emperor was waiting. While Davout was facing the attack directed against the right wing, Napoleon took advantage of the opening to hurl Soult against the heights of Prazen in the centre of the enemy's lines, cut the line of the Austrio-Russians, and rendered all resistance vain.

[1] 2 Sam. xxiii. 21 and 1 Chron. xi. 23.

time, had mustered all the young men fit for war, and he and they fought with indomitable energy.[1] His call to arms was probably answered by more than twenty thousand:[2] it was the horde, but yesterday so savage, sent by Israel to follow the Judges. But since his exile, the son of Jesse had so skilfully environed the contingents from the tribes, and brought them into such a state of discipline, that he did not fear to include them in an operation which one moment's shrinking, one badly transmitted order, would have rendered disastrous. As for the result, it was superior even to the effort, and of such importance that the battle of Rephaim marked the beginning of the decline of the hereditary enemy of Israel. From Ekron to Gath, the Philistines are attacked all along the frontier. After having been the successful aggressors for several centuries, they are forced to defend themselves; after having laid the Hebrews under the yoke of tribute, they in their turn are driven to beg for peace.[3] They buy it dearly, at the price of annual contributions and of the principality of Gath.[4] From that moment, and

---

[1] See above, pp. 148 and 149, and Josephus, "Ant. Jud." vii. § iv.

[2] See above, p. 148, n. 2.

[3] 2 Sam. viii. 1; 1 Chron. xviii. 1.

[4] 1 Chron. xviii. 1. This conquest is not spoken of in the books of Samuel, but mention is made there of battles waged around Gath, as well as in the parallel passages in the Chronicles. Moreover, Solomon, on ascending the throne, is lord over the principality of Gath under the title of suzerain prince (1 Kings ii. 39 and iv. 20; 2 Chron. ix. 26). Then, it is known that the city of Gath was fortified by Rehoboam (2 Chron. xi. 8) and re-taken from the Hebrews in the

for ever after, their military power fades away. After the schism, during the wars which stained the reign of weak King Hezekiah with blood, they tried one last effort. But they were crushed. They were no longer fit to cope with Israel, even with Israel dismembered and weakened.[1]

One last point remains to be settled. Is the turning movement the original conception of David ? It is impossible to say so for certain. Nevertheless, it is evident from many indications that the battle of Rephaim was a military achievement extraordinary if not unique in the annals of earliest antiquity. We must remember first of all the ignorance of the ancients, in the East as well as in the West, of anything but the elements of tactics and strategy, and that David could not possibly borrow from those who had nothing to give. To the observations already made on this subject must be added the following remark : the Philistines, aware of the strength of the royal army, put on their guard by its last successes, skilled in the art of war and connected moreover with Egyptian troops, the best in those distant ages, were disconcerted by the manœuvre of the Hebrews. Finally, note must be

---

reign of Joash by Hazael, King of Syria (2 Kings xii. 17). These are decisive reasons in favour of the version of the Chronicles, and they show clearly that David made himself master of Gath. As for the tribute, it is mentioned in several passages (1 Kings iv. 20; 1 Chron. ix. 26; xvii. 12). The Philistines were still paying it in the reign of Jehoshaphat.

[1] 2 Kings xviii. 7, 8.

made of the fact that this flank attack was considered so wonderful by contemporaries, that they attributed its idea to God himself, while David, in spite of the legitimate glory which he could have derived from it, was careful to invest Jehovah with the responsibility of the operation. David never invoked in vain the authority of Heaven, reserving it as a final resort whenever he wished to impose his will in opposition to that of his followers, to ensure the success of an unforeseen manœuvre, or to introduce a conception too daring to be understood by his soldiers. Such were the deliverance and then the abandonment of Keilah, the pursuit of the Amalekites after the sack of Zik-lag, and the preceding campaign against the Philistines.

David thus was ignorant of his precursors, supposing any had existed, and the honour and glory of the battle of Rephaim may with every reason be claimed for his memory.

A critical examination of the two last campaigns against the Philistines and the brilliant victory by which they were crowned, explains better than any commentary the extraordinary fortune of the shepherd of Beth-lehem. David there shows himself impervious to fatigue, indifferent to privations; he displays the qualities of a heroic Gibbor, of an incomparable strategist, and of an unrivalled tactician. He triumphs by his conceptions, stimulates by his example; his soul and the body over which it reigns combine for the success of Israel and the ruin of its enemies.

No writer, no commentator, had ever pointed out the importance, both from a military and historical point of view, of these two campaigns. And yet, a battle which terminated an ancient feud, which crushed for ever a warlike people, demanded a technical study. The reason for this silence is to be found in the fact that both admirers and detractors of David have always considered the installation of the Ark at Jerusalem and the restoration of the faith as the culminating acts of his life. The fame of the sacred *choregos* has obscured the glory of the strategist and of the successful besieger.

No special objections have been raised against the historical value of the passages relating to this last campaign. A few gaps and unimportant transpositions only have been noted. There is no need to add that the account of the battle of Rephaim can only be an analysis or transcription of documents dating from the time of David. No annalist would have been capable of inventing a military operation of that order and of describing it in so precise a manner.

IX

The Ark at Jerusalem—Organisation of the Faith and of the
Clergy

NOTWITHSTANDING his successes in arms, in spite of his wonderfully rapid elevation, the young sovereign did not lose his head. He was on his guard against the dizziness to which Saul had succumbed, and did not slacken in devotion to his heavenly protector or in obedience to the prophets — those implacable censors—those tutors of morality—those interpreters of a jealous God. It has been already said and demonstrated: the son of Jesse was religious and a sincere believer.[1] He was no saint in the sense nowadays attached to the word, still less a fanatic or a bigot; but few men have ever had more faith in their Creator and more gratitude for His goodness, few have shown a more marked desire to walk in his ways, and to acknowledge by a constant piety the mercies and blessings poured down by heaven. He remembered that Jehovah had taken him from the

[1] See above, pages 81, 82, 97 and 98, and note H in Appendix.

pastures and from his flock to make him shepherd of the people of Israel. He did not forget the one who had aided him in his enterprises, who had struck terror into his enemies, who had made his name as glorious as the greatest names upon earth.[1]

"Oh Jehovah, who shall sojourn in Thy tabernacle? Who shall dwell upon Thy holy hill? He that walketh uprightly and worketh righteousness . . . shall never be moved."

And as the righteousness of a king consists in the strict accomplishment of his duties towards his subjects, and as the well-being of the subjects is the reward and token of a virtuous king, it will be the constant endeavour of David to seek a safeguard against peril and a sure pledge of happiness for his people by keeping them in the fear of the Lord. He has felt the mighty force, the invincible power lying in the faith of a nation in a God sovereignly just; he has understood that the corner stone of any social edifice which is to be great, useful and lasting, must be a religion founded upon morality. And he will display all his energy, he will make use of all the resources of his eloquence in order to rekindle the spirit of piety, to bring union among the clergy, to restore the popular faith neglected since the reigns of Saul and Ish-bosheth, and to restore to Jehovah the undivided soul of the tribes. The work that he began in his youth when he defended his father's flocks against wild beasts, that work he now continues

[1] 2 Sam. v. 2; vii. 8, 9.

in favour of the people whose destinies have been placed in his hands, and, with this aim, he will make Jerusalem, not only the capital, but the pole of Israel's religion.

After the ark, so rashly brought into the field of battle at Aphek, had been taken by the Philistines, and later on carried back to Beth-shemesh, it had been left at Kirjath-Jearim, in the house of Abinadab, a member of the tribe of Judah. Samuel had judged the children of Israel: Saul and Ish-bosheth had reigned over them, and no one had troubled about the ark, forgotten in the neighbourhood of the uncircumcised, in a spot unworthy of its sanctity.

The indifference of the chiefs of Israel is easily explained. The accession of Samuel to the dignity of the shophetate corresponded to a sudden change in the direction of the religious power, which, from the hands of the priests who had grown up around a symbol, passed to the prophets whose existence was independent of any.[1] This transition, which is indicated in every verse of the books of Samuel, was facilitated by the disappearance of the ark, and followed on the numerous abuses of which the chiefs of the sacerdotal caste had been guilty. The priests had never been loved; they ended by thoroughly wearying the people, who looked upon the taking of their palladium and the death of Eli and his sons as a

---

[1] See above, chap. vi., pp. 100 to 102. For the historical criticism of the texts used for this study, see note L in Appendix on the organisation of the clergy.

punishment from heaven. The prophets took advantage of this disaffection, and their chiefs, who had become the directors of the conscience of Israel, far from seeking to restore an emblem which was the great force of their competitors, did their best to let it be forgotten. Then came the massacre of the priests of Nob, after which the cohen accompanied David in his wanderings, and a kind of schism arose among the clergy.[1] This weakened still further their waning influence over the tribes; and with each passing year the memory of the holy emblem of the covenant and the respect for the earthly throne of Jehovah, grew fainter among the people.

From that time divination played a preponderant part to the detriment of religion, and the struggle for influence between the priests and the prophets confined itself to a close rivalry between directly-inspired prophecies and the oracles of the ephod, whose importance had increased beyond measure ever since the taking of the ark. The Hebrews, instead of the pure and lofty worship they used to offer up to God, instead of the sacrifices they used to celebrate before the tabernacle as long as it contained the mercy-seat of the Lord, now went from the ephod to the seers, and wore themselves out in vain consultations of the future. Deprived of the ark, the faith was exposed to one more danger, for it lent itself to the multiplication of ephods and of cohenim, thus losing the discipline and unity which constituted its strength.

[1] See note L in Appendix.

Had not David, better inspired than his predecessors, felt that prophecy, consultations of the ephod, and religious observances celebrated at the many altars erected all over the country would not suffice to win back fickle hearts, and would not take firm hold of the wavering imagination of the Hebrews, it is quite possible that their religion, degraded by ceremonies of divination, and abandoned to the caprices of numerous sects, would have degenerated into idolatry. To satisfy the inordinate craving of the people for material representations of the divinity, and to make them forsake the gods of the strangers, the palladium of Israel that Ephraim had allowed to be ravished must be set on high, the great traditions of the Exodus renewed, and the ark restored to the prestige attached to it before it betrayed the hopes of the nation. The throne must be supported by the walls of the tabernacle : the representative of earthly power, and this symbol of the power of God, the royalty of earth and the royalty of heaven, must meet in one common abode, in the same metropolis, behind the same strong gates.

The ark of the covenant or *aron*, destined by David to become the pivot of the worship of Jehovah, consisted of a chest of *shittim* (acacia?) wood, surmounted by a winged figure at each end : it had been made both light and solid, so that there should be no difficulty in moving it. The chest and the cherubim by which it was crowned were covered all over with pure gold : rings fastened to the sides had staves passed through them which served for purposes of transport and were never removed from their place. The remark has been long ago made that in its construction the ark must have been strongly suggestive of the bark of Osiris. One of the wings of the cherubim was lowered and brought forward; the other, horizontal, was spread out over the chest.[1] It appears from this detail that the cherubim, despite their Semitic name, betrayed an Egyptian origin. The genii of Chaldæa and of Assyria have, in point of fact, their wings thrown back, these being the organs of flight; while the wings of certain deities on the banks of the Nile, and no doubt those of the Hebrew cherubim, were arranged to form a protecting shield.[2]

This unusual attitude of the cherubim, the antiquity of the tradition which secured respect for them when the priests and the prophets were denouncing the representations of real or fictitious beings, the adaptation of the sacred chest to incessant journeyings, as well as the choice of an object recalling the cult of Osiris, all confirm the essential points of the biblical tradition. The ark, in all certainty, dated from the time when the chiefs among Israel, on leaving Egypt, proposed to themselves to group the tribes, and determined to rally them round a material emblem of their protecting God.[3]

[1] Exod. xxv. 10-21; xxxvii. 1-9.
[2] For the cherubim, see note P in Appendix.
[3] Exod. xxv. 17, &c.; xxxvii.; Josh. vii. 6-15; 1 Sam. iv. 4; 2 Sam vi. 2.

The actual presence of Jehovah between the wings of the cherubim was admitted at a very early date, and remained an article of the faith. It was from this throne that the Lord communed with His elect. This was the origin of the idea that there was but one legal oracle, that the oracle was inseparable from the ark, and that only the cohen or chief of the clergy of the ark was pure enough and high enough placed in the sacred hierarchy to dare to present himself before God and ask Him questions. As for the other priests, and still more those Hebrews who did not fulfil a sacerdotal function, they would be struck dead, it was said, if they ventured to approach Jehovah.[1] Later on, the clergy became so jealous and anxious to increase their prestige, that they forbade the laity to approach the ark within a distance of less than two thousand cubits when it was taken out of the tabernacle.[2] The ceremonial of Eastern courts, and of many religions, notably that of the Mazdæans with regard to the sacred fire, ordain similar decrees.[3] The majesty of beings and of things is greatly increased by the mystery and the darkness which hide primary causes, and render them sensible only by their effects.

The growth of the intimate relations between

---

[1] 1 Sam. vi. 19; 2 Sam. vi. 6, 7. These different points have been more fully treated in note K, on the prophetic ephod, and in note L on the organisation of the clergy.

[2] Josh. iii. 4. About six hundred paces.

[3] The sacred fire could not be approached at a distance of less than thirty paces. See Dieulafoy, "Acropole de Suse," p. 415.

Jehovah, the ark, the ephod, and the cohen, can thus be traced. To the one and only God, a throne is given from which he can make known his will and pronounce his judgments. For God descended between the wings of the seraphim, there must be an organ and an interpreter to enter into communication with the material world. The organ was the prophetic ephod, the interpreter of the ephod was the cohen. In periods of trouble, and particularly after the taking of the ark, there were several cohenim, just as there have been several popes co-existent, and there were in the same way many ephods; but at the time when the ark was consecrated, and as long as it dwelt among the Hebrews, there is no doubt that there was but one legal cohen, the head of the clergy of the ark, and but one legal ephod, that handled by the cohen to interrogate God when he descended on the mercy-seat. There was the law, and there the truth; all beyond was sacrilege and sin.[1]

After the conquest of the Promised Land the ark had been installed in Shiloh,[2] but it was removed at times to other places. This was in accordance with tradition. Thus, it is doubtless present in Shechem when Joshua, shortly before his death, gathers together there the heads of familics and of races.[3]

---

[1] See notes K and L in Appendix.

[2] Josh. xviii. 1; Judg. xx. 18; xxi. 19, &c. (Gibeah was, in point of fact, taken in the early days of the conquest; see p. 12, n. 2.) 1 Sam. iii. 3; iv. 4.

[3] Josh. xxiv. 1. No formal mention is made of the ark, but it is said that at Shechem the elders and officers of Israel " presented

Later on, upon a serious occasion, it is transferred to Beth-el.[1] Then finally the Israelites, beaten by the Philistines, insist that the sons of Eli should bring it into the field at Aphek. The disastrous issue of the enterprise is well known. The priests intrusted with it died in its defence, the ark was taken, carried into the Temple of Dagon, and seven months later was brought back into Israelite territory, where it finally found a refuge in the house of Abinadab, a Judæan of Kirjath-jearim.

The ark was still in the rustic abode where it had been forgotten, when David, strengthened in his resolve to restore its cult and to make it the pivot of the faith, determined to seek it in person and to convey it to Jerusalem. He assembled the Judæans, summoned musicians and singers, and set out at their head on the road to Kirjath-jearim. "And they set the ark of God upon a new cart, and brought it out of the house of Abinadab."[2] As they had to go down a steep incline,[3] Uzzah, son of Abinadab, kept close to the wheels, holding himself in readiness to put the drag on, while his brother walked in front of the team. The oxen stumbled and shook the ark; Uzzah instinctively endeavoured to support it. "He

---

themselves before God." Given the belief in the actual presence of God between the wings of the Seraphim (see above, p. 182) this statement can bear no other interpretation than the one I have given to it.

[1] Judg. xx. 22.
[2] 2 Sam. vi. 3. The reason is given in the Septuagint.
[3] 1 Sam. vi. 21; 2 Sam. vi. 3, 4.

put forth his hand and took hold of it . . . and God smote him there for his error, and there he died by the ark of God."[1]

The authenticity of this mysterious death is but little disputed; there is more room for discussion as to its cause. Did the son of Abinadab succumb to a broken blood vessel, to an aneurism?—or was it that the cart, having been carried away by the slope, Uzzah slipped under the wheels in trying to wedge them up, and was crushed to death? It is not improbable. In any case, he perished in a manner highly opportune for the glorification of the ark. Jehovah smote the man, who, violating ancient custom, dared to approach his throne at the risk of touching it; and gave back to the ark the prestige which defeat and exile had greatly weakened. For the veneration of the multitude is always accompanied by a sentiment of fear; and the punishment of the sacrilege which had been committed, struck this necessary terror into the impressionable soul of the Israelites, that soul whose weaknesses and agitations have been laid bare to us in the history of Saul's life and the multiplication of false prophets.

After the chastisement of Uzzah, the escort, seized with terror, had dispersed and had scattered the dread news among the tribes. The abandoned ark was sheltered by a Levite of Gath named Obed-edom. He kept it for three months in his house, treating it with the utmost piety and respect, and as all his

[1] 2 Sam. vi. 7; 1 Chron. xiii. 10.

family were blessed by the Lord, every one took fresh courage. Then David once again assembled the people, but instead of confiding the sacred shrine to their care, he "called for Zadok and for Abiathar the priests" and gave it into their charge.

Although long before David the constitution of the clergy of the ark acknowledged one chief alone,[1] the Bible is not without good reason for calling Abiathar and Zadok by the same title of cohen. Abiathar bore it by right of inheritance. He was, by his father Ahimelech, the unfortunate chief of the priests of Nob, the great-grandson of the shophet Eli. Moreover he had charge of the ephod and, from this fact above all, was the superior of Zadok. The proof of this supremacy is that he alone was appointed chief guardian of the ark, and that in the following reign, when he had fallen into disgrace, the second cohen Zadok succeeded him in his office at Jerusalem.[2] With regard to Zadok, there would only be question of a title corresponding to an irregular situation, of an abuse born of those days of trouble, that David had been obliged to recognise because Zadok was a reputed descendant of the eldest son of Aaron, and particularly because the priests of Gibeon who owned Zadok for their chief had rallied to the new dynasty on this express condition.

It is probable, indeed, that from the day of the capture of the ark and of the death of Eli, Shiloh,

---

[1] See note L in Appendix.
[2] See below, p. 254.

the ancient religious metropolis and the residence of the cohen-shophet, had been abandoned. The priests had settled themselves at Beth-el, then at Nob, towns in the neighbourhood of Shiloh, and had taken with them the tabernacle, the tables which bore the offerings, and the shewbread, the altars attributed to Bezaleel, the sacred treasure, and finally the ephod. Nob then became for a very short time the spiritual capital of Israel. But after the murder of the priests of Nob and of Ahimelech, their chief Abiathar, son of Ahimelech, had fled to David, while Zadok transferred to Gibeon all the ceremonial appurtenances that Abiathar had been unable to take with him. Nob, in its turn, was deserted.[1]

Gibeon, which had been a Levitical city for a long time,[2] would thus have become the religious centre of the kingdom of Saul and would have all the more increased in importance from the fact that Abiathar, attached to the person of the son of Jesse and following him in all his wanderings, had in a manner abdicated. It was the high position that Zadok occupied among the priests of Gibeon,[3] a position retained by him until the day of his summons to Jerusalem, that doubtless gave him the right to bear the title of cohen. This would explain the presence of the two chiefs of the priesthood at the ceremony, as also the anxiety of the king to command their

---

[1] See note L in Appendix; and for the ephod, altars, &c., notes K and N.
[2] Josh. xxi. 17.   [3] 1 Chron. xvi. 39.

attendance, with the object of amalgamating the two divisions of the clergy by compelling them to participate in the transport of the ark.

"Ye are the heads of the fathers' houses of the Levites, he said unto them; sanctify yourselves, both ye and your brethren, that ye may bring up the ark of the Lord, the God of Israel, unto the place that I prepared for it. For because ye bare it not at the first the Lord our God made a breach upon us, for that we sought Him not according to the ordinance."[1]

Obeying the orders of the monarch, the two cohenim, followed by their acolytes, formed themselves into a sacred cohort; and the people, recalled to their reverence for the prescribed rites that they had forgotten —they had lived for so long far away from the ark— assembled behind the ministers of the Lord in one of those sumptuous processions whose splendours are indicated in Assyrian bas-reliefs.

When the sacred emblem reached Jerusalem, there rose up from the streets and from the terraces a hymn of joy, a triumphal concert in which human voices blended with the music of harps and the blasts of the trumpets made famous by the taking of Jericho.

---

[1] The facts are given in the Second Book of Samuel (vi. 1–12). The details are derived from the Chronicles (1 Chron. xv. 12–14), particularly those relating to the presence of the two cohenim. (Perhaps the part they played was exaggerated there, but the interest of the passage lies in the mention made of them, and in the accordance which it establishes between other verses of the Books of Samuel and of the Kings; see below, pp. 287 and 288.)

THE ARK AT JERUSALEM

" Sing unto God, sing praises to His name : Cast up a highway for him that rideth through the deserts. His name is Jah, and exult ye before Him.

They have seen Thy goings, O God, even the goings of my God my King into my sanctuary.

The singers went before, the minstrels followed after,

In the midst of the damsels playing with timbrels.

Bless ye God in the congregations,

Even the Lord, ye that are of the fountain of Israel.

There is little Benjamin their ruler,

The princes of Judah and their council,

The princes of Zebulun, the princes of Naphtali.

Sing unto God, ye kingdoms of the earth ;

O sing praises unto the Lord ;

To him that rideth upon the heavens of heavens, which are of old ;

Lo, he uttereth his voice, and that a mighty voice.

Ascribe ye strength unto God ;

His excellency is over Israel,

And His strength is in the skies.

O God, Thou art terrible out of Thy holy places ;

The God of Israel, He giveth strength and power unto His people.

Blessed be God."[1]

David himself, dressed like a priest in a simple ephod of linen, offered up burnt sacrifices in the way of the procession,[2] in order to purify its path, and

---

[1] Psalm lxviii.

[2] The Mazdæan religion also ordains the purification of the path in front of the sacred fire. In Persia even at the present day a sheep is immolated before a king or any very exalted personage entering a town for the first time. The immolation of victims before the ark had the same reason. The Bible states that a bullock and a fat calf were sacrificed at every six paces. This would have been an excessive butchery had the journey been a long one. The Chronicles (1 Chron. xv. 27) speak only of a sacrifice of seven bullocks and seven rams.

overcome with joy and intoxicated with various emotions, danced and played before the ark. He brought it in this manner to the tabernacle erected according to the ancient ordinance, offered burnt offerings and peace offerings before the Lord, blessed the people, and to "every one of Israel, both man and woman, he dealt a loaf of bread, a portion of flesh, and a cake of raisins." Then, before retiring, he appointed a cohen and priests to minister before the ark as in olden days in Shiloh, to worship Jehovah the Elohim of Israel, to pray to Him and magnify His name. Thus ended this joyful and glorious day, one of the most solemn ever recorded in the annals of the Hebrews.[1]

In the accounts of the rejoicings, the immense concourse of the people, the number of sacrificial victims, the splendour of the pageant, all pale before the personality of David. As a king, he has conceived the political design of restoring the cult of the ark in order to cement the union of the tribes, he has guided this return of the people to traditions that had been neglected or misunderstood, and has formed the escort and organised the details of the triumphal entry into Jerusalem. But directly the procession has started the king is effaced; and it is as a priest that he assists at the sacrifice and penetrates into the tabernacle, that he presides at the installation of the ark, the symbol of the covenant of Jehovah with the sons of Jacob. He bears no token of royalty, no

[1] 2 Sam. vi.; 1 Chron. xv. and xvi.

THE ARK AT JERUSALEM

attribute of power : he has donned the priestly ephod,[1] and, as a prophet seized with the spirit of God, he sings and dances with the other prophets. When Michal, the daughter of Saul, reproaches him for appearing in the costume of a simple priest and for compromising the royal dignity in the eyes of his servants, he bares his soul to her in his answer and expresses all the ardour of his faith. "It was before the Lord, which chose me above thy father, and above all his house, to appoint me prince over the people of the Lord over Israel ; therefore will I play before the Lord. And I will be yet more vile than thus, and will be base in mine own sight ; but of the handmaids which thou hast spoken of, of them shall I be had in honour." [2]

The reproaches of Michal and David's answer have not been properly understood. Commentators declare that David could never have debased himself by dancing before the ark, and consider this episode as a legend. They think that it arose in the prophetical world towards the time of Josiah, and that it was an indirect criticism of the antipathy of Amon and his wives to the faith of Jehovah ; that it pointed a rebuke to the courtiers whose self-seeking drew them away from religious observances.

This mistake would never have been made by an Oriental brought up in a mode of life still closely resembling that of biblical days. If the truth were

---

[1] See for the priestly ephod, or *ephod bad*, note M in Appendix.
[2] 2 Sam. vi. 21, 22, 23 ; 1 Chron. xv. 27.

before his eyes he would recognise it at once. In the opinion of an Israelite, a child, a young girl, a servant, irresponsible or insignificant members of the community might take a tambourine and disport themselves to the rhythm of the music, without trangressing against the rules of decorum ; from Miriam, sister of Moses, to Salome, daughter of Herodias, examples abound of women bursting forth into dance and song.[1] But a personage of note, a man of note or of "big bones," as the Persians have it, owed it to his dignity to move slowly, to walk or rather glide over the ground without gestures and without sound, in order that his demeanour might correspond to the gravity of his thoughts and the seriousness of his duties.[2]

In reality, David had been affiliated by Samuel to the prophetical brotherhoods.[3] His mind, more vigorous than that of Saul and cast in another mould, seemed to have braved contagion without any evil effects. On that day, overcome either by his joy or by the general excitement, he fell no doubt into a transport whose outward characteristics closely resembled those of the ecstasy of the prophets. He acted instinctively, without reflection. The daughter

[1] Exod. xv. 20 ; Judg. xi. 34, xxi. 21 ; 1 Sam. xviii. 6, 7.

[2] Dancing was condemned by purists when there was a question of men indulging in it (Exod. xxxii. 6, 7, 19). As a matter of fact, the only ones to dance were the common people and the prophets, and even then it was necessary that the former should be drunk (Judg. ix. 27) and the latter in a state of ecstasy (see above, pp. 103–105).

[3] See above, pp. 70, 71.

of Saul, brought up in a species of court where ideas of dignity and etiquette were already prevalent, was none the less shocked. Michal's anger was consistent with her conventional education; while the people, who were in direct sympathy of ideas with the prophets, and whose enthusiasm was untrammelled by forms and ceremonies, thought very differently. David won their approval because on this day, as on all others, he had obeyed the inspirations of his heart.

The entrance into Jerusalem of the ark of the covenant consecrated the religious downfall of Shiloh, Beth-el and Nob, weakened the influence of Gibeon, and in this manner ruined the prestige of the ancient sanctuaries in the territory of the children of Joseph. This was natural and inevitable. But the ephod, whose importance should have increased now that it was kept near the throne of God, lowered its voice. It seemed as if Jehovah refused to inspire his former oracle and preferred to avail himself of the prophets. There is, in fact, a very interesting manifestation of the struggle between the seers and the priests, of that struggle which had made the cohen Eli chief magistrate over the people, and which was terminating in the success of the prophets. The decline of the ministers of the ark in their capacity of interpreters of the ephod had, however, an unexpected result.

Although dating from the first days of the Exodus, and in spite of its having been strengthened at Shiloh during the period of the Judges, the priesthood participated to a certain extent in the prevalent anarchy.[1] It suffered also from the disfavour in which the cohenim and the servitors of the tabernacle were held by the people, who either despised them on account of some early stain or were envious of their privileges. Then also the sons of Levi, attracted by the advantages accruing to this tribe, had become legion. Like the so-called descendants of Mahomet who were allowed to share in the tithe, they increased in swarms without its being possible to trace back their ancestry. Finally, ever since the taking of the ark and the massacre of the priests at Nob they had divided themselves into at least two sects. The one, it has already been said,[2] recognised as its chief Abiathar, great-grandson of Levi, the other was under the orders of Zadok, a reputed descendant of the eldest of the children of Aaron. This led to incessant quarrels, which injured the priests and religion in general. As long as they had remained the only delegates of the authority of heaven, they had not felt the necessity for reform. Confronted with a rival power they made it their aim to limit the encroachments of the prophets. By degrees they abandoned all prophetic prerogatives to the latter, but in accordance with the intentions of David they consolidated themselves around the ark and opposed to their competitors a hereditary caste, strict

---

[1] See note A in Appendix on the tribe of Levi, and note L on the organisation of the clergy.
[2] See above, pp. 185-188.

and rigorous in its hierarchy. Each race, each family was carried back to some traditional ancestor, and their members were appointed according to their presumptive origin, to the different offices of the tabernacle and the subordinate duties of the scribes. The accident of birth, however, created no rights, but only made a man eligible; it was necessary for the exercise of sacerdotal functions, but was not sufficient by itself.

The details given by the Chronicles with regard to the number and the duties of the priests and of their acolytes, the judges, singers, and guardians of the tabernacle, relate to a period subsequent to the building of the temple.[1] It is none the less certain that the transport of the ark to Jerusalem, as well as the stimulus of a rival power, rekindled the zeal of the priests, favoured their concentration, and furnished a motive for their consecration to the ministry to the practical exclusion of the practice of divination. David must have lent his aid to this reform. He had prepared for it by giving back to the priests the guardianship of the throne of God;[2] and the introduction among the members of the clergy of a hierarchy modelled upon the hierarchy of the army was a measure so attractive to his spirit of order and in such complete harmony with his instincts, that it is impossible to think he was not privy to it.

[1] 1 Chron. xiii.-xxvi. See note L in Appendix on the organisation of the clergy. [2] See above, p. 186, and below, p. 254.

The son of Jesse cannot claim to have organised the faith in the same sense that he organised victory. In the domain of God his action was less personal: it was none the less decisive and salutary. For by restoring the cult of the ark, to the profit of the priests, and by subordinating Gibeon to Jerusalem and the cohen Zadok to the cohen Abiathar, then again by introducing a certain discipline among the Levites, while leaving to the prophets the more or less exclusive privilege of divination, he abolished every pretext for a rivalry as hurtful to the reputation of the ministers of the faith as it was to the dignity, the grandeur, and, above all, the unity of religion. David did not plant the sacred tree in the midst of Israel, but by relieving Jehovism of its greedy suckers and its dead branches he prepared for its blossoming. For this he cannot be too highly praised.

It is thus that Jerusalem became the home of religion when the oracle of the ark grew dumb, and that the house of Levi was consolidated when it lost the privilege which had seemed to be its greatest force. Destiny loves at times to mock at human wisdom, and takes pleasure in proving the vanity of our calculations.

X

Internal Administration of the Kingdom—The Palace—The great Works

AFTER securing peace within, and banishing fear to the confines of his kingdom, after surrounding himself with a formidable army, after strengthening the throne by alliances with powerful neighbours and thus disarming his worst enemies, David had brought the ark into an asylum which would protect it from every insult; he had favoured the progress of the priesthood, and had aroused the Israelites to the fear of the Lord.

He had thus established on a firm foundation the two pillars of the empire, religion and the army, knowing well that upon their solidity depended the duration of the monarchy and of his house. But the maintenance of the faith and above all the expenses of a standing army necessitated a financial prosperity which could only be effected by means of a centralised administration and absolute justice, a social organisation which was repugnant to the old Israelite spirit, so enamoured of an independence bordering upon anarchy. David, nevertheless, in spite of general opposition and although he could not call tradition to his aid, created its principal machinery. One must needs marvel at the strength and versatility of this extraordinary genius.

First of all, to each of the tribes whose autonomy causes him anxiety, he gives a military chief, judges, and a royal prefect; their respective duties being to recruit and command the militia, to settle civil disputes and repress crime, to collect the taxes in kind and to watch over the public spirit.[1] At Jerusalem dwells the head of the prefects, Adoram, who is at the same time entrusted with the operation of the levies, and who will be stoned to death by the people in the reign of Rehoboam.[2] The hatred of the populace for collectors of taxes and for the chiefs of police is not a thing of yesterday. The other dignitaries are: the *sarsaba* or generalissimo of the army, Joab, son of Zeruiah; the *sar* or commander of the Gibborim, Abishai, brother of Joab; the *sar* of the guard of the Cherethites and the Pelethites, Benaiah, son of Jehoiada, who appears to be independent of the generalissimo; the *sapher* or chief of the secretaries, Seraiah[3]; the *mazkir* or chief chancellor,

[1] 1 Chron. xxvii. 16-22; 1 Kings iv. 7-19.

[2] 2 Sam. xx. 24; 1 Kings iv. 6; xii. 18; 2 Chron. x. 18. This office was divided in the reign of Solomon. The superintendence of the levies was retained by Adoram; and that of the tribute was given to a son of Nathan named Azariah (1 Kings iv. 5).

[3] 2 Sam. viii. 17. A little later on (2 Sam. xx. 25) the holder of the same office is called Sheva. Is this another person, or is the change of name the work of a careless copyist?

ADMINISTRATION OF THE KINGDOM

recorder, historiographer, Jehoshaphat, the son of Ahilud; the tutors of the princes, Jonathan, uncle to the king, and Jehiel, son of Hachmoni; the cohenim Zadok and Abiathar, and David's chief almoner, Ira the Jairite.[1] The greater number of them form the royal council, which is completed by Ahithophel,[2] Jehoiada the son of Benaiah, and Abiathar, the two latter occupying a secondary rank among its members.[3] Solomon had only to live and to complete the work. Its programme was traced out in every detail.

The impost in kind, which it is difficult to convert into money, is applied to the maintenance of the table, of the house, and of the guards of the king. This system is still in force among the great Arab *sheikhs* and the Persian *naïbs*. Like the military levy, it rests for one month a year upon each of the twelve administrative provinces. Other expenses are deducted from the revenues of the monarch's domains or from his reserve in specie. The administration of this fortune, whose origin dates from the expeditions against the Amalekites, the Syrians, the Moabites and Edomites,[4] requires a numerous

---

[1] 2 Sam. xx. 26. This very special office must not be confused with that of the cohen of a sanctuary. In the reign of Solomon, it is filled by Zabud, son of Nathan (1 Kings iv. 5), who is described as "the king's friend."

[2] 2 Sam. xv. 12, 31, 34; xvi. 16–23; xvii. 1–23; 1 Chron. xxvii. 32–34.

[3] 2 Sam. viii. 16, 18; xx. 23–26; 1 Chron. xviii. 16, 17; xxvii. 32–34.

[4] See above, pp. 87–91, and below, chap. xi.

staff and explains the titles and the duties of the treasurers, of the officers in charge of the barns, the storehouses and the camels, of those placed over the tillers of the ground and entrusted with the care of the stables of asses and mules.[1]

These officials are responsible for the pay of the Gibborim and that of the Cherethites and Pelethites, for the arming of the troops, the construction of engines of war, and for the expenses of the great works undertaken at Jerusalem. A stair is cut in the rock which, from the valley of the Kedron, leads into the upper town [2]; the fortifications are strengthened and repaired, the citadel is perfected, an armoury is built,[3] the palace is completed. Everywhere, under the direction of Phœnician masters and mechanics, an army of workmen is in activity.[4]

How these constructions, although nothing remarkable in themselves, how this court with its officers and its armed guards, how all the excitement and

---

[1] I Chron. xxvii. 25-31. We do not see horses make their appearance yet. David himself, out of the enormous number that he took from Hadarezer, only reserved enough for a hundred chariots and had the others killed, for want of being able to make use of them (2 Sam. viii. 4). It is not until the reign of Solomon that the Hebrews make up their minds to breed horses and employ them (1 Kings iv. 26; 2 Chron. i. 14; ix. 25, 28).

In the reign of Saul, the management of the services enumerated above was confided to one man alone, Doeg the Syrian (1 Sam. xxi. 7; xxii. 9, 18). This fact shows how greatly royalty had increased in importance under the impulse of David.

[2] Nehem. xii. 37.

[3] Song of Songs iv. 4.

[4] See above, p. 24, n. 3, and p. 142, n. 4.

movement surrounding the king must have dazzled the Israelites! The credit of the throne increased beyond measure, for every new achievement was a fresh and visible manifestation of the royal power, that went straight to the eyes of the people and struck their imagination.

David dreamed of many other projects. He was ashamed to inhabit a palace of cedar-wood and stone, while the ark of the covenant remained in a tent of skins. In imitation of the Philistines and of the Phœnicians, he wished to build for his God a dwelling both durable and magnificent.

Was it war, or was it the dread of heavy expense disproportionate to his resources, that prevented the realisation of his desire? Already in the days of Solomon this was the explanation given; it is nevertheless inexact. Long before his death, the monarch had made an immense hoard of precious metals, and had amassed the treasure which later on supplied the gold, silver, and brass work lavished on the temple of Solomon.[1] As for the wars undertaken or sustained during the second half of the reign, he was not sufficiently absorbed by them to neglect a project dear to his heart.

He was restrained by considerations of a very different nature. As has already been explained,[2] the pastoral tradition respected in Shiloh held that the safeguard of the people, nomads in their habits,

[1] 2 Sam. viii. 7, 8, 11 ; 1 Chron. xviii. 14–18; xxix. 1–6.
[2] See above, p. 19, p. 20, n. 1 and n. 2, and p. 25.

was the ark, an emblem easily transported, mobile as the sons of Israel. By substituting a monument of wood and stone for a tent of skins or for a sanctuary of a very simple character, he would run the risk of offending the guardians of religious observances. Then also, the Israelites looked upon the neighbourhood of the ark as a signal mark of favour ; to live in its shadow was considered as a very great privilege. If the king should erect the Holy of Holies in the neighbourhood of his dwelling, would he not arouse the dormant susceptibilities of the tribes of Joseph, would he not be accused of monopolising the God of Israel, of procuring for the capital alone the blessings attached to the presence of Jehovah ?

From the persistence of Nathan [1] in thwarting his plans, David must have perceived that the building of a temple would augment the prestige of the sacerdotal caste, and that by favouring the priests he would estrange the prophets and would be in danger of destroying the balance that he endeavoured to maintain between the two rival powers. He was too wise to err even from excess of zeal ; he invoked a command from Heaven, abandoned his projects, and

---

[1] 2 Sam. vii. 1–12 ; 1 Chron. xvii. 1–11. The Bible, when making Nathan speak, only states the command of God to David not to build the temple. In another verse (1 Chron. xxii. 7, 8) it makes David say that his blood-stained hands were not pure enough to erect the sanctuary of Jehovah, that this honour was destined for a king of rest and peace, such as Solomon was to be. Finally, it professes by the mouth of Solomon (1 Kings v. 2, 3) that David could not build the temple on account of the many wars in which he was engaged.

left their execution as a legacy to his descendants. Only after a pestilence that devastated the tribes, he raised up to the Lord an altar of sacrifice,[1] thus leaving behind him a token of his intentions and a formal command to realise them.

[1] See note N in Appendix.

XI

The Great Wars—Victories over the Aramæans, Edomites, and Moabites—Battles of Medeba and Helam

UNTIL now David had engaged in wars that were strictly necessary; except for the siege of Jerusalem and the last expedition against the Philistines, they might all be called defensive. In his much-occupied youth he had always stood firm against the passion for fighting. In middle age he makes acquaintance with inaction and monotony, and does not know how to resist their attacks; his conscience hardens, his heart closes to pity. Then he remembers his army lying in idleness, looks across the frontiers, and conceives the design of increasing the heritage of Israel at the expense of its hereditary enemies. The occupation would be worthy of his thoughts were it not that war, noble and fruitful when undertaken for purposes of defence or of vengeance, becomes criminal indeed when purely aggressive.

Moab had lived in peace with Israel ever since the first years of Saul's reign;[1] David was connected

---
[1] 1 Sam. xiv. 47.

with Moab through his ancestress Ruth,[1] and in the days when he dreaded the exposure of his family to the cruel retaliations of Saul, he had taken his father and mother to Mizpeh and had confided them to the care of the King of Moab.[2] Nevertheless he did not hesitate. In contempt of old associations and of the ties created by hospitality, he crossed the Jordan, fell upon the Moabites and laid them under tribute. Benaiah, the son of Jehoiada, had covered himself with glory during this campaign. As a reward the king gave him the command of the Cretan guard,[3] and also, perhaps, his seat in the council. At the end of the war the prisoners were fettered and cast upon the ground side by side, then they were measured with a rope and were divided into three equal sections—two marked out for death and one for life. David was not naturally cruel, but in acknowledging the services of Benaiah and in putting the men of Moab to the sword his object was to exalt the courage of the army and to strike terror into the peoples whom he next intended to attack; he wished to point a lesson that all around might read. Shortly after he was on his way to the north, threatening Hadarezer, King of Zobah.[4] The Aramæans of Damascus hastened to the latter's aid. The Hebrews

---

[1] Ruth iv. 9, 10, 13, 17-22, although the Book of Ruth is not considered as being of any historical value.

[2] 1 Sam. xxii. 3.

[3] See above, p. 193, and notes 1 and 2.

[4] 2 Sam. vii. 3, 4; 1 Chron. xviii. 3. It was a small Aramæan principality with which Saul had already been at war.

defied the allies, occupied the country, and left garrisons behind them. And as this expedition against a people of great wealth was exceedingly fruitful in booty, they returned to Jerusalem laden with rich spoils, bringing with them some hundred horses from the stables of the King of Zobah, the first that are mentioned in the military annals of Israel. Then came the turn of the Edomites. An army under the orders of Abishai, brother of Joab, totally defeated eighteen thousand of them in the valley *of Salt;* they shared the fate of the men of Moab and of Aram. For six months the country was under military occupation. Massacres and banishment at last overcame all resistance.[1]

Then the weak were afraid when they saw the fate of the strong, and they offered themselves in bondage. Thus did Toi, King of Hamath, who sent his son to David to congratulate him and to buy his good will. He brought with him vessels of silver and vessels of gold and of brass. The conqueror accepted his homage, added the tribute of the King of Hamath to the precious metals taken from the Moabites and Aramæans, and consecrated them unto the Lord. He thus swelled the treasure that he would leave to Solomon for the erection of the temple of Jehovah. The excuse was hardly sufficient for so many massacres, so many useless wars.

---

[1] 2 Sam. vii. 13; 1 Kings xi. 14-17; 1 Chron. xviii. 12; Ps. lx. The battle took place at the entrance to the country of the Edomites and of the mountains of Seir, in the lowlands south of the Dead Sea.

VICTORIES OVER THE ARAMÆANS

In the meantime, Nahash, King of the children of Ammon, died, and his son Hanum reigned in his stead. David, to whom the deceased monarch had shown kindness, hastened to send an embassy to express his sympathy. This was an act of simple courtesy, necessitated by his personal relations with the father of the new sovereign.[1] On similar occasions the courts of Egypt and Assyria always pursued this course. Hanum, alarmed at the recent expeditions of the Hebrews, mistook the intention of their king. He looked upon the arrival of the mission as the prelude to an attack, saw spies in the members of the embassy, and threw them into prison. Then he had them shaved on one side of the face, and their garments cut short till just below the waist, and sent them to the frontier.

The ambassadors, sick with shame, reached Jericho, informed their master, and received permission to wait there till their beards had grown. Such an outrage could not rest unpunished. The Ammonites saw this. At their call, the Aramæans of Zobah, of Maacah, and of Tob,[2] either thirsting for vengeance or anxious to stop the progress of the Hebrews, came to their aid in large numbers. It was agreed that the Ammonites should take up a position in front

---

[1] Nahash was the prince (1 Sam. xi. 1) who besieged the town of Jabesh and was driven away by Saul (see above, p. 48). No details are known with regard to these points.

[2] 2 Sam. x. 7. In the Chronicles (1 Chron. xix.) the geographical names and the composition of the allied army are given a little differently.

of the stronghold of Medeba, formerly conquered from the Reubenites,[1] and that the Aramæans should hold themselves in the distance, ready to come down upon the assailants in the rear.

The plan was well thought out. If the Israelite army had directed its efforts against either of the two divisions it would have been attacked from behind and defeated to a certainty. The generals brought up in David's school were too wise to fall into the snare. Joab advanced upon the Aramæans with the pick of his troops, and confided the reserves to his brother Abishai, with the orders to keep the Ammonites in check. At the first encounter, the auxiliaries, seeing themselves forestalled, fled without striking a blow, while the Ammonites, thus deserted, retired behind the walls of Medeba. The Hebrews did not dare to attempt its siege, and returned to Jerusalem.

Joab was victorious, but he had not inflicted a very severe defeat upon the enemy. A new coalition was formed, inspired by Hadarezer, King of Syria. David, anxious to strike a crushing blow, took the command himself and started for Helam, where his adversaries had concentrated their troops. The battle was a fierce one. The allies lost their chariots and forty thousand horsemen; Shobach, their commander-in-chief, was killed, and the kings who had come to the help of Hadarezer made humble submission and implored the yoke of Israel.

[1] Josh. xiii. 16.

BATTLES OF MEDEBA AND HELAM

It would seem as if this victory should have brought the war to a close. This was not the case. Conquerors are compelled to tread one and the same path. When once on the fatal road of aggressive war they march without halt or truce, tormented by an implacable desire. Success condemns them to success until the moment when, pursued by reverses, they fly before the storm, turn back, and, worn out and breathless, reach the point they started from. It is the revenge of morality, of that morality that is disdained and mocked at by those whose passions it condemns, but whose decrees seize and strike both the men and the peoples who violate its laws.

David was yet far from his decline. Nevertheless he knew already the necessity of conquest as a result of former conquests; he bore the burden of his useless triumphs. After provoking a defensive alliance among the peoples of the east and of the north, he had crushed the Aramæans and had condemned them to a long impotence; now he had to reach the Ammonites, the real culprits of the coalition, to punish them severely and to take their capital. Though the enterprise was very difficult and necessitated the siege of a place surrounded by strong defences,[1] it was no longer beyond the scope of Joab and the Hebrew engineers. The king gave over the conduct of the affair into their hands.

It was during the course of the first operations

[1] See above, p. 139, n. 3.

that death came to Uriah the Hittite,[1] an officer of the Gibborim, whose end has thrown a tragic gloom over a siege remarkable in so many points, and the success of which shows to what a degree of science and skill the Israelites had attained in an art that, but a while ago, was new to them.

[1] Uriah was in command of a company of the Gibborim (2 Sam. xxiii. 39). His name proves that he had embraced the religion of Jehovah, and the description "Hittite" that there were still some Canaanites among the officers of David. This was not the case under Solomon (1 Kings ix. 20).

XII

Bath-sheba

THE drama which was played out before the walls of Rabbah in Ammon, has been the subject of such ancient and heated controversy that debate on the subject has wandered far astray. Historians have treated David with scant justice. Some have abased the Psalmist king, in order to exalt the merits of repentance, others have sullied his memory so as to attack the Christ in the person of the most illustrious ancestor assigned to him by the Bible. Impartial criticism of the actual facts and the analysis of the sentiments they reveal have been secondary considerations.

What was the nature of David's sin when examined according to the standpoint of the country and the age in which he reigned?

What was the part played by David in the preparation and the guidance of the events by which Uriah's death was preceded? Was he the author of the crime or its accomplice? Might he not have been but an instrument in the hands of his mistress?

These are the moral and historical points which should be settled before sentence is pronounced. In forming judgment we must resist the fascination of the monarch's striking personality and concern ourselves also with the favourite; we must scan the chief episodes of her existence and seek in them for light.

Bath-sheba was the daughter of a Benjamite called Eliam.[1] The acts of her life, the success of her manœuvres, indicate a woman violent, ambitious and passionate; but they denote also one of the strongest characters even in that age so rich in energetic temperaments—a nature incapable of any scruples, a powerful and unfettered mind, a born actress, a consummate tragedian. Moreover, arrogant as many women are because their moral nature presents sharp edges that have been worn away in men by friction with their fellows, Bath-sheba was one of those from whose hands a husband or lover is predestined to accept the distaff if he receives no arms to gratify their lust for vengeance or to further their desires.

She had been married very young to one of the thirty captains of the Gibborim, a Hittite who was probably a convert to the religion of Jehovah.[2]

[1] 2 Sam. xi. 3. The name of Bathsheba's father is written Amniel in the Chronicles (1 Chron. iii. 5). That of the favourite of David, in the same verse, is spelt Bath-shua, while in the books of Samuel and of the Kings it is given as Bath-sheba.

[2] See above, p. 210, n. 1.

Uriah was apparently a valiant soldier, a disciplinarian, inured to fatigue, more in love with his profession than with the joys of his own home, a sword turned into a man, with the tenderness of a bar of iron and the soul of an instrument of war. The couple occupied one of the portions of the palace assigned to the superior officers, and from her dwelling the young woman could look on David when every evening after the noon-day sleep he walked upon the terraces. The inferiority of her husband's position in comparison with that of the princes and the great dignitaries of the crown, a natural taste for luxury and power, intensified by her surroundings and by the impossibility of satisfying it, gave her no rest. Queen by right of beauty, queen by right of wit, she dreamed of becoming queen by the favour of the master whose image haunted her thoughts. Only, she would have to hasten and profit by the absence of Uriah, who was away at the siege of Rabbah in Ammon. Despite her efforts to attract the attention of the monarch, David, who was on the downward slope of life,[1] and on whom the pleasures of the harem began to pall, took no notice of her manœuvres. Disappointed and vexed, but steadfast in her design, determined in her hope, she waited till the king came out upon the terrace. The sun was setting; it was that delightful moment of the East, when before sinking below the horizon its

[1] He was from fifty to fifty-two years of age. See below, p. 246, n. 1.

rays caress the earth, when light grows golden and pearly shadows languidly stretch themselves out, inviting the world to repose. Then she appeared, divested herself of her garments as if about to bathe, unbound her hair and slowly perfumed the billowy tresses that fell in all their dark splendour over the ivory fairness of her young beauty.

Her audacity had its full measure of success. Surprised by this apparition, his eyes dazzled by the radiant and unexpected vision, the king made inquiries among his household. All knew Bath-sheba. They informed him that she was the wife of an officer of the Gibborim, serving under Joab at the siege of Rabbah in Ammon. David sent for her and soon obtained his desire. His fancy satisfied, he would perhaps have forgotten all about her, if some weeks later she had not announced to him that she was pregnant. At each of their interviews, Bath-sheba, tender, graceful, captivating, took a greater hold upon his heart. In bearing a child of the king, she had formed the only real ties ever known in the East; and she meant to take good care to draw them so close as to make them indissoluble.

The sovereign, wishing to protect her honour, recalled the Hittite. When Uriah arrived in Jerusalem, he feigned to question him, asked after Joab and the troops, made inquiries as to the progress of the siege, and purposely kept him until evening. Then, at the time for the last repast, when night was come, he sent him back to his wife and had meats from the royal table carried to them. He did not doubt that after so long an absence Uriah would be anxious to see Bath-sheba once more. David reasoned like a lover. The Gibbor, partly out of soldierly bravado, and also perhaps because he found at home a cold reception and closed doors, did not second the projects of his master. He returned to eat and drink with the officers of the guard, told them his deeds of prowess, learned the court news, and went to sleep in their midst.[1]

It has been supposed that the Hittite had been informed of his wife's conduct, and that he feared by passing the night by her side either to offend the king, who was now become his rival, or on the other hand, to lend himself too easily to the desires of the monarch. But this supposition tallies neither with the heroic death of the Gibbor, nor with the rough ways of Joab's companions, nor with the violent jealousy of the Hebrews which is manifested in the terrible sentence pronounced against erring women. Uriah, had he known the truth, would not have allowed his complaisance or his despair to make him court death beneath the walls of Rabbah in Ammon, he would have been content with stoning his wife. Besides, none of those aware of Bath-sheba's condition, even supposing that there were any in the secret, would have dared to divulge the mysteries of the royal harem. These are subjects never broached by an Oriental, even when they do not concern an

[1] See below, p. 217, n. 1.

awe-inspiring master. Finally, David, who was on his guard, would never, even in veiled terms, have confided the decree of death to Uriah which he soon after committed to his care, if he had thought the latter had any suspicion of the truth.

However it may be, the king called the Hittite to him and did not conceal his surprise at his action.

"And Uriah said unto David, The ark, and Israel, and Judah abide in booths; and my lord Joab, and the servant of my lord are encamped in the open field; shall I then go into my house, to eat and to drink and to lie with my wife? As thou livest, and as thy soul liveth, I will not do this thing."

These excuses were also evasions. In resorting to them the husband of Bath-sheba was silent with regard to the repulse he had probably received. In spite of this answer, David did not lose courage; perhaps the harm done was not yet irremediable? He invited Uriah to his table, made him drink until he was intoxicated, and ordered him to be conducted home, hoping that wine would soften his scruples. All in vain, the king had over-reached himself. The Hittite fell down like a log and was unable to leave the palace, where he passed the night once more.

The biblical annalist, scrupulously exact, but very sparing of detail, contents himself with summarising events, and does not mention incidents which in his eyes are of secondary importance. It is thus that he is silent with regard to Bath-sheba.[1] Nevertheless, had she wished to see her husband, she would have had small difficulty in making him prolong his visit to Jerusalem, her woman's wit would have succeeded where the somewhat clumsy plots of the monarch failed. But it is easy to imagine the welcome given by the king's mistress to this inopportune husband. If she had received him her dearest hopes would have been ruined and the edifice raised at such cost would have been shattered. She was mother to a child of the king—she did not wish to let the Gibbor call himself its father. She made capital doubtless of Uriah's dilatoriness in seeking her, reproached him for his libations with the body-guard, made his want of eagerness an excuse for non-compliance with his demands, or invoked other reasons based upon the observance of the law. In short, she succeeded in getting rid of him, but the danger had been imminent —if she did not lose her husband, her manœuvres would bring forth no fruit.

That very evening, more beautiful than ever in her emotion, excited by the wish to consecrate her victory, Bath-sheba threw herself at the king's feet, and with eyes full of tears, her voice shaking with anguish, trembling and desperate, she reminded him of the punishment meted out to the faithless

---

[1] The intimate aspects of the part played by Bath-sheba are, generally speaking, only hinted at. But the gaps in the story can easily be supplemented by the help of a study of the manifestations of Bath-sheba's will and of surface events with which she was concerned.

wife.[1] It was death, ignominious death beneath the stones gathered from the wayside; and it meant the destruction of the being whose life was bound up with hers. Would he suffer that at the gate of his palace, under his very eyes, near his heart, she and their child should perish in fearful tortures, she whom he had led astray from her duties, and the child, that innocent victim, who was his own flesh and blood? To save them, to purge the sin, it was necessary that a formal marriage should consecrate their guilty union.

"But Uriah?" the sovereign must have objected.

He would return to Rabbah in Ammon. In a siege, danger is born afresh each day. Every step forward is paid for with much bloodshed. Why not confide to Uriah the glorious mission of leading the next attack? Instead of exposing a father, a son, a brother, an Israelite, whose life assured the life of his dependants, were it not better to appoint a stranger without family ties, a Hittite? Then she must have prepared excuses for him, citing no doubt the example of Saul, who exposed him, David himself,

---

[1] Throughout the East, adultery is an unpardonable crime. Even in the present day, in Persia, the nearest relatives of the guilty woman kill her, often by casting her off the top of a minaret. All the Old Testament reflects this sentiment (Genesis xx. 2; xxvi. 11; Exod. xx. 15; Lev. xviii. 8; Numb. v. 11, &c.; Deut. v. 18). As to the penalty incurred by an offending wife, it was that of being stoned to death. Stoning, for that matter, was common among the Hebrews, and was even prescribed against animals (Exod. xvii. 4; xxi. 28; Lev. xx. 14; cp. with Josh. vii. 25; Lev. xx. 2, 27; 1 Sam. xxx. 6; Matt. xxiii. 37, &c.)

to perils far more grave out of spite and to satisfy an unjustifiable grudge.[1]

And the monarch, whose body and soul revolted against the thought of looking on powerless at the execution of a woman bearing a child of his race, at the death of so beautiful a mistress—David, weak because he was madly in love and because his original fault placed him in a cruel dilemma, allowed himself to be persuaded. He would not abandon Bath-sheba to the anger of Uriah, he would not cause her death, he would not permit the stoning of a prince of the blood royal. Besides, the siege was dragging on, the ardour of the troops needed rousing, the enemy must be intimidated, the assault must be prepared for by a brilliant action.

Uriah received orders to return to the camp. He was the bearer of a message to Joab.[2] Here again, the Bible, very concise and very impartial, gives only the purport of the king's commands.

"Set ye Uriah in the forefront of the hottest battle, and retire ye from him, that he may be smitten and die."

It is certain that David, whatever may have been the impatience of Bath-sheba, did not proclaim his secret, and would certainly not have confided it to the Gibbor in such a thin disguise. He still hesitated to

---

[1] See above, p. 69.

[2] The fact of this message being in writing should not arouse any feeling of surprise. The Hebrews made use of alphabetical script long before the time of David. See note I in Appendix.

sacrifice Uriah, and even if he had had no scruples, prudence would have restrained him. The remainder of the story shows moreover that he contented himself with hints. He complained of the slowness of the operations, and stimulated the zeal of the troops. "We must make an end of Rabbah in Ammon and not let it humiliate the army of Israel," he must have written to Joab. "I send thee Uriah the Hittite, I have looked on him with favour and have had him in my thoughts. Put him at the head of a detachment, and at the first opportunity, let him break into the city at any cost. These are my orders."

Uriah was once more encamped before the walls of Rabbah in Ammon. Proud of his reception by the king, anxious to prove his worthiness, dreaming of a glorious fate, he joyfully accepted the task of beating back a sortie. He behaved with his accustomed valour, drove back the Ammonites at the point of the sword, and endeavoured to follow them behind their defences. While he was obstinately trying to carve a passage with his sword or to break down the gate, he was struck by an arrow shot from the ramparts and fell dead upon a heap of the slain.

Rabbah in Ammon was a fortress of the Chaldæo-Susian type, surrounded by massive walls and defended by a deep and wide moat into which flowed a branch of the Jabbock. Among its works it comprised a citadel which commanded the enceinte. The siege and the taking of such a place[1] necessitated

[1] See above, p. 139, n. 3.

preliminary operations of a slow and arduous character, which were barely sketched out at the moment when Joab received orders to push the attack. All attempts were bound to end in failure. Nevertheless, the sarsaba was alarmed. Had he misunderstood or exceeded his instructions? He dispatched one of his officers to vindicate him in the eyes of David.

"If the king's wrath arise, and he say unto thee, Wherefore went ye so nigh unto the city to fight? knew ye not that they would shoot from the wall? Who smote Abimelech the son of Jerubbaal (Gideon) at the siege of Thebez?[1] Did not a woman cast an upper mill-stone upon him from the wall, that he died at Thebez? Why went ye so nigh the wall? Then shalt thou say: The men prevailed against us, and came out unto us into the field, and we were upon them even unto the entering of the gate. And the shooters shot at thy servants from off the wall: and some of the king's servants be dead, and thy servant Uriah the Hittite is dead also."

These words, and the precautions taken by Joab, all indicate that the instructions sent from Jerusalem were not explicit. Had the husband of Bath-sheba returned home safe and sound, the king would perhaps have given more precise orders. And even that we may be permitted to doubt. Yielding to the suggestions of an unprincipled woman, David was led to hope for the death of Uriah, but he wished that

[1] Judg. ix. 53.

fate should have a share in bringing it to pass, so greatly did he fear to bear the responsibility alone. He heard of the catastrophe without showing sign of anger or of joy, and reassured the messenger, "Thus shalt thou say unto Joab: Let not this thing displease thee, for the sword devoureth one as well as another; make thy battle more strong against the city and overthrow it. . . ."

Meanwhile the authoress of the plot, the true culprit, having learned of her husband's death, filled the palace and the town with her lamentations. She rent her veils and her tunics, put on the mourning garment of sackcloth, abjured perfumes and ointments for her body and her lustrous tresses, and mourned for her dead, fasting for the space of a week.[1] Then as Uriah had died like a hero, fighting for the king, she was received into the harem of the sovereign till the end of her period of mourning. When it was over, David hastened to take her for his wife.[2] Shortly afterwards she bore him a son.

Bath-sheba was a mother. She was assured against the reverses of fortune and the inconstancy of the

[1] Gen. l. 10; 1 Sam. xxxi. 13; 2 Sam. i. 11, 12; xiv. 1, &c.; Isaiah xxxii. 11; Joel i. 8; ii. 13; Amos viii. 10. The mourning garment or *sak* was made of white or brown woollen stuff, the natural colour of the fleece and of a very coarse web. Hence the name of sac, or *sacco*, adopted by all the inhabitants of the Mediterranean coasts, after trading with the Phœnicians, for the bags destined to contain corn and flour, &c., and which were made of the same stuff.

[2] The duration of the period bound by law to elapse before a widow could re-marry is unknown. It cannot have been very long 1 Sam. xxv. 38, 39.)

king. But, unless she confessed her fall, her child would have no right to the throne. When she remembered the humble dwelling which had been the home of her youth and compared it to the palace in which she now lived, her remorseless soul was filled with ambition. She dreamt of an exalted rank, and to attain it she did not scruple to publish a sin which was to her a source of pride. Then everybody explained for himself the mystery of Rabbah in Ammon and the mad attack on a gate. Uriah and the heroes fallen beneath the walls of the city of the Ammonites had paid for Bath-sheba's elevation with their lives.

The opinion of the Israelites we do not know. Perhaps they murmured, but if so it was under their breath, for David was loved for his glory and feared for his strength. The prophet Nathan alone, interpreter of a higher conscience, feared not to face the monarch and to raise his voice in the royal presence.

"There were two men in one city," said the man of God, "the one rich and the other poor. The rich man had exceeding many flocks and herds, but the poor man had nothing, save one little ewe lamb, which he had bought and nourished up: and it grew up together with him and with his children; it did eat of his own morsel and drank of his own cup, and lay in his bosom, and was unto him as a daughter. And there came a traveller unto the rich man, and he spared to take of his own flock and of his own herd, to dress for the wayfaring man that was come unto him, but took the poor man's lamb and dressed it for the man that was come unto him."

"That man that hath done this is worthy to die: and he shall restore the lamb fourfold," replied the king, whose anger was kindled and who resolved to punish the author of this detestable action. Nathan interrupted him: "King, thou art the man . . . thou hast smitten Uriah the Hittite with the sword. . . ." And after reminding him of the blessings which he had received and threatening him with bitter punishment he added, "Thou didst this secretly, thou shalt suffer for it before all Israel, and before the sun."

David had sinned blindly and weakly in taking to his bed the wife of one of his officers. His first offence was a venial one from a royal point of view, but it had placed him in a cruel position. He had to choose between Bath-sheba's life and that of Uriah, to decide between desire and duty; and while desire pleaded with the lips of the beloved, duty had been left with no one to urge its cause. Nathan's reproaches unsealed his eyes. Instead of defying the man of God, instead of ordering him from his presence or punishing him as Saul had treated Samuel and the priests of Nob, the king acknowledged his guilt and humiliated himself. His confession surprised the prophet, his contrite attitude appeased him, and he promised David the pardon of the Lord. "Howbeit, because by this deed thou hast given great occasion to the enemies of the Lord to blaspheme, thou shalt yet be punished."

David's first great sorrow was the illness of the child of his guilty love ; the monarch saw in it retribution for his sin. But while he humbles himself before the Lord, Bath-sheba exalts herself in the eyes of men ; while he retires to the harem and fasts, lies on the ground and beseeches the divine mercy, the favourite profits by this prostration to dismiss every woman of whom she is jealous, to stifle all rival influences. And when she loses her child, when the token of her sin is no more, she proclaims her grief with such violence, she succeeds so well in exciting pity, that all other mournings disappear in the shadow of her misfortune. Uriah is forgotten, the unfortunate men immolated at his side and sacrificed to hide a crime are no more wept for ; all sympathies go straight to the woman who instigated, the woman who benefited by the crime.

Later on she becomes once more a mother. Then, as exacting in her joy as she was exaggerated in her grief, she wishes the Almighty to take her child into favour, and she chooses, as tutor and support to her son, Nathan, her declared adversary. She sends for him, disarms his anger, and wins him over by the tokens of her respect and by the graces of her piety, just as she had fascinated David by the charm of her beauty and the gifts of her mind. And the prophet yields to her prayers ; he accepts the charge of guiding the child in the ways of the Lord, and he adds to the name of Solomon ("Happy," "Frederick") the surname of Jedidiah ("Beloved of God," "Theophilus").[1]

Then in order to endow the boy with the gift of a joyful birth the siege of Rabbah in Ammon is pursued with the greatest vigour; the outer defences and the lower town are taken by storm, and the citadel capitulates to David, who has made his appearance at the seat of war.

It was the crown of the king of the Ammonites that was placed on the head of the newly-born, it was the blood of those cut in pieces or crushed beneath iron harrows, it was the crimson liquid and the purple scum overflowing the brick-kilns into which the vanquished had been thrown that anointed the forehead of the infant prince.[2] And after the fall of Rabbah the other cities of the children of Ammon were besieged in their turn and shared the fate of the capital. Bath-sheba would suffer neither intrigues nor revolts to spring up around the cradle. She wished her son to sleep in peace, untroubled by sedition or by war.

The birth of Solomon increased still further the signal favour enjoyed by the favourite. From the depths of the harem she gives orders, rules, and prepares herself to reign in the name of her child. The order of succession to the throne is not yet determined by law, but custom assigns extensive

---

[1] 2 Sam. xii. 24, 25.
[2] 2 Sam. xii. 30, 31; 1 Chron. xx. 2, 3.

privileges to the eldest of each family.[1] Moreover, certain of the princes have a numerous following at court. Of these are Ammon, son of Achinoam of Jezreel, and Absalom, who was born to the monarch by Maacah, daughter of Talmai, King of Geshur. The hour has come to attack them, and the struggle between the favourite and the rivals of Solomon is waged in bitter earnest.

Little is known of what is behind the scenes of the drama in which the eldest of the princes lost his life. The Bible, always sparing of confidences, contents itself with innuendos. It states that Ammon assaulted Tamar, his half-sister, under odious but most strange circumstances; that the victim appealed for vengeance to her brother Absalom, that he killed the offender and fled from Jerusalem, and that these events were provoked by a singular personage, a cunning and vicious courtier named Jonadab.[2] The result was that of the two pretenders to the crown the most formidable was dead; the other had fled from court in order to escape punishment.

Was it really on his own initiative that Jonadab had counselled and prepared the crime of Ammon, and had sown the seeds of hatred in the royal family? It seems as if the court thought otherwise, and that Bath-sheba was accused of having woven this new plot. Then a change took place in the minds of most men. The most powerful grew

[1] See above, p. 27, n. 2.
[2] 2 Sam. xiii. 3-5, 32, 34.

alarmed, and Joab himself, although privy to the murder of Uriah—Joab, the accomplice of the favourite and her friend—set himself from this day forth to combat her influence and to seek for a rival capable of counterbalancing her preponderance. He could only see Absalom to oppose to the wife of David, and he worked for three years to obtain his pardon.

The prince, who had taken refuge in Syria [1] with his grandfather Talmai, King of Geshur, hastened to Jerusalem. "He dwelt two full years in Jerusalem; and he saw not the king's face. . . ." At last, at the instance of Joab, the king consents to receive him. "He came to the king, and bowed himself on his face to the ground before the king: and the king kissed Absalom." [2] The monarch, who adored his son,[3] would have consented to a reconciliation long before this if the favourite had not stifled the impulse of his heart.

Taught by experience, Absalom at once took up an attitude of defence, and posed as the heir-presumptive, surrounding himself with an escort, and seeking to obtain an ally against Bath-sheba in the favour of the populace. He took up a position in front of the gates of the palace and stopped every man who had a suit to bring before the king; and he won all hearts by his manner and kind words.

[1] 2 Sam. xv. 7, 8.
[2] 2 Sam. xiv. 28–33.
[3] 2 Sam. xviii. 12, 28–33.

"Of what city art thou?" he would say to them. "See, thy matters are good and right; but there is no man deputed of the king to hear thee. Oh, that I were made judge in the land, that every man that hath any suit or cause might come unto me, and I would do him justice."

Did any one come near to do him obeisance, he would put forth his hand and take hold of him and kiss him, stealing thus the hearts of all the men of Israel. In the meantime he bought over valuable assistance, sometimes only paying in promises, and he succeeded in gaining a body of adherents whose ranks were swelled by the general discontent and by disappointed ambition.

When he saw that the moment was favourable Absalom pleaded a vow and proceeded for its fulfilment to Hebron. He surrounded himself there with former followers of Saul, whose tears flowed at the memory of their lost independence, and with men from the South who could not forgive David for having deserted them for Jerusalem. Mingling with them, he inflamed their resentment, stirred up their anger, and to a certainty represented the favourite to them as the author of their misfortunes and the evil genius of his father. The companionship of Ahithophel, a member of the privy council,[1] and then an escort of two hundred men taken from the king's guard, gave an official character to his action. Thanks to this misunderstanding, of which skilful

[1] 2 Sam. xv. 12, 34.

use was made, and to cunningly propagated falsehoods, the conspiracy became very serious.

Moreover, David himself greatly contributed to the first successes of the insurrection. Without making any hostile demonstration, the monarch had left his capital, preceded by the Cretan guard and the Gibborim, and followed by some faithful friends and without any doubt by the favourite, as is shown by the rest of the tale.[1] He had fled, bare-footed, with bowed head and eyes bathed in tears, loaded with insults and accepting them without a murmur in a spirit of penitence.

No doubt the king recognised the finger of God in the revolt of Absalom as in the death of the first-born of Bath-sheba, and he went out to meet his trials with the resignation and the courage that are the fruits of sincere repentance. Nevertheless, it may be questioned whether, considering the general feeling and the fact that the insurgents had half the nation at their back, the abandonment of his capital was not above all, an extremely skilful manœuvre. A prince who had raised so high the fortunes of the Hebrews, could not allow them to be ruined by a conspiracy. Duty commanded him to defend the work by which the people were to benefit and to crush a revolt

[1] It is known that Absalom, acting on the advice of Ahithophel, took possession of David's harem " in the sight of all Israel " (2 Sam. xvi. 20–22), and also that David, on his return to Jerusalem, put away from him the women he had left behind in his house, shutting them up unto the day of their death and keeping them in widowhood (2 Sam. xx. 3). Now Bath-sheba was never thus disgraced.

by which the enemies of Israel alone could profit. On the other hand, he had no illusions as to the gratitude of the inhabitants of Jerusalem. Knowing that thanklessness is the tribute paid by great cities to their benefactors, he feared to be caught, with his friends and his guards, between Absalom's army on the outside and a popular rising inside the town, while by hastening away, he would draw the rebels from the cradle of the insurrection, would baffle any ambuscades, and would re-establish his influence and reconstitute his army. David was carrying out a manœuvre whose value he had learnt from its repeated success.[1] In the same prudent spirit, he commanded that the ark should be carried back to the tabernacle instead of allowing it to follow him. The Hebrews, surprised at his abandonment of an emblem which shared its renown with its possessor, and which established the legitimacy of his cause, saw in this order an act of humility and a fresh proof of contrition. In point of fact, it was an excellent pretext for leaving in the capital the two cohenim, Zadok and Abiathar, their families and their priests, who would all work upon the minds of the people and bring them to their allegiance, and who would keep him informed as to the projects of his son. He even took care to send back Hushai, one of his most faithful friends, charging him to insinuate himself into Absalom's good graces, in the hope of paralysing the influence of Ahithophel, whose spirit of intrigue

[1] See above, pp. 145 and 146.

and acute intelligence he greatly dreaded. He did not hide from himself the extreme gravity of a revolt in which Judah and the important tribes over which Saul had formerly ruled were taking part; and he neglected no means of action, no measures that were prudent. The approach of battle had revived David. Although following closely upon his steps, even the favourite played for the time being a passive part. At least, the effects of her influence are little felt during this period. At the moment of preparing and directing resistance the king took counsel only of his own wisdom. The conqueror of the Amalekites and of the Philistines awoke in the plenitude of his strength and of his genius.

Ahithophel saw this; he wished to pursue the fugitive with ten or twelve thousand men, take advantage of his dismay and attack him without delay. This advice was sound. But Hushai, who felt that David was lost if it should be followed, pointed out that the king and his men, "chafed in their minds like a bear robbed of her whelps in a field," would not allow themselves to be surprised without fighting desperately—that they were "mighty men" and "men of war." He counselled that "all Israel should be gathered together, from Dan even unto Beersheba, and should march on David, lighting upon him as the dew falleth upon the ground," and that if he withdrew into a city then all Israel would "bring ropes to that city and draw it unto the river, until there was not one small stone to be found there." This proposition was both cunning and tempting, for it flattered the indolence of Absalom's followers, and gave them leisure before burdening them with duties. His opinion won the day. Then Ahithophel, feeling that David, with breathing time before him, would return victorious to Jerusalem—chose rather to die as a man of honour than in the hands of the executioner. He saddled his ass, rode home unto his city, set his house in order and hanged himself.

Some weeks later, Absalom crossed the Jordan in pursuit of the royal army, and pitched his tents in the land of Gilead, in front of Mahanaim, where David had taken up his position. Amasa, the general of the insurgents, was the son of an Ishmaelite named Jether, or Ithra, who had had relations with David's sister Abigail [1] before the rise in fortunes of the house of Jesse. The king, on his side, had chosen as his lieutenants, Joab, Abishai, and an officer of the Gibborim called Ittai the Gittite.[2] The two armies watched each other for some weeks; both sides dreaded to come to blows. However, the rebels, whose first operations had brought them back to the right bank of the Jordan, at last began the attack. The battle was waged in the forest of Ephraim and was disastrous for them. Twenty thousand men, according to the Bible, "were slaughtered," either during the battle or the pursuit.

---

[1] 2 Sam. xvii. 25 ; 1 Chron. ii. 17.

[2] This was a new-comer (2 Sam. xv. 20) who owed his post of honour to the fidelity and loyalty of which he had given proofs when David retired from Jerusalem (2 Sam. xv. 21, 22).

Absalom, finding himself hemmed in on all sides, chose a spirited mule and fled through the forest. As he was riding under the thick boughs of a great terebinth, his head caught between the low hanging branches, while the mule that was under him went on. He remained hanging between heaven and earth.[1] A soldier saw him and ran to Joab with the news. The sarsaba "took three darts in his hand and thrust them through the heart of Absalom, while he was yet alive in the midst of the oak. And ten young men that bare Joab's armour compassed about and smote Absalom and slew him." This story shows how troublesome and yet how loyal a subject was Joab. He had protected Absalom against Bath-sheba, but he killed the favourite's rival for having offended against the king.

While the battle was taking place on the right bank of the Jordan, David, who never commanded in person in a civil war,[2] had seated himself between the gates of the two enceintes of Mahanaim.[3] He was

---

[1] The Bible does not give us to understand that Absalom was hanging by his hair. It is certainly said that he had hair in abundance (2 Sam. xiv. 25-28), but the text specifies that he was caught by the neck between two branches and half suffocated, and that he was nearly dead when Joab arrived. From the time of Josephus it has been related that his long, streaming hair, was caught by the branches of a terebinth as he galloped past. [2] See above, p. 121.

[3] This passage is very interesting from a military point of view. Mahanaim, like Rabbah in Ammon, is a place fortified according to Chaldæo-Susian principles; that is to say, possessing two enceintes with strong gates (2 Sam. xviii. 24) surmounted by casemates (2 Sam. xviii. 24) and flanked with towers occupied in time of peace by sentinels who kept a watch over the surrounding country (2 Sam. xviii. 24).

waiting anxiously for news, when a watchman perceived a messenger approaching at full speed. He brought tidings of the victory. The sentinel soon saw a second one hastening. He confirmed the great success of the royal troops, and announced that Absalom had fallen on the field of battle. The monarch forgot the triumphs of his arms when he heard of the death of his second son. He went up into the casemates over the gate and wept bitterly, giving way before everybody to despairing grief. " Oh, my son Absalom, my son, my son Absalom. Would God I had died for thee, O Absalom, my son!" Joab, however, who arrived some hours later, complained that David wrought confusion and discouragement among his defenders. Urged by him, the king consented to go back to his seat between the gates of the two enceintes, and the soldiers, called to his presence, marched past before him.

One person alone must have had feelings of unmixed joy in this day of mourning and of triumph. This was Bath-sheba, whose intrigues were crowned with success and who saw the obstacles to her progress disappearing one by one. Little she recked of trailing her robes in blood-stained tracks if the path she followed only led to her end. One last step lay between. Taking advantage of the prostration into which despair had thrown David, she worked upon him till he named her son Solomon as his successor on the throne, in the presence of the prophet Nathan, whom she had called as witness to the royal will. If her voice had been silent during the war, this success shows that her influence was once again paramount.[1]

Absalom dead, the insurgents had made a partial submission. It seems as if harmony would once more reign in the pacified monarchy. It was not so. Before re-crossing the Jordan and returning to Jerusalem, David, who had good reason to mistrust the fidelity of the tribes formerly devoted to Saul, wished to make sure of the Judæans. They had given the signal for revolt, they were even now sulking; but if their heads were hot, their hearts at least were good and faithful. He sent Zadok and Abiathar to remind them of the ties that bound them together. "Ye are my brethren," they were to tell them in the name of the king, "ye are my flesh: wherefore then are ye the last to bring back the king?" Then to Amasa, chief of the insurgents, they were to say privately: "Art thou not my bone and my flesh? God do so to me, and more also, if thou be not captain of the host before me continually in the room of Joab."[2] The intervention of the cohenim was completely successful. Amasa was won over and exhorted his fellow-tribesmen to forget their

---

[1] 1 Kings i. 13, 17. Cp. 1 Kings i. 13, 14. The Bible does not specify the moment when the favourite obtained this promise, or rather, there is a gap in the text. But it dated back in all probability to a period not far distant from the very hour which brought the news of the death of Absalom, David's favourite son and the only obstacle to the recognition of Solomon as his heir.

[2] 2 Sam. xix. 11, 12, 13, 42.

grudges, and the Judæans, oblivious of their grievances, rushed forward to welcome the son of Jesse.

Seeing them so numerous and enthusiastic, and witnessing the reception given to the last comers, the representatives of Benjamin and Joseph took umbrage and expressed the fear of being sacrificed to the powerful tribe. In vain were they told that Judah "had not eaten at all of the king's cost, nor had been given any gift";[1] the quarrel increased in bitterness. The monarch was not yet back in his capital ere the malcontents, for want of a prince of the house of Saul, elected as their chief Sheba the son of Bichri, a Benjamite.[2] War was once more aflame; no longer between David and his sons, but between the children of Jacob. It was a fresh manifestation of the ancient antagonism of the north and south, a new phase of the struggle between Joseph and Judah, a break to the truce which David's strength and skill had forced them to respect. It was felt that a reconciliation would never more be durable, that a tearing apart would take place south of Ephraim. In this empire whose unification had been so laboriously accomplished, the germ of schism was already to be found.

The command in the campaign which was about

[1] 2 Sam. xix. 42.
[2] 2 Sam. xx. 1. Further on (verse 21) it is stated that Sheba was a native of the hill country of Ephraim. This would mean that Bichri was a Benjamite, but that he was dwelling in the land of Ephraim at the time of his son's birth. The fact is, however, of no great importance.

to open naturally devolved upon the sarsaba. Natures so imperious as those of Bath-sheba and Joab could not long exist in harmony with each other. For some time past their interests had divided them as much as their passions. The favourite wished for the exercise of power in order to transmit it to her son; the sarsaba refused to share the king's confidence with any rival. Bath-sheba dominated David by love, Joab by his services and loyalty. In the beginning of their contest, the general had won a victory over the favourite by obtaining Absalom's pardon ; but his advice had had such fatal consequences, and he had afterwards shown such arrogance in massacring the prince in direct defiance of orders, and in forcing David to put aside his mourning and review the victorious troops, that Bath-sheba had not much difficulty in setting him aside. The king's first choice for Joab's successor was that of Amasa. Amasa was among the number of the Judæan chiefs who had betrayed the royal cause. He had commanded Absalom's army ; but he had atoned for his offences by helping Zadok and Abiathar in their negotiations with the south, and on that occasion he had received great encouragement if not formal promises. Perhaps also he found an auxiliary in the favourite, who knowing herself to be disliked by the men of Judah, devoted to the elder sons of the king, endeavoured to cajole these powerful adversaries and to draw them over to her party. She had acted thus with the prophet Nathan and had transformed his formidable hostility into friendship.

Although Amasa was in his turn superseded by Abishai for his slowness in mustering the troops, Joab could not forget the affront. When Amasa came to meet him, to join in the pursuit of Sheba, he pretended to embrace him, drew his sword suddenly, and drove it through him. It was thus that Abner had been killed. "He that favoureth Joab, and he that is for David, let him follow Joab," said the spectators of the crime. This was the only funeral oration pronounced over the dead. A few days later the murderer had driven back the insurgents into Abel of Beth-Maacah, and he pursued the attack with such determination that the terrified inhabitants fell upon Sheba, cut off his head and cast it into the lines of the royal army.

The surrender of Beth-Maacah put an end to civil war without interrupting the course of the crisis through which the monarchy was passing. The revolt of Absalom had been succeeded by the rebellion of the northern tribes. The rebellion was followed by a pestilence, the pestilence brought about a disastrous famine. There is no need of a direct intervention of heaven to explain this ill-starred period. Life rewards each man according to his deserts. Very often punishment strikes the guilty one in the privacy of his feelings, remaining hidden to the unobservant multitude; sometimes it is made manifest as a salutary example. Such was the tempest let loose upon the royal house after the death of Uriah.

The monarch whom prosperity had weakened recovers his strength in the face of evil fortune. His soul is tempered anew by adversity, and his genius, instead of being dulled by trials, regains the force and penetration of the distant days of his youth. He suppresses Absalom's rising, he crushes the partisans of Sheba, he struggles against famine and pestilence without ever losing constancy or courage. And the destinies of Israel resume their glorious course under the guidance of the repentant and forgiven king.

During the last years of trial there took place an incident imputed as a sin to the king for reasons whose significance it is hard to understand. This was the numbering of the military forces of the north and of the south. Joab, who was charged with this office, remonstrated with David, but the king's will prevailed, and the sarsaba, at the head of his chief officers, went through the country counting the men who were able to bear arms. Why should this measure, so frequent in the pastoral period, have become criminal to such a degree that God sends pestilence upon the land as a punishment for the king who has ordained it?[1] The Bible does

---

[1] Josephus, who cannot understand the reason for the anger of Jehovah, alleges that David had omitted to pay half a shekel per head for each person numbered, to the priests, as had been decreed by Moses. The fact that it was a prophet who reproached the king shows how ill founded is his conjecture.

not tell us. It relates the observations made by Joab, the reproaches of the prophet Gad, and the wrath of Jehovah. Here again it is possible to supplement its silence and to fill in the gaps in the narrative.

The king was old, every one awaited his death. The timid endeavoured to surprise the secrets of destiny in order to attach themselves to the successor of David ; the bold had made choice of a pretender and had helped him to usurp authority in the hope of sharing his spoils. With the former it was a question of divining the future—with the latter, that of bending it to their will. It is not only from yesterday that men rush into politics.

In the midst of these court intrigues and conflicting interests two parties with their staff and their troops had grown up. At the head of the one was Bath-sheba, the other was lead by Joab ; the erstwhile accomplices being now decided enemies. It is extremely probable that the explanation of the pestilence as an effect of the wrath of Jehovah was a simple manœuvre and an episode of the struggle waged around the throne. The numbering had been undertaken at the instigation of Bath-sheba, who was anxious to know the respective forces of the tribes both hostile and favourable to her influence at the approaching hour of the succession, whilst her adversaries, considering this census to be a dangerous tool in skilful hands, endeavoured to force the sovereign to change his decision. It is in fact noticeable that Nathan, the accustomed critic of the royal actions, who had, however, drawn closer to Bath-sheba since the birth of Solomon, is silent at this juncture. Joab is the first to entreat his master to abandon his project; then comes the prophet Gad, one of David's first partisans, and the friend of Joab's early days,[1] who, speaking in the name of God, represents the pestilence as the expiation of a sin against Jehovah. These indications of the part played by Joab and the prophet Gad on this occasion, are for that matter confirmed by the existence of the plot woven by David's early companions against Bath-sheba and her son Solomon. Before having recourse to violence, the conspirators tried to frighten the old king, and to guard against further concessions—to defend him against his own weakness.

Joab, who was the soul of this conspiracy, set up against Solomon Adonijah, the son of Haggith, who since the deaths of Amnon, Chileab and Absalom, was now the eldest of the princes. Joab's choice must not be considered as a protestation of his virtue. He had often proved himself to be without scruples. But he knew that the favourite was proud, resentful and passionate; and had fought against her because she hindered his ambitions and had stolen from him the affection of the king. At the present moment he

---

[1] 2 Sam. xxiv. 11-14. It was Gad, an envoy of the fervent followers of Jehovah, who had gone to make overtures to David at the time when he was flying from the anger of Saul (1 Sam. xxii. 5 and above, p. 73).

was influenced by the fear of reprisals as much as by jealousy. Around Adonijah and the sarsaba were grouped the princes and the greater number of the soldiers. The weakness of the party lay in its *secular* character; for Bath-sheba had won over the majority of the prophets and the priests, who triumphed in the repentance and submission of David. Feeling his inferiority on this point, Joab had endeavoured to conciliate Abiathar, cohen of Jerusalem, and the rival of Zadok, cohen at Gibeon.[1]

On her side, the favourite, strong in a promise extracted from David in favour of her son, was able to count upon some devoted friends and faithful servants. There were first of all the prophet Nathan, Solomon's governor, Zadok the cohen at Gibeon, who was anxious to obtain the religious supremacy for himself and for his house, Benaiah, a general greatly renowned ever since his campaign against Moab,[3] and whose devotion was all the more sincere from the fact that Joab had sacrificed him to his brother Abishai, and then the priests, the prophets and also the Gibborim and the Cretan guard, where Benaiah had served by turns as an officer and as the chief in command.[4] And finally, she was in negotiation with

[1] See above, pp. 186, 187, 188; and below, note L in Appendix.

[2] See above, p. 236, n. 1, and cp. 1 Kings i. 13, 17, with 2 Sam. vii. 12; 1 Kings ii. 15. The phrase relating to the inheritance promised by God to Solomon, to the detriment of his elder brothers, is not repeated in the corresponding passage in the Chronicles. (1 Chron xvii. 11, 12.) [3] See above, p. 205.

[4] Cp. 2 Sam. viii. 18; xxiii. 20; 1 Chron. xi. 22, with 2 Sam. viii. 2.

the men of Judah. Joab, who knew that the latter were hostile to the new influences paramount at court, and who thought that they would put their hopes in Adonijah, born at Hebron while David was still reigning there,[1] had forgotten that the blood of Amasa lay between Judah and himself, and had not troubled to make atonement for his crime, while the favourite, hearing that they complained of not having eaten at all "of the king's cost" during the reign of David,[2] had continued the policy which she inaugurated by raising up Amasa against Joab, and had promised them compensation, pledging herself to except them from taxes the day that Solomon should ascend the throne. On these conditions, the southern chiefs had promised her, if not their support, at least their neutrality.[3] When interests of great gravity are at stake, many a feud, many a personal dislike, is forced to be dumb. In short, the mother of Solomon could rely on the majority of the priests, on the prophets, and on the flower of the troops. She lacked, however, the support of the most popular and illustrious general in the army.

[1] 2 Sam. iii. 4. Adonijah became the eldest on the death of Absalom (2 Kings i. 5).

[2] See above, p. 237, n. 1.

[3] The officers of Judah are called to the banquet given by Adonijah (1 Kings i. 10), but at the decisive moment, they do not take up the defence of the prince, whom they certainly could have saved if they had so chosen. Their conduct is explained by the fact that on the accession of Solomon, Judah is freed from tribute and has none of the royal collectors dwelling in its territory (1 Kings iv.). These privileges must have greatly aggravated the hatred of the north for the south, and must have done much to hasten the schism.

The forces of the two rivals were about equal; victory would be for the one most rich in skill and daring.

Adonijah, incited by Joab, whose leading virtue was not that of patience, wished to take his adversary by surprise. Like Absalom, he gathered round him a large escort of chariots, horsemen and runners to clear the way. Like his brother, he called his partisans to a solemn sacrifice. The place was by the stone of Zoheleth, near the fountain of En-rogel,[1] which flows at the foot and to the south of the rocky promontory on which Jerusalem is built. And there, before his brothers, before Joab and Abiathar, in the midst of the Judæan officers, witnesses rather than accomplices, he asserted his rights to succeed David. Their manœuvres having miscarried owing to the vigilance and cunning of the favourite, the conspirators now unmasked and made ready to enter on a path of violence. Nathan was the first to hear of their assembly. He knew not what would be the result, but could very easily guess. He hastened to Bath-sheba and made known his fears. The triumph of Joab and his associates meant death for her and for her son. Stones soon strike the bottom when they roll down a rapid slope without an obstacle to stay their fall. Immediate action was all-important,

---

[1] Nowadays the well of Job, *bir Eyoub*, situated at the junction of the valley of Hinnom and of the Kedron. It is also called the well of Nehemiah. It is thirty-eight mètres deep. It was doubtless a place of general meeting, as all fountains are in the East.

the blow must be parried ere it was aimed. Adonijah must be struck before he could appeal to the people.

The mother of Solomon was not the woman to shrink from strife.

In a brief interview Bath-sheba and Nathan decide to go before the king and remind him of his solemn promise to leave the crown to Solomon. She will enter David's presence alone, and soften his heart by her prayers; then the prophet will follow and lend her the support of his moral authority.

The old man was sitting in his chamber, in the company of a young girl whom they had brought to the king to minister unto him and to bring warmth into his frozen limbs. Bath-sheba recoiled from these duties of a slave. When he saw before him the woman who was to this day beloved and to this day beautiful,[1] and noticed her altered countenance, her streaming tears and body shaken by sobs, he was moved himself, and demanded the cause of her grief.

"My lord, thou swarest by the Lord thy God unto

---

[1] A passage in the Chronicles which is not contradicted anywhere, represents Solomon as quite young when he ascended the throne (1 Chron. xxix. 1). It may be that he was from nineteen to twenty years of age, since one of his wives had already given him a son, Rehoboam, who was a year old when David died. (Cp. 1 Kings xi. 42, with xiv. 21.) From these data we may infer that David, who breathed his last at the age of seventy years, was from fifty to fifty-one years old when he fell in love with Bath-sheba. A tradition exists that Solomon was only twelve years of age when he became king (Migne, "Patr. gr.," vol. i. col. 596). This tradition is in slight contradiction with the Bible, but it confirms the fact that Solomon was very young when he succeeded to the crown, and that Bath-sheba was certainly not more than forty when the king's death left her a widow.

thine handmaid, saying, Assuredly Solomon thy son shall reign after me, and he shall sit upon my throne. And now, behold, Adonijah reigneth; and thou, my lord the king, knowest it not: and he hath slain oxen and he hath sacrificed oxen and fatlings in abundance, and hath called all the sons of the king, but Solomon thy servant hath he not called.

"And now, my lord the king, the eyes of all Israel are upon thee, that thou shouldst tell them who shall sit on the throne of my lord the king after him. Otherwise it shall come to pass, when my lord the king shall sleep with his fathers, that I and my son Solomon shall be counted offenders."

She was still speaking when Nathan was announced. The man of God had forbidden David to raise a temple to Jehovah, he had confronted him on the morrow of the death of Uriah, he had dared to reproach him for his crime and by the sheer force of audacity had gained an absolute ascendancy over his soul. The favourite having retired, he entered the presence and made complaint that David had said nothing to him of his intentions with regard to Prince Adonijah, and that he had not been invited to the festival of the coronation. He declared his astonishment that neither Solomon, the servant of the king, nor Zadok the priest, nor Benaiah the son of Jehoiada had been called to consecrate an act of such solemnity.

Bath-sheba's lamentations and Nathan's speech made a great impression on the monarch. Bath-sheba, when she invoked a solemn promise and the right of the king alone to appoint his successor, when she reminded him of the danger to Solomon and the peril to which she herself would be exposed should the conspiracy compass its ends, had roused his anger; Nathan, who pointed out that his wishes were ignored during his own lifetime, that his power was set at defiance, and that his death was an object of desire, amply justified his wrath. There was no longer room for doubt. Though the mother of Solomon, anxious for the fate of a beloved son, might be capable of misrepresenting or of exaggerating what had happened, Nathan, a holy prophet, would never deceive him. Then he found at the back of Adonijah all the malcontents, all the culprits guilty of the late disorders. He hesitated no longer. In the plenitude of his will and of his rights he had sworn to bequeath to Solomon the inheritance of his authority; he would fulfil his oath, and in order to prevent any further competition, the royal will should be proclaimed before the people. Sending instantly for Zadok and Benaiah, he ordered them to accompany his son to the fountain of Gihon, situated in the valley of the Kedron, to the southwest of Jerusalem,[1] to anoint him there king over Israel and to announce his accession with flourishes of trumpets.

[1] The fountain of Gihon, nowadays called the fountain of the Virgin, fed two large reservoirs (2 Chron. xxxii. 30; xxxiii. 14). It was, like the well of En-rogel, a favourite gathering place of the people.

Benaiah in the name of the army, Zadok in the name of God, acted at once upon their master's orders. They mounted Solomon on David's own mule, gathered together a large number of priests and of prophets, called the Gibborim and the Cretan guard, and reached the valley of the Kedron. In the same way that Samuel had consecrated David Nathan poured the holy oil on Solomon's forehead and anointed him in the name of the Almighty. Then the trumpets rang out and the cheers of the crowd cried in answer to their music, "God save King Solomon." Preceded by harps and pipes, followed by the rejoicing crowd, the procession turned back towards the palace, its numbers swelled at every step by new arrivals. On their return, David had the throne of state placed by the side of the bed of his old age, invited Solomon to take his seat there, and in accents weakened by the approach of death but rendered firm and assured by force of will, he announced the accession of his heir. And as he feared that the preference shown to the last of his children might excite comment among the people, he invoked the commands of God and the precedents celebrated in the annals of Israel.[1] Had not Judah, the fourth son of Jacob, been raised above his elders[2]; had not he himself, the youngest of Jesse's eight sons, been singled out in preference to his

---

[1] 2 Sam. vii. 12; 1 Kings ii. 15; 1 Chron. xxviii. 5; xxix. 1; Josephus, "Ant. Jud." vii., xi.

[2] See above, p. 27, n. 2.

brothers? The Almighty alone knew what was good for His children.

"Thy God make the name of Solomon better than thy name, and make his throne greater than thy throne," replied the officers. Then David bowed himself upon the bed in one supreme effort, and was the first to do obeisance to the new king: "Blessed be the Lord, the God of Israel, which hath given one to sit on my throne this day, mine eyes even seeing it."[1]

Now he could die in peace. The royalty of the house of Jesse, which had been established on the frail base of his personal ascendency, and which had been maintained at the cost of incessant effort, was now founded indeed. Thus to his last day David continued to give proofs of a decision, a resolution and a wisdom, surprising in a youth, and extraordinary in an old man.

Meanwhile Adonijah and his associates were rejoicing. The sacrificial feast was drawing to a close. Suddenly shouts and trumpet blasts fill the air with clamour. "Wherefore is this noise of the city being in an uproar?"[2] cries Joab. That very instant, Jonathan, the son of Abiathar the priest, appears among the feasters. He brings startling news. While Adonijah has been tarrying and wasting precious moments, Bath-sheba, always vigilant, has caused Solomon to be crowned! Seized with terror, the conspirators disperse in all directions, and Adoni-

[1] 1 Kings i. 48.   [2] 1 Kings i. 41.

jah, the king of an hour, flies back to the town, hastens to the tabernacle [1] and grasps the horns of the altar raised before it. It would not befit Solomon to inaugurate his reign with a sanguinary execution. He makes a show of pardon, accepts his brother's homage, and sends him back to his own palace.

Some weeks later, David, who felt that his days were drawing to a close, called his son to him, and after a few august words of exhortation that summed up the entire teaching of his life, he commanded him to build the temple of the Lord, and to discharge for him certain debts of gratitude. Then his eyes were closed and he slept with his fathers. He was about seventy years of age and had reigned for over seven years in Hebron, and for thirty-three in Jerusalem.[2]

David was dead. But Bath-sheba, who for many long years, and especially since the return to Jerusalem, had been more or less at the head of affairs, soon showed that she would not loose her grasp of power. After the funeral ceremonies, the first time that she entered the presence of her son, Solomon rose up to meet her, bowed down to her and kissed her feet. He caused a throne to be placed near his own, and she sat on his right hand, thus sharing in his sovereignty. What intense joy must it not have been for the widow of Uriah, the favourite of David, to receive the honours of royalty, to don at last the

---

[1] See above, p. 203, and also note N in Appendix.
[2] 2 Sam. ii. 10, 11 ; v. 4, 5 ; 1 Kings ii. 21, and see above, p. 246, n. 1.

diadem which the dead monarch would have feared to place upon her brows![1]

Bath-sheba had committed or suggested many crimes—her violent entrance into the royal house had compromised its very existence. These reservations once made, it must be allowed that her love of intrigue and passion for power were served by a rare intelligence, an inflexible will, and a virile energy, and that her elevation contributed to the stability of the new reign.

Her first commands were decrees of death or exile against the heads of Adonijah's party. She struck at Joab, even at the cost of violating the sanctuary where he fled for refuge; she exiled the cohen Abiathar whose sacred character protected him from execution. Adonijah had been killed a little while before for having had the audacity to ask for Abishag, the young Shunamite who had tended David in his old age. Shimei, one of the last descendants of Saul, and noted for his hostility towards the house of David,[2] shared the same fate. Before giving orders for these rigorous measures, the queen-mother put forward a verbal will and testament made by David

---

[1] Compare with this greeting her reception by David (1 Kings i. 1–16). There is more in this behaviour of Solomon than the mere observance of a rule of etiquette. To begin with, the prerogatives of the queen-mother had not yet been determined by custom, Bath-sheba being the first favourite whose son was crowned; and even supposing the contrary to have been the case, the Bible would not have troubled to chronicle a detail of the ceremonial code.

[2] 2 Sam. xvi. 5–11.

on his death-bed.[1] Nothing could be less certain
than the authenticity of the savage recommendations
she professed to execute.[2] David's whole life, the
nobility of his character, the loftiness of his soul, and
also many passages in the Bible all rise up in direct
contradiction.[3] The woman who had killed Uriah,
who had plotted the deaths of Amnon and of Absalom,
because they stood in the way of her son's advance-
ment, struck without mercy at those who had been
independent enough to brave her anger, or to seek to
do her harm. Bath-sheba was listening to the voice
of her own animosities, she was wreaking personal
vengeance rather than obeying the last wishes of the
king.

In any case, in order to free Solomon from every
anxiety, and to assure for him the tranquil enjoyment
of power, these punishments were necessary. In a
certain sense they were even just. Joab, Abiathar,
Adonijah, Shimei himself, had been guilty of conspiracy or of treason, and antiquity had but one mode

---

[1] The Bible states that these orders were given by Solomon. It
may be so, but in any case he was so young that he cannot be held
responsible for them. During the whole of his after life he was a for-
bearing and clement prince. Neither his instincts nor his tastes were
cruel.

[2] It may be that David would not have dared to kill Joab himself,
but had he wished to punish others, such as, for instance, Shimei, he
would never have left the office to his son.

[3] The forbearance shown by David to Saul must be remembered
(1 Sam. xxiv., xxvi.; see above, p. 81), and also to Shimei himself
(2 Sam. xvi. 5-11), and his admonitions to his followers on those
occasions. David bore no malice and was only cruel upon extremity,
and when forced to punish by superior considerations.

of dealing with such crimes: death, which chastises the culprit and disables him for ever. Mercy—forgiveness of injuries—magnanimity in triumph—all these are virtues inaugurated by the Gospel. Before the days of Christ they would not have been understood, and would even have been despised from the fact that in primitive societies, where the action of the law is but weak, the punishment of offences is a social duty.

Alone among the conspirators, Joab perhaps deserved another fate. He had been a skilful lieutenant and a faithful friend. None had lent David more efficacious aid in good and evil fortune. But arrogant, bloodthirsty, violent, he would not tolerate a rival influence near the king. In a fit of jealousy he had assassinated Abner, general of the troops of Saul, and Amasa, chief of the men of Judah, though David had pledged his good faith to the one and was uncle of the other. He had massacred Absalom in violation of the king's orders; he would have struck down the favourite had Adonijah's conspiracy been successful.

In the course of these events Benaiah, the executor of Bath-sheba's decrees, inherited the office of sarsaba of the royal armies, and Zadok was made cohen at Jerusalem in the place of Abiathar.[1] Nathan remained in high favour, as is shown by the exalted situations occupied by his sons at the court of Solomon.[2] The partisans of the favourite thus re-

[1] See note L in Appendix. [2] 1 Kings iv. 5.

ceived the reward for their fidelity and payment for their services.

Henceforward no more mention is made of Bath-sheba. Did she survive David for many years? Did she follow him soon to the grave? It is impossible to say, so profound is the silence with regard to her name, while those of her *protégés* recur at different times, either in the Book of the Kings, or in the Chronicles, or in the writings of Josephus. Solomon, after making use of his mother and lavishing upon her the tokens of his affection, as long as her experience and her energy could be of any avail, perhaps one day showed himself to be her worthy pupil, and relegated to the depths of the harem a councillor whom he knew to be arbitrary and greedy of power, or who proved to be too compromising. This child, the beloved of her soul, this son whom she had raised so high in spite of wars and rebellions and the obstacles created by his birth—had he no gratitude for all her efforts and for the crimes committed for his sake? If such were the end of Bath-sheba, the disillusion must indeed have been cruel, and retribution, though tardy and unexpected, was none the less just and terrible.

The personages of the fatal drama which was played out before the walls of Rabbah in Ammon and in the palace at Jerusalem have accomplished their destiny. It is now time to determine their different responsibilities, and to mete out blame in proportion to their guilt.

It must first of all be noted that the adultery of a sovereign with one of his subjects, as well as the murder of the husband, are acts authorised by the Asiatic conception of absolute power. These odious crimes, unpardonable from our point of view, were often committed at the courts of Memphis, of Nineveh, and of Susa, and are repeated nowadays in the harems of Mussulman sovereigns without exciting universal reprobation. It is apt to be forgotten that the oriental autocrat disposes of maidens and of women in the same manner that he does of wheat, of the soil, of lambs and of sheep, of the fortune, the blood, and the very existence of the beings living under his dominion. A creature apart from the world beneath him, he violates laws, or rather frees himself from their control, without remorse. In so doing he exercises more than a privilege—it is a sovereign right. He is the living law, he can do anything with impunity—for public opinion does not exist, nor are there any institutions that could give it voice. His edicts are considered oracles of heaven; his will is that of a god. He is only approached in an attitude of worship. Was not David himself addressed as an *angel of God*.[1]

The beings sacrificed to the monarch's interests or passions are the victims of a calamity analogous to fire, flood, or pestilence. They suffer, they lament, and if they accuse the master they complain in the same way that they rail at the gods in a moment of

[1] 2 Sam. xix. 27.

anger in order to relieve their pain, mostly without design or will to reach the inaccessible author of the scourge. The respect for the will or the caprice of the monarch goes so far that Xerxes kills with impunity his brother Masistus, whose wife he has desired, and takes by force the wife of his own son; [1] that Artaxerxes II., copying his ancestor, compasses the death of his own son Darius, whose favourite he admires; [2] that the religions of Egypt and of Persia, so pure and strict in many respects, authorise incest in order to palliate the guilt of princes,[3] that the ephoræ throw the cloak of their authority over the amorous fancies of their kings.[4] Rome herself would never have been thrown into an uproar by the crime of Sextus and the suicide of Lucretia had the people not been tired of foreign masters and anxious for a pretext for driving them away. In the days of antiquity the priests, the law, the magistrates are either the king's slaves or his accomplices. In every age and in every clime the conscience is perverted by the abuse of unlimited power and by the servility of the human race. The great prophets of Israel are solitary

[1] Herodotus, ix., 108–113.

[2] Plutarch, "Life of Artaxerxes," xxxix.–xliv.

[3] See the life of Queen Hatasu or Hatchopsitou (Maspero, "Hist. anc. des peup. de l'Orient," 4th ed., p. 193). Cambyses married his own sister under these same conditions (Herodotus, iii., 51), Artaxerxes II. his daughters (Plutarch, "L. of Art.," xxxix.–xliv.). Without pretending, like Xanthus of Lydia and Ctesias, that the grossest incest was practised by the priests, the "Avesta," which has codified customs of extreme antiquity, does not forbid the unions of blood relations.

[4] Herodotus, vi., 61–63.

in their attitude towards the kings of the earth; the torah alone will make no difference between the powerful and the weak. But these teachers of Israel have not yet raised their voice— the law is not yet promulgated; it is but a few superior minds that are inspired by its commandments. Nevertheless David is guilty just because he is one of these elect; and the precautions which he takes to conceal his sin, his anxiety to justify the death of Uriah, and the sincerity of his repentence, are the very proofs of his transgression. His remorse denounces him—it is a confession.

In any case, in the eyes of the majority of the Israelites, the king did not commit a very grave offence and certainly not a crime. He sinned, but it was against Jehovah and his own conscience. Another sovereign would have taken Bath-sheba from her husband, would have killed Uriah without scruple had he dared to complain, and have felt neither pity nor regret.

In addition to these considerations based on the general condition of manners and of morals, the indulgence manifested by the priests and prophets, and especially the words put into Nathan's mouth by the Bible,[1] show once again how mistaken critics have been as to the nature of the sin for which the king was blamed by his most enlightened and strict contemporaries, and for which he bitterly reproached himself.

[1] See above, pp. 224 and 225.

Nathan condemns him for having taken the poor man's ewe lamb, but it is especially on account of the duplicity with which this act has been accomplished, and because he has despised the word of the Lord, that the prophet threatens him with the divine anger. And as the king is penitent and his heart is filled with remorse, the man of God pardons him, becomes again his counsellor and his friend, and does not even dream of demanding the repudiation of Bath-sheba as a token of repentance and of reparation. For the fear of Heaven, the abhorrence of falsehood, and the glorification of perfect frankness, are safeguards of society, and become cardinal virtues in communities where the prevention of crime is as difficult as its recognition. With similar motives, the Mazdean religion, whose origin belongs to the dark ages, attaches immense value to the practice of such virtues and makes of them the corner-stone of its doctrines.

The memory of Bath-sheba's lover is of course for ever tarnished; nevertheless it was David who taught an ignorant world the greatness of humility and the efficacy of repentance. His unmurmuring readiness to make expiation proclaimed that morality was one and that all men were equal before its laws, paving the way long beforehand for the truths which would triumph with the Gospel, and preserving future generations from the evils engendered by a false conception of royalty. On all these points he was a pioneer. This is not the moment to discuss the age and origin of the *Miserere*,[1] but if the disciple of Samuel did not compose this sublime psalm of penitence, he certainly inspired it by his conduct.

Here lies the real sin of David. If we take into account the surroundings and the times in which he lived, the precepts he had gathered in his intercourse with the prophets and the loftiness of his own mind, his love for Bath-sheba and the orders given to expose Uriah are but the venial aspects of the crime—the true offence lies in the deceit that was practised, and in his disobedience to the teachings of the prophets.

To what extent was David's responsibility involved? The facts speak for themselves.

Bath-sheba makes her appearance as a passionate woman, ardent and ambitious, alarmed at no obstacles, undismayed by failure. And in addition it had pleased nature to endow her with most precious gifts. She was a politician, a strategist, a *charmer*. After fascinating David, she fascinates the prophet Nathan, the cohen Zadok, Benaiah, the chief of the Gibborim; she fascinates the men of Judah, she beguiles her contemporaries to the point of exciting their pity for her misfortunes; she fascinates her friends and her enemies, her partisans and her adversaries.[2] And those who choose to resist

---

[1] Psa. li. in the Hebrew text, l. in the Greek.

[2] The error which has arisen is so complete that former exegetes, assimilating Lemuel to Samuel, attributed to Bath-sheba the precepts replete with beauty and wisdom which are found in the first verses

she threatens, she strikes, she kills. Her hand can be traced in every plot, in every crime whose object is to isolate David and to extinguish rival influences. Such was the woman concerned in the drama of Rabbah in Ammon. This woman alone could reap advantage from her fall. Bath-sheba alone was interested in Uriah's death, for she only was building up dreams of power on a child to be born of her relations with the king.

Who will dare to call her innocent?

David was the instrument that served her turn. The king, desperately in love, terrified at the thought that she ran the risk of death, and that the unborn child would perish with her, abandoned himself to her influence, promising to marry her and to rid her of her husband, just as later on, in answer to her prayer, he decreed that Solomon, the son that she had given him, should ascend the throne in preference to his elder brothers.

It may perhaps seem strange that the man who was master of the maidens of Israel, and who ought to have been cured of guilty fantasies by the satiety of satisfied desire, should have experienced love, unique all-absorbing, and should have fallen under the dominion of a woman in the very autumn of his life. The fact, however, admits of no denial. Bath-sheba appears, and until the last day of David's life her

of the thirty-first chapter of Proverbs, and that supreme counsel of the mother to her son, to fly from the pitfalls laid by vicious women (Prov. xxxi. 3).

sway over him is so complete that for her sake he proves false to a virtuous past, and, deaf to the voice of his conscience, sacrifices at her pleasure his wives and his children, the auxiliaries of his glory and the supporters of his power.

Many causes predisposed him to this weakness. Polygamy, first of all, which renders vain the ties that should result from marriage, then also the flattery and the inaction that marked the decline of an existence so active and fraught with interest in its commencement, and finally the impaired vitality due to advancing years in conjunction with fatigues and emotions undergone in early life. But the principal reason, the one that triumphed over all, was the perfect beauty, the enthralling charm, and the supreme cleverness of the favourite. It was she who offered herself to David and lured him to his fall, she it was who enervated her lover's will—upon her must rest the responsibility for the crime.

As for the indulgence shown to Bath-sheba, notwithstanding her intrigues and the innocent blood that stained her hands, it is only too easily explained.

In her own day it must be attributed to the ignorance of the greater part of the nation with regard to the part she played in the death of Uriah. Later on, the despair which she feigned touched the populace, always inclined to champion a pretty woman and hostile by instinct to the masters whom it serves. The mode of thought in Hebrew Society at this period must also be taken into consideration.

On one hand marriage was reduced to a formality, on the other the caprices of the monarch were a law in themselves so long as they were not opposed to the general interests of the people bound up with those of God. Many centuries were yet to run their course ere legislators, taught by a long experience of life, would decree the unity and indissolubility of the bonds contracted between man and woman, and the equality of all before the law of morality.

Nowadays, the question is considered from another point of view, equally favourable to Bath-sheba. To begin with, by whitening the memory of the favourite, that of David is blackened in proportion, and it has already been explained how harmony has arisen on this point between the historians and exegetes of the schools most opposed in their views. Finally, the detractors of David, the enemies of this biblical ancestor of the Christ, are full of indulgence and even tenderness for the elegant vices. Already Saul, that crowned madman, has been set up against the hero of the biblical epic; one step further, and we shall see Bath-sheba, no longer excused but glorified. Her capabilities for passion will be brought forward, her need for a luxury incompatible with the plain existence offered by an officer of the Gibborim; compassion will be lavished on her hourly martyrdom by the side of a rough soldier. And if ever there should come a reaction in favour of David, if in spite of his virtues, his merits, and his compromising descent, the rehabilitation of the son of Jesse should one day be brought about, an excuse will be found in his very sin; it will be remembered that his love for his mistress was so great that it led him to bury Uriah under the walls of Rabbah in Ammon.

CONCLUSION

WHEN Saul died the enemy was in the heart of Israel, anarchy, like a pestilence, ravaged the tribes, poverty and misery reigned supreme. Ruin was imminent. At the time of the death of David, there were caravans going from Egypt to Assyria without ever quitting the empire of the Hebrews. Moab, Edom, Aram—those ancient enemies—were under Israelite governors; Philistia, reduced to impotence, was for ever dismembered. The Phœnicians were making offerings to obtain or to preserve a friendship fraught with profit. From Hamath and Damascus to Arabia Petræa and the frontiers of Mizraim all men obeyed David, provided him with soldiers or paid him tribute.[1] Jerusalem was glutted with precious metals.[2] And everywhere, from Dan even

---

[1] 2 Sam. viii., x., xi., xii. 26–31 ; xxi. 15–22.

[2] There is no means of strictly estimating the weight of the precious metals accumulated by David in his treasuries. It would be over thirty-two thousand tons. It is easy to understand that the fruits of his various campaigns must have been abundant. He had brought over to Jerusalem the greater part of the gold and silver of the Ammonites, the Moabites, the Aramæans, and the Amalekites, to say nothing of the metals which were sent to him as more or less voluntary gifts or as annual tribute.

to Beersheba, the people were as numerous as the sands of the sea; drinking, eating, rejoicing in safety, every man under his vine and under his fig-tree.[1] Power had succeeded slavery, youth had followed on decrepitude, opulence on misery. The life of one man had sufficed to work this miracle.

Of the qualities revealed by this marvellous achievement, the most surprising are those of extreme prudence in conjunction with supreme audacity and hardihood. From the beginning to the end of his life, David remains the youth who, for his first encounter, dares to challenge Goliath, and at the same time the captain who, though ever victorious, is yet patient enough to await at Hebron the end of the reign of Saul, the death of his son, and the offer of the crown. General, diplomatist, poet, and administrator, he realises the perfect type of the monarch—he is beyond doubt the greatest genius of the biblical world. His accession had a flavour of the marvellous, and the reign which achieved the constitution of a state out of such hostile and independent elements as the tribes, and the discipline of a people so inclined to anarchy, impatient of restraint and always ready to revolt, was one long miracle.

Such was David, without exalting his qualities or palliating his weaknesses. This is the unscrupulous brigand, the drunkard, the descendant of a courtesan, the thief, the bandit, the rogue, the assassin, depicted by certain schools because our religious traditions

[1] 1 Kings iv. 25.

have given eternal sovereignty to his race. Had he but lived some centuries earlier among an idolatrous and fiction-loving people, he would not have been counted as an ancestor of a God—he himself would have been placed in the ranks of the Immortals.

NOTES

NOTES.

A.—On the tribe of Levi.

In Jacob's dying words to his children (Gen. xlix. 5), the third son of Jacob and Leah is relegated to the last rank and is excluded from the family of Israel. The cause of this great fall is unknown. It may be that the Levites were punished for having violated a treaty of alliance and for having thus exposed the tribes to just and terrible reprisals. It is, in fact, stated that Simeon and Levi, to avenge the insult offered to their sister Dinah by Shechem, son of Hamor, had massacred all his family—although they had amply atoned for the offence and had even adopted the religion of the Israelites (Gen. xxxiv. ; xlix. 5, 6, 7). It is difficult to discover the real truth; but the decline of the tribe is a certain fact. Later on the Benjamites suffered analogous chastisement inflicted by the common consent of the tribes (Judg. xix., xx.).

It is probable that after having lost even the right to possess property, the Levites insinuated themselves into the subordinate offices of the primitive faith, then were *associated*—hence the name of *Levi*—with the sacerdotal functions of the heads of families, and finally were appointed for the transport and the guardianship of the ark of the covenant. (See note L.) The reprobation weighing on the tribe of Levi is still to be traced in the days of David.

Nevertheless, as in their capacity of guardians or of servants of the ark, the Levites had acquired certain enviable privileges, their numbers increased in such proportions, and there were so many intruders in their ranks, that they were obliged to make a resolute stand against the invasion, reserving for themselves the highest sacerdotal dignities and limiting the number of offices. In David's reign and at his instigation the first revision no doubt took place. See above, pp. 193, 194, 195.

B.—JEHOVAH AND ELOHIM.

From the days of the patriarchs, the best Hebrews adored a one and only God, a being ethereal and divine. The march of progress was slow. Monotheism took root with difficulty among the masses of the people. In course of time rites and ceremonies were regulated and became more complicated: but the religion, both originally and in its subsequent history, was clear and absolute, spiritual on the surface and at heart, with no real affinity to the religions of the countries in which the Hebrews had lived and those of the peoples to whom they were closely related. Supposing that the latter had served in the past the same God that was worshipped by the Israelites, they must have hastened to fall into idolatry. The confused rudiments of a primitive paganism that some have endeavoured to find in the monotheism of the Israelites appear to be foreign to its original conception, and are connected either with idol worship, which had an invincible attraction for the tribes, or else with divine personages quite distinct from the God of Israel, but designated by analogous words among the peoples speaking a Semitic tongue. Such are, in the Aryan languages, the derivatives of the root *div*, "the splendour of the pure sky," which apply equally well to the inhabitants of Olympus or to the one God of the Christians. The God of Abraham, of Moses, and of David, whatever His name may be, is one and one only, without division and without sex, with no beginning and no end, the founder of no divine race, the son of no other gods. He is not confounded with the vault of Heaven, the stars, or the great forces of nature; neither is He hidden beneath a pantheistic envelope. He is as foreign to Zeus, Ahura-mazda, and Varuna as to Bel, Moloch, Osiris, Dagon, or Chemosh. The thunder, the fires of heaven, the whirlwind, hail and rain, even the messenger *Malachi*, entrusted with His orders for the earth, never become divine beings independent of or emanating from a first God ; they never rise or fall in the celestial hierarchy. They are the manifestations of His will and of His almighty power. This superior conception of divinity which was peculiar to the Israelites is a phenomenon all the more inexplicable from the fact that the sons of Jacob borrowed from strangers, in addition to their civilisation, the ceremonial furniture, the insignia of the priests, and certain portions of the sacerdotal garments.

To this divine idea correspond two principal designations or definitions, sometimes joined, sometimes distinct: Elohim and Jehovah. The first, which is a plural, "the Gods," used as a singular, is but the integration or unification of the divine atoms scattered in infinite space; and was often replaced by the personal pronoun in the third person singular, "He." The second designation explains itself by the Hebrew verb *haia*, or by the corresponding Aramaic form *hawa:* "I am that I am." "I am" became a substantive and a proper name. Which of these two designations is the most ancient? There has been much discussion on this point. At one time it was thought to be Jehovah, at another time Elohim. It has even been said that the latter was usual among the priests and in the northern tribes, while the name of Jehovah had been introduced later on by the tribes of the south and vulgarised by the prophets. But the Hebrews, no doubt, before there existed either prophets or priests, were already offering prayers to Elohim and Jehovah. And besides, how can the above hypothesis be reconciled with the fact that the name of Jehovah is so intimately connected in tradition with the constitution of the priesthood and the tribe of Levi? In addition, the name of Jehovah is Aramaic in form and seems to have been that of a God worshipped in Padan-Aram (Schrader, p. 23, &c.), the last station of the Israelites before their descent into Palestine. It might, therefore, have come from the north. It is evident that there is no certainty upon these points.

When the terachite tribes who were to form by their union the nucleus of the Israelite nation federated themselves for the defence of their common interests, it may be that they belonged, for the greater part, to two distinct branches. The families of each of these two groups expressed their impressions of divinity by a traditional and different name for the Creator. The ones worshipped Jehovah, the others Elohim. But on their alliance they must have determined the identity and unity of their heavenly master, and Elohim and Jehovah thus became synonymous. A work of adaptation must have taken place then similar to that necessitated by the fusion of the beliefs of the Iranians of the south and of the north, when to the Persian pantheon of the forces of nature was added the Median pantheon of moral qualities worshipped as divinities and it was endeavoured to identify Ahura-mazda, the "living Creator of all," with Çpentô-mainyus, the "White" or "Holy Spirit." Primitive minds are content with these paradoxes. Even at the present day the average peasant, a firm monotheist when he prays to God, becomes a polytheist if he thinks of his favourite saints. But the essential point, that which appears to admit of no dispute, is that the God of Israel, Elohim or Jehovah, was for his worshippers the one and only God, without beginning and without end, without ancestors and without posterity.

C.—Israelite Artists.

It is probable that neither the Judæan nor the Danite worked with their own hands at the objects for which they are honoured by tradition; they would have had to excel in too many different arts to be able "to devise cunning works, to work in gold, and in silver, and in brass, and in cutting of stones for setting, and in carving of wood, to work in all manner of workmanship . . . to make all the furniture of the tent . . . and the finely wrought garments . . ." (Exod. xxxi. 3, 4, 5, &c.; xxxv. 32, 33; xxxix.). They were doubtless entrusted with the superintendence of Egyptian artists and workmen, whose skill and experience were very different from those of the Hebrews, but whose name and nationality had to disappear so that it should not be thought that the sacred objects were touched by impure hands. Later on a similar fiction was adopted, representing the author of the two pillars of brass and of all the metal work that adorned the temple of Solomon as the son of a woman of Israel, though he was in fact a Phœnician (1 Kings vii. 13, &c.).

D.—The Historical Value of the Eighth, Tenth, Twelfth, and Thirteenth Chapters of the First Book of Samuel.

The books of Samuel have been reconstituted by means of divers texts and have undergone various revisions or mutilations before receiving the canonical form. But even if it were possible to analyse them, it would still be imprudent to condemn one source in favour of another. I have explained myself on this head in the Preface. Thus, in my opinion, no serious argument is advanced against the historical value of the verses relating to the action of Samuel in the establishment of royalty (whether in chap. viii., chap. x. from verse 17, chap. xii., or chap. xiii., verse 1 and verses 9 to 15). Samuel, it is objected, could not possibly have known the disadvantages of royalty, since the Israelites had not yet made the experiment of that form of government. But had he not the example of the neighbouring monarchies? Had not Abimelech, son of Gideon, reigned to all intents and purposes over the tribes to which Samuel belonged? (Judg. ix.). Jotham, in his apologue of the trees, had expressed similar ideas long before the prophet.

In reality, the authenticity of the facts related in the eighth and fifteenth chapters is denied, because it is not wished to admit that Samuel took any part at all in the transformation of the patriarchal system and had, in consequence, motives for raising up David against Saul. It is thus possible to suppress or to dispute chapter xvi., which is devoted to the consecration of David, and which contains an enumeration of the moral qualities which are denied to him by his critics.

I have not heeded reasons of this nature, which have but the value of *tendenz* arguments, while the tale told by the Bible is more human and less factitious than the account offered as a substitute. I have explained myself on this point. See above, pp. 45, 46 and 47.

E.—Historical Value of the Fifteenth Chapter of the First Book of Samuel.

It has been alleged that chapter xv., which relates the campaign against the Amalekites, was composed in order to abase royalty before the prophets. The argument is a feeble one. If the historical value of this chapter be contested, it is only in order to deny that Samuel had any motives for discontent, any plausible reasons for dethroning Saul and setting David in his place. In reality, the anger of Saul against Samuel as well as the first symptoms of the evil to whose attacks the king is at that moment subjected, are observed and described to perfection. Moreover, the war against Amalek was a political necessity (see above, p. 59, n. 1 and 2, and pp. 87 and 88); numerous allusions are made to it in a chapter considered quite authentic (xiv. 48; see also xxviii. 18). It is the same with chapter xv. as with chapters viii., x. and xii., which, although containing no traces of a doubtful origin, have also found no favour simply because they explain and prepare for chapter xvi., in which David is anointed by Samuel; and because it is wished at any cost to deny this consecration, its cause and its effects. To deny in such a case is a resource. It would appear that proof is only needed to support an affirmation.

F.—HISTORICAL VALUE OF CHAPTER XVI. OF THE FIRST BOOK OF SAMUEL.

I have already said that chapter xvi. finds no favour in the eyes of certain exegetes, and is suspected in its turn of being derived from a doubtful source. It is accused, above all, of being in contradiction with the character of Samuel, such as it has been imagined towards the end of the nineteenth century, and not such as it was in reality. (See above, p. 43.) I will not stay to show that while the historical value of this chapter is disputed, numerous extracts are unhesitatingly taken from it (Renan, "Hist. du Peup., &c." v. i., p. 413, n. 2 and 3). It forms in reality a whole, if not homogeneous, at least very compact, with the chapters accepted by critics (chapter ix., from verse 28, chapters xi., xiv., chapter xvii., verses 1 to 10; chapters xviii., xix., &c.). It supplies, like them, information of absolute truth with regard to the prophets and the attacks of Saul (see above, p. 100); it is the connecting link between the lives of Saul and David, and their necessary and logical preface. (See notes D, E, G, and above, p. 61, n. 3; p. 66, n. 1; p. 71, &c.) Finally,

I have shown in the first part of this study, the efforts of centuries which could not but end in the constitution of the monarchy in the favour of a son of Judah. So that chapter xvi., however closely it may be examined, does not possess the prophetical character attributed to it and in virtue of which it has been condemned. These explanations and the remainder of the story will, I hope, be found convincing by minds unwarped by prejudice.

G.—HISTORICAL VALUE OF THE SEVENTEENTH CHAPTER OF THE FIRST BOOK OF SAMUEL.

Objection has been made to the verses in chapter xvii. relating to the duel between David and Goliath—firstly, on account of the improbability of such a contest, then because of the four references found in other chapters to combats nearly identical (2 Sam. xxi. 15–22 ; xxiii. 21) and the attribution of the victory over Goliath to a Benjamite, named Elhanan, son of Jaare-oregim (2 Sam. xxi. 19). Contradictions are also discovered in the text. Thus, though David has been the king's harpist, Saul speaks as if he did not know him and only sees him for the first time. (1 Sam. xvii. 55–58.) It is strange, say the critics, that David, after having served as armour-bearer to the king, and being moreover described as a Gibbor in chapter xvi., should be ignorant of the use of arms and should content himself with a sling (1 Sam. xvii. 38, 39). Finally, Jerusalem is spoken of, although the town is not yet in the hands of the Hebrews.

I have answered the first objections (see above, pp. 58 to 68, p. 109). As for the name of Jerusalem, it has either been used by a careless copyist or is an anachronism of no great importance, unless the low town to which allusion is made denoted an encampment below Jerusalem, perhaps established on the celebrated plateau of Rephaim where the Philistines will return later on with such determination. I will add that, agreeing with Reuss ("La Bible Hist.," i., p. 289, n. 4), I consider that the tent mentioned in verse 54 and to which David brings the armour of Goliath, is the tabernacle where he finds them later in his hour of need.

H.—THE FAITH OF DAVID.

The history of David has been until now presented in a false aspect because the Bible has inscribed this great prince among the ancestors of Christ. It was not only necessary to disparage Jesus by depicting his ancestor as the descendant of a courtesan, as an assassin, a bandit (see above, p. 266), it had also to be shown that the man from whom Jesus was descended was an unbeliever, or that he had no preference for either Jehovah or Baal. To arrive at this conclusion appeal has been made to the circumstance that the same son of David is called "Eliada" in the books of Samuel (2 Sam. v. 16) and "Beeliada" in the Chronicles (1 Chron. xiv. 7). And from this it is concluded that as El is replaced by Beel or Baal, it mattered little to David to which of these two gods he addressed himself. Keeping strictly to facts, I have shown on the contrary how great was David's faith and how sincere his love for Jehovah. (See above, pp. 81, 82, 176 to 178.) There would, therefore, be no need to touch again upon the subject, were it not interesting to note the frailty of the accusation brought against David.

The Israelites, inclined towards idolatry and living in the midst of idolaters, often adopted names compounded with those of strange gods. Sometimes, when they returned to the religion of Jehovah, they changed the name. It is thus that Jerubbaal (he who fears Baal) caused himself to be called Gideon. Some men, to proclaim their faith, substituted for the name of the strange god a form of the names of the God of Israel. Beeliada, son of David, becomes Eliada. On the other hand, other Israelites, though conforming to the national religion, attached no more importance to their name than did the early Christians when they retained the names which had become traditional in their family. In the lists of saints we find Babylas (Gate of Bel), Barnabas (son of a prophet), Bartholomew (son of Tholmai), Delphina (priestess of Delphi), Denis (priest of Bacchus), Mark, Marcellus, formed from the name of Mars, Olympias (the Olympian), Sulpicius, Tatiana (of the *gens* Sulpicia, of the Tatius family), Waltruda (presiding spirit of the forest), Radegund (goddess of combat), &c. Is it believed that because of these names derived from those of Roman,

Greek, German, Chaldæan or Hebrew gods, their owners, most of whom suffered martyrdom, were pagans, or at least very eclectic in matters of religion? Yet that is the conclusion that might just as logically be arrived at, if it be inferred from the name given to a child of David by the Chronicles (whose authenticity is generally considered doubtful by those who quote it in this case) that the father worshipped Moloch Baal, and Jehovah without distinction.

I.—ON WRITING.

It is generally agreed nowadays that the Hebrews were acquainted with the art of writing long before the time formerly assigned to its use. Moses, who was really an Egyptian by education and by name, was able to note down his thoughts, and long before the days of David, the genealogical lists and the numberings of the tribes were graven upon stone. If hieroglyphics were known to a chosen few they were afterwards abandoned, for they lent themselves with difficulty to the transcription of Hebrew words. The Cadmean alphabet in use among the Sidonians and the Canaanites, analogous to that of the celebrated inscription of Mesa, was doubtless preferred to them. The objections once considered irrefutable and so long advanced against the authenticity of the traditions speaking of lapidary inscriptions, thus fall to the ground. (See Exod. xxxiv. 28, 29, and xl. 18; xxvii. 14; xxxix. 6, 14; 1 Sam. x. 25.)

It must, however, be acknowledged that writing thus understood was of very limited usage. And accordingly, the very ancient inscriptions which have been mentioned are described by the Bible as very short. The tables of the law are called the "ten words of the covenant" (Exod. xxxiv. 28, 29; xl. 18). The breastplate bore only the name of Israel and those of the ten tribes, designated perhaps by hieroglyphics (Exod. xxxix. 6 and 14), which remained in use for some time, as is shown by the animals representing the tribes which figured on their respective standards (Numb. ii. 2). Finally, the laws for royalty, "laid before the Lord" by Samuel (1 Sam. x. 25), must have been summed up in a few very concise precepts, given the small dimensions of the sacred code. The result was that the Hebrews for a long time preserved the habit of cultivating their memory and of confiding to it the rhythmic chants which it was able to retain with fidelity. This is why we see that even in the reign of David, at a period when writing was made use of for the transmission of political or military documents (2 Sam. xi. 14), children would learn by heart a number of poems, which they recited or sung on solemn occasions.

Memory and short inscriptions suffice to assure a regular transmission of the historical and legendary annals of a people. There is thus reason to believe that from the moment that writing became common (perhaps in the eleventh century), exact and trustworthy information concerning the Exodus, the Judges, Samuel, and particularly the lives and reigns of David and Solomon, was noted down, and precious documents relating to the most ancient periods were recorded.

J.—On the Song of the Bow.

The Song of the Bow (2 Sam. i. 18, &c.) and fragments of the elegy pronounced over Abner's tomb (2 Sam. iii. 33, &c.) are wonderful pieces, surpassing even the Song of Deborah. I know well that some deny to David the poetical gifts ascribed to him by the Bible (1 Sam. xvi. 18, 23 ; xviii. 20 ; Amos vi. 5), but in general his authorship of these works is not disputed. They formed part of the Jasher written either in the reign of David or at least in that of his successor, and on the other hand, the tradition based on contemporary documents is so unanimous that it would be certainly very daring to attempt to reform it at a distance of thirty centuries without a single proof and against all probability.

Furthermore, by a contradiction worthy of note, if the virtues and moral qualities of David are disputed, no exception is taken to the physical gifts attributed to him by the most contested chapters.

K.—The Ephod of Divination.

The prophetic ephod was the instrument given by their religion to the priests for the consultation of Jehovah. (Judg. viii. 27 ; xvii. 5 ; xviii. 14, 17, 18, 20, 33 ; 1 Sam. x. 22, 23 ;

xiv. 18, 20, 36–41 ; xxi. 10 ; xxiii. 6, 9 ; xxx. 7 ; Hosea iii. 4 ; Isaiah xxx. 22.) The first mention of this ephod occurs in the story of Gideon (Judg. viii. 27), but as the text speaks as if there were nothing unusual in its adoption for such purposes, and as the ephod in practices of divination was inseparable from the *urim*, whose use dates according to the Bible from a period much earlier than that of Gideon (Exod. xxviii. 29 ; Numb. xxvii. 21 ; Judg. i. 1), it is probable that the ephod became the organ of the ark at a very early day. This opinion is also supported by the very close analogies between the pectoral of the Chief Judge in Egypt and the *essen* or oracle of the priests of Jehovah (Josephus, " Ant. Jud.," iii., viii. 9), which formed an integral part of the ephod, as will be shown below. It can be felt that there is a liturgical relationship between the ark itself, borrowed from the religious furniture of Egypt (see above, p. 181), and the ephod, and that they had a common origin.

As the mouthpiece of the ark, the ephod was unique, and was only handled by the priests who had access to the tabernacle, when they came before the Lord (Numb. xxvii. 21 ; Deut. xxxiii. 8 ; see above, pp. 183 and 184). It was a necessary consequence of the sacred mystery surrounding the ark. But the unity of the ephod had also the object of centralising the faith, of drawing the faithful round the ark, of maintaining the purity of doctrine, of combating idolatry and of drawing closer the religious ties which the custom of sacrificing on any high place, under any green tree (1 Kings iii. 4 ; xiv. 23), tended to loosen. As soon as the faith was organised there was but one legal ephod to express the will of the one God of Israel, just as there had always been but one ark. While the ark is at Shiloh, a town of Ephraim, it is at Shiloh that the ephod speaks. Hence Gideon, who judges Manasseh (Judg. vi. 11), while Manasseh has strained relations with Ephraim, only enters into communication with God through the medium of the prophets (Judg. vi. 8), of celestial messengers (Judg. vi. 11, &c.), or of dreams, unable as he is to go to Shiloh. Finally, weary of this precarious situation, he installs an ephod at Ophrah near the altar which he had erected there (Judg. vi. 24–26), as much for the sake of having within his reach an instrument of divination as in order to compete with the oracle of Ephraim. In any case, this act of his was considered so blameworthy that it was supposed to have prevented the descendants of Gideon from the exercise of the hereditary power which seemed destined for them (Judg. viii. 27). The Danite ephod (Judg. xvii. and xviii.) and many others no doubt had a similar origin. But their oracles, like those given forth by the ephod of Gideon, were judged impious and sacrilegious on the same grounds as those of idols (Judg. viii. 27 ; xviii. 31) and the predictions of false prophets and magicians, and had, besides, but an ephemeral fame. On the other hand, it will be noticed that the altars, the vases of gold and silver made for sacrificial purposes by Gideon or by Micah, were not considered to violate the law because they served to celebrate a rite that every Israelite might perform.

One more proof may yet be given, and that a decisive one, that there was but one ephod recognised by the law. After the Battle of Aphek, when the ark was taken by the Philistines, the ephod had remained the only link between Jehovah and the priests. It was perhaps the period of its greatest authority. Saul, eager for its counsel, never failed to have its company on his expeditions (1 Sam. xiv. 3, 18, 19, 36). But after the massacre of the high priest at Nob and of his acolytes, Abiathar, the only one who escaped from death, seized the ephod and took refuge with David (1 Sam. xxii. 18, 19, 20 ; xxiii. 6). From that day, the son of Jesse had the benefit of the consultations of heaven (1 Sam. xxiii. 2, 4, 6, 9 ; cp. 1 Kings xxviii. 6), while Saul was reduced to evoking the shade of Samuel (1 Kings xxviii. 11, 12, &c.). If I have cited this last example, in spite of its resemblance to the preceding ones, it is because it confirms the passages relating to the embarrassments of Gideon before he consecrated his ephod, and because it belongs to a portion of the Bible whose authenticity cannot be denied.

What was the aspect of the ephod—of what elements was it composed—how did it give forth its oracles?

The ephod was an object of no great bulk, easily handled and transported (1 Sam. xiv. 3, 18, 19, 36; xxiii. 2, 4, 6, 9 ; xxx. 7 ; 2 Sam. v. 19, 23, 24, 25, &c.; cp. with following note). As a rule it was placed in the tabernacle, near the ark (1 Sam. xxi. 10), but for certain rites, the Bible says that the cohen "wore on his heart" or "put on" the ephod (Exod. xxviii. 29 ; Judg. xvii. 5 ; 1 Sam. xxx. 7). This custom afterwards became general, no doubt during the period which elapsed between the capture of the ark and its installation at Jerusalem.

The *ephod bad* (see note M) or special ephod worn by the priests admitted into the tabernacle and authorised to ask questions of the Lord, contained an opening in the place just over the heart, which was closed by the oracle. This sacred badge, copied without doubt from the pectoral of the Chief Judges of Egypt, was composed of twelve precious stones of different colours, placed in rows and fastened on a piece of stuff by means of threads or hooks of gold (Exod. xxviii. 15-30, 40, 41 ; xxix. 5, 8, 9). The biblical texts and certain authors even specify that the *urim* and *thummim* were contained in the oracle. (Exod. xxviii. 30 ; Lev. viii. 6-9 ; Deut. xxiii. 8 ; Eccl. xlv. 12-13, Latin text; Diodorus of Sicily, i. 48, 75 ; Élien, "Var. hist.," xiv. 34 ; Philon, "Vita Mosis," iii. 11 ; " De monar.," ii. 5). The rabbis add that the urim pronounced their decrees according to their place on the twelve precious stones. These details are very valuable, for if they are compared with the characteristic name of oracle given to the "breastplate" which the cohen or chief of the priests placed upon the *ephod bad*, as well as with the small weight and volume of the ephod, and the very name of *ephod bad* given to the garment of the priests, and then the synonymous expressions used by the editors of the Bible, such as to put on the ephod, to put the ephod on the heart (Exod. xxviii. 29), to put the *essen* or oracle on his heart (Lev. viii. 6-9), there is ample authority for the identification of the ephod with the "breastplate" and the *urim* and *thummim* combined. The instrument of divination must thus have consisted, as is explained by the Bible, of a pectoral formed of twelve precious stones of different colours arranged in checquers on a cloth and forming the *essen* or oracle properly so-called, which contained in a pocket or special compartment two objects something like dice, the *urim* and *thummim*.

When the priest asked a question of Jehovah, he would throw the urim, casting lots (1 Sam. xiv. 41, 42), and their relative position upon the checquers would dictate the answer of God.

Despite the texts of such clearness which I have just cited, despite the analogies with the pectoral of the Chief Judges of Egypt, despite an unvarying tradition, it has been alleged that the ephods of Gideon and Micah, and by analogy, the lawful ephod, must have been heavy and cumbersome objects, and arguments have been found in their weight for their identification with statues or at all events with a bas-relief representing the Egyptian sun encircled by two uræus. The heads of the uræus would have been jointed and moved by strings which the priest held in his hand; and according to his making the head incline towards the right or the left, the ephod would give *urim* or *thummim*. First of all, the argument would not be conclusive, for it would be a question of idolatrous ephods which their owners would desire to be all the richer on account of their being destined to supplant the one at Shiloh. But then there is a still better reason against this theory; there is not one word, not one allusion in the Book of Judges to authorise the thought that the sacrilegious ephods differed in volume or weight from the ephod of the law. As to the figured representation adorning it, it is conjectural, and is contradicted by the Bible, by the authors, by the tradition of the synagogue. It has no doubt been imagined in order to speak of the strings which worked the heads of the uræus, and to render the ephod ridiculous by comparing it to a sort of puppet.

The triumph of the prophetical body caused the abandonment of the ephod. Four centuries before our era it was already forgotten. It was the ephod which had dethroned direct divination; it was the prophets who ruined in their turn the supremacy of the ephod. Its history summarises the struggle of influences and the antagonism between the two religious powers which dominated Israel, the priests and the prophets, between the organised sacerdotalism reserved for one caste, and an open and independent corporation doubtless more directly connected than the clergy with the ancient faith of the patriarchs.

L.—The Organisation of the Clergy.

During the patriarchal period, when altars made of earth or of unhewn stones rudely put together sufficed for the ceremonies of a very simple faith, sacerdotal functions were exercised by the eldest of each family. Every head of a family was a *cohen* (Exod. xiii. 2, xx. 24, 26; Numb. iii. 12, 40, 41, 45, viii. 16, 17;

Judg. ii 5, xxi. 2, &c.). This condition of things was prolonged until the day when the Hebrews adopted the ark as the symbol of their religion. Egyptian influence is so clearly manifested and so direct in descriptions or traditions concerning the ark, the sacrificial altars, and the tables of unleavened bread, the costume of the priests, the oracle of the ephod (see above, pp. 181, 281, and below, p. 292), the formation of a sacerdotal caste, perhaps even the name of Moses; and, on the other hand, there are so many and close moral bonds existing between the ark, the ephod, and the constitution of a privileged clergy, that the transformation of the pastoral cult into a religion of which the ark of the covenant was to become the pivot, must have been effected at a period when Egyptian influence was still preponderant.

The heads of families continued to celebrate isolated sacrifices; the right to do so was even allowed to every Israelite, but there was constituted for the service and transport of the ark a species of corporation which became the kernel of a professional clergy.

When Moses obtained the dictatorship, thanks to the support that seems to have been afforded to him by the tribe of Levi (Exod. xxxii. 26-29), of which he was doubtless a member, he wished to reward his fellow-tribesmen, and instituted them guardians or accredited bearers of the ark and privileged members of the new priesthood. It was a means of putting an end to the opprobrium with which they were covered (see note A), and of securing for them, if not a regular revenue, at least a certain source of profit (Exod. xiii. 2; Numb. iii. 22, 33, 40, 41, 45, viii. 16, 17, 18). At the same time he introduced the summary hierarchy of the tribes into the Levitical priesthood (Exod. xx., xxix. 9, 44). If it be certain that neither Moses nor his successors realised for several centuries afterwards the organisation indicated in Leviticus, Numbers, Deuteronomy, and the Chronicles (Lev. viii.; Numb. viii. 6-26; Deut. xviii. 5, 6, 7; 1 Chron. xxiii., xxiv.), neither can it be doubted that the clergy of the ark comprised several hierarchical degrees, and either claimed or had granted to them certain privileges. There is no need for texts for the assurance of this fact.

The first chief of the clergy or first *cohen* named by the Bible was Aaron (Lev. viii., ix.). He was said to be the eldest brother of Moses, and *nassi* or chief of the race of Kohath, issue of the second son of Levi (Numb. iii. 5, 6, 7). Whether Aaron is a legendary personage or not, Moses, who did not possess the gift of oratory, certainly had among his near relatives a skilful, bold, and eloquent lieutenant, who was of great service to him. It would even seem as if the privileged office, obtained by this lieutenant as a reward for his aid, and which according to very ancient custom should have been held by the elder branch (see above, p. 27, n. 2) was granted to him by special favour, to the detriment of the chief of the race of Gershom, who was the head of the tribe of Levi (Exod. i. 2-10, vi. 16, 18, 20, vii. 12, viii., xxix., xl. 12, 13; Numb. iii. 10, 17, 27-32; Deut. xviii. 5; 1 Chron. vi. 1, 2, 3, 49, xxiii. 6-13; Eccl. xlv.). Evidence exists that this measure was an ancient one, that it was unpopular and had to be imposed by force. We know the number of risings that Moses suppressed, and the decrees of death he pronounced in order to assure to his near relatives in particular, and his fellow-tribesmen in general, the possession of their new prerogatives, and to prevent encroachment on their sacerdotal functions (see p. 290). The priests, even for the purpose of intimidation, would never have invented such occurrences, some of which are greatly to their discredit; they would rather have been inclined to attenuate them. It had needed the authority and energy of Moses to make the other tribes agree to the favour shown to the tribe of Levi, and to impose Aaron upon them to the exclusion of the heads of nobler or older races of the tribe of Levi (Numb. iii. 10, xvi. 1, &c., xviii. 7). These violent proceedings became the origin of or pretext for new scenes of violence, and thenceforward, and for a long time afterwards, the cohenate had to be gained by hard fighting. It is thus that by an unjust substitution, preceded or followed by the execution of his elder brothers, the Bible shows us Eleazar, Aaron's third son, succeeding his father (Exod. vi. 23; Lev. x. 1, 2, 6, 12; Numb. iii. 2-12, 32, iv. 16, xviii. 2, xx. 26, 28, 29, xxv. 7-13, xxvi. 1-3, xxvii. 19, 21, 22; Josh. xiv. 1, xxi. 1, xxii. 13, 31, xxiv. 33; 1 Chron. vi. 4, xxiv. 1, 2) in conjunction with Ithamar, his younger brother, who has taken part against the elder ones (Lev. x. 12; Numb. iv. 4, 5, 19, vii. 8, viii. 13, 19, xviii. 1, 2, 7; 1 Chron. vi. 49). For some generations the cohenate seems to have remained in the house of Eleazar (1 Chron. vi. 3–5, 50 ; Josephus, "Ant. Jud." viii. § 1, 3), but starting with Eli, the presumed descendant of Ithamar, and after fresh intrigues and fresh troubles, the sacerdotal authority appears to have been exercised by the chiefs of the younger branch, that of Ithamar. Josephus ("Ant. Jud." v. § xii. 2, and viii. § i. 3), and even more so the comparison of the different verses in the First Book of Samuel and in the Chronicles seem conclusive on this point (1 Sam. ii. 12–17, 22–24, iii. 11–14, iv. 11, 20, and 21, xiv. 3, xxii. 20, xxiii. 6 ; 1 Chron. xxiv. 3). Nothing is known with regard to the situation of the chiefs of the race of Eleazar during this period. It may be that they had already constituted at Gibeon a clergy whose cohenim they had made themselves ; but in any case, not possessing the support of the ark, they had no position recognised by the Law.

Then came the disaster of Aphek. The ark was taken by the Philistines, the sons of Eli were killed in its defence. Eli himself was struck with apoplexy on hearing of the disaster. It was a terrible blow to the fame of Shiloh, where the ark had had a more or less permanent abode ever since the days of Joshua. Accordingly, Ahimelech, son of Ahitub, one of the victims of the Battle of Aphek, and great-grandson of Eli, and afterwards his successor as cohen, determined to emigrate. He installed himself first at Beth-el, but only remained there a short time, finally settling in the town of Nob, a little to the north of Jerusalem, where he brought the tabernacle, the tables of shewbread, the altars of Bezaleel, and a treasure of consecrated objects, among which was the sword of Goliath (see note G and above, pp. 186, 187, 188), and the lawful ephod (see note K, and 1 Sam. xxi. 4, 6, 8, 9, xxii. 9, 10, 13, xxiii. 6). Nob then became the religious capital of Israel, where a large number of the clergy dwelt around their chief (1 Sam. xxii. 11, 18, 19). But after the murder of the cohen and of the priests ordained by Saul, Abiathar, the only one of the sons of Ahimelech who had escaped massacre, took the ephod with him and fled to David. Nob was in its turn deserted (1 Sam. xxii. 20, 21, xxiii. 6).

After the double misfortune which had fallen upon the ancient clergy of the ark, namely, the disaster of Aphek and the massacre of Nob, and following on the war waged by Saul against David and the southern tribes, disorder reigned in the sacerdotal caste. It is probable that after the disaster of Aphek the priests of Gibeon who claimed descent from Eleazar, and who protested on that ground against the elevation of Eli to the direction of the sanctuary of Shiloh, had gathered the discontented round them and had already constituted a distinct and powerful clergy. These same priests took advantage of the flight of Abiathar and the abandonment of Nob to obtain possession of the sacred objects, such as the tabernacle, the tables for the shewbread, the altars of Bezaleel (1 Chron. xvi. 39, xxi. 29, 2 Chron. i. 3, 5, 6). From that time there was a schism among the priests. While Abiathar, the Ithamarist cohen and the direct heir of Eli, followed David's army, and in his capacity of guardian of the ephod was the only one able to interpret the lawful oracles, the priests of Gibeon, also in possession of consecrated articles, saw their credit increase daily. They attracted the pious Israelites who were not able to follow the cohen attached to David's person in his perpetual wanderings, and they were about to make Gibeon the religious metropolis of the north when the triumph of David, reflecting on the Ithamarist clergy, of whom Abiathar was the chief, ruined their hopes. At that moment they had for cohen Zadok, head of the race of Eleazar (1 Chron. vi. 3-5, 50). They felt that the conqueror would crush them if they did not make submission; and, led by Zadok and the head of the tribe of Levi (1 Chron. xii. 27, 28; Jos., "Ant. Jud.," vii. § 11. 1), they sought his presence, stipulating no doubt for the recognition of their cohen, the maintenance of the sanctuary of Gibeon, and the right of retaining the sacred articles that they had gathered there, as the price of their allegiance.

This situation, which David was obliged to tolerate, was, however, not a very lasting one. It came to an end as soon as the transport of the ark to Jerusalem enabled the monarch to subordinate Gibeon to Jerusalem and Zadok to Abiathar (2 Sam. xv. 24, 29, 35, xx. 25; 1 Kings ii. 26, 27, 35; 1 Chron. xvi. 39), without directly attacking either the credit of Gibeon or the title of Zadok. Abiathar, the Ithamarist cohen, installed alone at Jerusalem, retained the high priesthood of the ark until the end of David's reign, and the conspiracy of Adonijah in which he was led to participate by his hatred of Zadok (1 Kings i. 7, 19, 25, 42). The chief authority then returned to Zadok (1 Kings

ii. 26, 27, 35 ; 1 Chron. vi. 3-5, 50, xxiv. 3), who remained henceforth the superior of Abiathar (1 Kings iv. 4 ; 1 Chron. vi. 8-15), and who became the ancestor of the family of Sadducees from which the high priests issued (1 Chron. vi. 8-15).

In substance the following is in all probability the organisation prepared for by Moses, elaborated when the ark was permanently established at Shiloh, but perfected when it was installed by David in Jerusalem.

At the head was the chief of the priesthood of the ark, quite distinct from the chief of the tribe of Levi. He inherited the title of cohen formerly given to the heads of families. In times of disturbance and during periods of fighting there were probably several cohens, just as there have been two and three popes existing at the same time, and it would seem as if at least two families shared the right to supply them ; but when order was restored, and by the very essence and definition of the office, there could only be one cohen because there was but one ark.

The cohen alone had the right to wear and interrogate the lawful ephod, though his sons shared in a large number of his prerogatives, and particularly in the privilege of entering the tabernacle, of accompanying the ark, and of taking hold of the ephod in case of need (Exod. xxviii. 29, xxxix. 1-30 ; Lev. xvi. 4 ; Numb. xxvii. 21 ; 1 Sam. ii. 12-17 (see Hebrew text) ; iv. 4, 11. See note K). Setting aside the texts out of Exodus and Leviticus quoted above, we find more proofs in the maledictions pronounced against Gideon and the priest of Micah (p. 282), and above all in the example of Saul and David, who have recourse to the cohen when they wish to consult the Lord by means of the Urim and Thummim (1 Sam. x. 21, xiv. 3, 18, 19, 36, &c., xxiii. 2, 4, 6, 9, xxx. 7 ; 2 Sam. v. 19, 23, 24, 25). If it be mentioned there is no room for hesitation even in the case of Joshua. When the son of Nun begs for an answer from God, it is understood that he receives it by the intermediary of the cohen Eleazer, represented by the Bible as the son and heir of Aaron (Numb. xxvii. 21 ; Josh. xxi. 1). This privilege of the cohen, as I have already said in speaking of the ephod and the ark (pp. 182, 183, and note K), was the necessary corollary of the unity of the ark, of belief and of the faith.

After the cohen and his sons came the auxiliary priests, who wore the *ephod bad* of ordinary priests (see note M) as a sign of their functions, and who occupied their positions in their supposed capacity of chiefs or sons of chiefs of the Levitical families (Exod. xxviii., xxix. ; Lev. viii. 6, 13, ix. 1, 9, 12, 18 ; 1 Sam. ii. 12-17, iv. 4, 11). The exceptions that have been brought forward all tend to confirm the rule rather than to destroy it. Thus during the period when the ark was abandoned and its cult neglected even to forgetfulness, its guard and its escort were undertaken by Israelites who did not belong to the tribe of Levi, and David was able to enter the tabernacle ; but as soon as the ark returned to Jerusalem, and quite as much in order to fight against the progress of the prophets as to follow the inspiration of David, the ancient traditions were resumed, and their severity and rigour were even exaggerated.

In an inferior position to that of the priests came lastly the servants of the ark and of the tabernacle, recruited at least in theory among the descendants of Levi. However exalted or however humble the prerogatives of the Levites admitted into either of these two categories happened to be, they were soon left without rivals in their claims to them. The prescriptions of the Exodus (xxviii. 29, xxx. 1–30), of Leviticus (viii. 4, ix. 5) and of the Book of Numbers (iii., iv.), whatever may be their date, are confirmed by traditions too numerous not to rest upon a foundation of truth, and are too much in harmony with the egoism of those installed in office not to be allowed some credence. I will quote the terrible laws decreed against those who sought to encroach on the rights of the Levites (Numb. iii. 10, 38, iv. 18–20, xvi., xviii. 7, 21, 22, 23), the sanguinary executions which sanctioned them (Numb. xvi.), the military expedition sent by Joshua against the Gileadites who had raised an altar and had dared to create an unlawful priesthood around it (Josh. xxii. 9, &c. ; Hosea xii. 11), and the instantaneous deaths which were said to have twice signalised the transport of or even the mere approach to the ark by non-Levites (1 Sam. vi. 19 ; 2 Sam. vi. 6, 7 ; cp. 10, 11, 17).

M.—THE EPHOD BAD.

The *ephod bad* or linen ephod was a species of short stole worn by the cohenim and their acolytes (see note L). The model had been brought no doubt from Egypt. It is known that the Egyptian priests clothed themselves in garments of linen. The *ephod bad* seems to have been distinctive of the sacerdotal functions. Thus David dons an ephod when he dances before the ark and performs the rites of the faith (Exod. xxviii. 4; 1 Sam. ii. 18, xxii. 18; 2 Sam. vi. 14; 1 Chron. xv. 27; Hosea iii. 4; Josephus, "Ant. Jud.," iii. § viii.). The ephod of the cohen was a little different from that of his acolytes. It was open on the chest, and this opening was closed by an oracle or "breastplate" strongly reminiscent of the pectoral of the Chief Judges in Egypt (see note K on the *ephod of divination*, which must not be confounded with the *ephod bad*).

N.—ON THE ALTAR.

High places were generally chosen for the celebration of sacrifices. The altar, erected just before the offering of the holocaust, rested on the ground without steps and without foundations, and was formed of unhewn stones (Gen. xii. 7, 8, xxii. 2, 9; Exod. xx. 24–26; Deut. xxvii. 2–6; Josh. viii. 31; Judg. xxi. 2, &c.; 1 Sam. x. 8, xiii. 9, 10, xiv. 35, 36, xv. 11, 12; 1 Kings i. 9, iii. 4, xviii. 19, 31, 32; 1 Chron. xvi. 39; 2 Chron. i. 3). In accordance with the spirit of the religion it had thus a provisional character. Nevertheless there were some altars that were built in a permanent manner in order to consecrate certain celebrated sites. Among this number were those of Shechem (Gen. xii. 6, 7), of Beth-el (Gen. xii. 8), of Mount Ebal (Deut. xxvii. 2–5; Josh. viii. 31), of Ophra (Judg. vi. 24), of Hebron (2 Sam. xv. 8, 12), of Araunah's threshing floor (2 Sam. xxiv. 21), of Gibeon (1 Kings iii. 4; 1 Chron. xvi. 39; 2 Chron. i. 3), of Samaria or of Mount Carmel (1 Kings xviii. 2, 19, 31, 32).

The ancient religion of the Aryans, still practised by the Persians in the days of the Achemenidæ, also enjoined that sacrifices should be offered up in the open air and preferably on high places, on altars built just before the ceremony with raw material gathered on the ground (Dieulafoy, "Acropole de Suse," p. 401-403). I will add that the Persians, like the Israelites, raised up permanent altars on sites accounted holy. There are some still existing in Persia which date from the middle of the sixth century B.C. (Dieulafoy, "Art. Ant." v. iii. p. 8).

The cult of the ark soon necessitated, in addition to a table for the offerings, two portable altars, one for the sacrifices celebrated before the tabernacle, the other for the incense burned inside the sanctuary (Exod. xxvii. 1, 2, 6-8, xxx. 1-6, xl. 5, 6, 24, 26, 27 ; Lev. iv. 7, xvi. 17, 18, 24, 25). Both were made of wood overlaid with metal. Such was the origin of the table of shewbread and of the two altars erected in the temple at Jerusalem (2 Chron. iv.).

The Mazdæan rites passed through the same phases and arrived at the same result. For the same reasons which had led the Hebrews to place the altars opposite to or inside the tabernacle, altars were first of all placed before the closed sanctuary, which was inaccessible to the faithful and in which burned the divine fire or the secondary fires produced by it. Since the reign of the Parthians, and especially during the reign of the Sassanidæ, these two altars and a table for offerings were arranged in a special enclosure forming part of the fire temple, and became the centre of the public cult (Dieulafoy, "Acropole de Suse," p. 403).

In remembrance of the time when sacerdotal functions were exercised by the heads of families, every Israelite could offer up a holocaust to God (Numb. xv. 13, and note L). Mazdeism was not so liberal. It was forbidden to perform any religious ceremony without the presence of a magian (Herod. i. 138).

The striking resemblances which I have pointed out with regard to the origin and transformation of their altars do not, however, denote any analogy between the conception of the God of the Hebrews and that of the gods of the Aryans, especially between Jehovah and Ahura-Mazda (see note B), but they indicate influences whose direction and scope now begin to be recognised, and to which the express prohibition against the conception or representation of Ahura-Mazda in a material form (see note P) should perhaps be attributed.

O.—THE CHERUBIM.

The unconquerable propensity of the Hebrews to idolatry had caused the issue and maintenance of the edict against the representation or modelling of images, which would have at once become the pretext for fresh sins (see above, p. 25, n. 1). But in such a prohibition there was also a lofty philosophical and religious idea—the impossibility for the creature, for a finite and ephemeral being, to conceive the Creator, infinite and eternal. This is why Mazdeism, although inferior to Jehovism in its conception of its God, also interdicts the representation of the master of the world by means of a material form or emblem. The original sacred fire, the fire *Bahrâm* itself, is a divine emanation, but it is not God (Dieulafoy, " Acropole de Suse," p. 392, n. 3).

The most formal and celebrated exception to this rule was that of the Cherubim placed above the ark (Exod. xxxvi. 3, 16). They alone escaped the zeal of the iconoclast prophets and kings. The rabbis and the Christian exegetes account for this exception by the fact that the cherubim sheltered the throne of the Lord with their wings. In reality two distinct causes saved them. The first was the antiquity, the power, and the sacredness of the traditions relating to the ark (see above, pp. 180 to 182). The second was that except for the priests and certain of the Levites, nobody saw these figures. When the ark was carried out no one was allowed to approach, and it could only be looked at from a great distance (see above, p. 182, n. 2).

Later on, under the influence of foreign artists, the Hebrews abated their severity. Cherubim, lions, oxen were scattered in profusion in the ornamentation of the temple and on the consecrated objects exposed to the view of the public (1 Kings vi. 29, 32, 33–35, vii. 25, 29, 44 ; Ezek. xli. 18–20, 25), but never at any time did there exist an emblematical or pictured representation of Elohim.

THE END.

www.ingramcontent.com/pod-product-compliance
Lightning Source LLC
Chambersburg PA
CBHW071958220426
43662CB00009B/1182